Japan and the United States:
Economic and Political Adversaries

Other Titles in This Series

Oil Money and the World Economy, Yoon S. Park

The New International Economic Order, edited by Karl P. Sauvant and Hajo Hasenpflug

International Business in the Middle East: Case Studies, edited by Ashok Kapoor

The Sogo Shosa: *Japan's Multinational Trading Companies,* Alexander K. Young

Debt and the Less Developed Countries, edited by Jonathan David Aronson

Kuwait: Trade and Investment, Ragaei El Mallakh

Foreign Investments and the Management of Political Risk, Dan Haendel

U.S.-Mexico Economic Relations: Current Issues and Future Prospects, edited by Barry W. Poulson and T. Noel Osborn

Extraterritorial Antitrust: The Sherman Act and U.S. Business Abroad, James B. Townsend, Jr.

International Trade and Agriculture: Theory and Policy, edited by Jimmye S. Hillman and Andrew Schmitz

The Lending Policy of the World Bank in the 1970s: Analysis and Evaluation, Bettina S. Hürni

Westview Special Studies in International Economics and Business

Japan and the United States: Economic and Political Adversaries
edited by Leon Hollerman

The current economic policy debate between the United States and Japan, increasingly assuming the attributes of an adversary proceeding, has roots in divisive issues that have simmered for years. In this first book to specifically address these issues, U.S. and Japanese scholars, government officials, and business executives provide a basis for understanding and resolving the difficult questions central to the U.S.-Japan controversy. Their approach is exceptionally well-balanced, reflecting their diverse backgrounds and differing points of view.

Leon Hollerman, professor of economics at Claremont Men's College and Claremont Graduate School, is the author of *Japan's Dependence on the World Economy.*

Japan and the United States:
Economic and Political Adversaries

edited by Leon Hollerman

Westview Press / Boulder, Colorado

Westview Special Studies in
International Economics and Business

All rights reserved. No part of this publication may be reproduced or transmitted in any form or by any means, electronic or mechanical, including photocopy, recording, or any information storage and retrieval system, without permission in writing from the publisher.

Copyright © 1980 by Westview Press, Inc.

Published in 1980 in the United States of America by
  Westview Press, Inc.
  5500 Central Avenue
  Boulder, Colorado 80301
  Frederick A. Praeger, Publisher

Library of Congress Cataloging in Publication Data
Main entry under title:
Japan and the United States: economic and political adversaries.
  (Westview special studies in international economics and business)
  1. United States—Foreign economic relations—Japan—Addresses, essays, lectures.
2. Japan—Foreign economic relations—United States—Addresses, essays, lectures. I. Hollerman, Leon. II. Series.
HF1456.5.J3J37   382'.0952'073   79-18646
ISBN 0-89158-582-6

Printed and bound in the United States of America

Contents

List of Tables ix
The Contributors xiii
Introduction, *Leon Hollerman* xv

1. Interventionism and Foreign Trade Statistics in Occupied Japan, *Leon Hollerman* 1

2. Technological Superiority: A Milestone in the Postwar Japanese Growth, *Mieko Nishimizu* 13

3. Japanese-U.S. Relations in Science and Technology, *Takeo Sasagawa* 39

4. U.S. Trade Problems with Particular Reference to Japan, *Eleanor M. Hadley* 57

5. Japan's Foreign Trade Policy, *Hiroshi Kato* 79

6. ASEAN and Its Relations with Japan and the United States, *Saburo Okita* 97

7. The Future of Japan-United States Trade Relations, *Hisao Kanamori* 111

8. The Evolution of United States–Japan Relations, *Philip H. Trezise* 147

9. The U.S.-Japanese Alliance—Cornerstone or
   Trouble Zone? *Robert A. Scalapino* 161

10. Locomotive Strategy and U.S. Protectionism:
    A Japanese View, *Leon Hollerman* 189

11. The Politics of Economic Relations
    Between the United States and Japan,
    Leon Hollerman 213

Tables

2.1	Output in the United States and Japan, 1952 to 1974	19
2.2	Factor Input in the United States and Japan, 1952 to 1974	23
2.3	Japan's Technology: Catching Up with the United States, 1952 to 1974	28
4.1	Ratio of Gross Fixed Capital Formation to Gross Domestic Product, 1970 to 1977	64
4.2	Growth Rates of Gross Capital Stock During Selected Periods	66
4.3	Ratio of Personal Savings to Disposable Personal Income, 1970 to 1977	68
4.4	Output per Hour in Manufacturing in Selected Countries, 1960 to 1976	75
5.1	Quarterly Trends in Manufacturing Productivity in Major Industrial Countries, 1976 to 1977	88
5.2	Hourly Wage Rates in Major Industrial Countries, 1977	89
5.3	Social Welfare Expenditures in Japan, 1966, 1971 and 1975	89
6.1	Japan's Direct Investment in ASEAN Countries, 1960 to 1976	100
6.2	Trade Matrix, 1972	101
6.3	Trade Matrix, 1977	102
6.4	Matrix of Export Share in 1972 and 1977	104
6.5	Matrix of Import Share in 1972 and 1977	105
6.6	Exchange Rates of ASEAN Currencies and the Yen, 1972 to 1978	108

7.1	The United States' Share of Japanese Trade, 1873 to 1977	112
7.2	Japan's Imports During Selected Years, 1960 to 1977	114
7.3	Regional Distribution of Japan's Imports, 1965, 1970 and 1977	115
7.4	Japan's Imports from the United States, 1960, 1970 and 1977	116
7.5	Japan's Imports of Principal Raw Materials from the United States, 1960, 1970 and 1977	117
7.6	Japan's Imports of Food and Animal Feed from the United States, 1960, 1970 and 1977	119
7.7	Japan's Machinery Imports from the United States, 1960, 1970 and 1977	120
7.8	Japan's Imports of Machinery by Specified Country of Origin, 1970 and 1977	121
7.9	Japan's Exports, Total and to the United States, During Selected Years, 1960 to 1977	122
7.10	Regional Distribution of Japan's Exports, 1968, 1970 and 1977	123
7.11	Japan's Exports to the United States, 1960, 1970 and 1977	124
7.12	Share of Japan and of Less Developed Countries in the United States Light Industry Product Market, 1965 and 1977	125
7.13	The Balance of Japan's Trade with the United States, 1960 to 1977	127
7.14	Annual Rate of Growth of Japan's Gross National Product, 1961 to 1970, and Forecasts, 1978 to 1985	129
7.15	Adaptation of the Japanese Economy to Changes after the Oil Crisis, 1970 to 1978	131
7.16	Japan's Industrial Structure, 1965 to 1985 (Summary)	131
7.17	Japan's Industrial Structure, 1965 to 1985 (Breakdown)	132
7.18	Economic Growth and Dependence on Foreign Trade, 1970 to 1985	134
7.19	Japan's Trade Structure in 1985	135

Tables *xi*

7.20	Japan's Imports from Southeast Asia, 1970 and 1977	138
7.21	Japan's Exports to Southeast Asia, 1970 and 1977	139
7.22	Principal Destinations of Japan's Exports, 1960, 1970 and 1977	141
7.23	Principal Commodities Traded between Japan and the United States, 1960, 1970 and 1977	142
8.1	Japan's Gross National Product, 1965 to 1978	156

The Contributors

Eleanor M. Hadley is assistant director of the International Division of the U.S. General Accounting Office in Washington, D.C. She is the author of *Antitrust in Japan* (1970).

Leon Hollerman, professor of economics at Claremont Men's College and Claremont Graduate School, has written numerous journal articles on the Japanese economy and is the author of *Japan's Dependence on the World Economy* (1967).

Hisao Kanamori is president of The Japan Economic Research Center in Tokyo. He is a former senior economist with the Economic Planning Agency of Japan.

Hiroshi Kato is professor of economics at Keio University in Tokyo. The most recent of his three books, *Umarekawaru Nippon* (The Rebirth of Japan), was published in 1976.

Mieko Nishimizu, assistant professor of economics and public affairs at the Woodrow Wilson School of Public and International Affairs of Princeton University, is the author of numerous articles and papers comparing U.S. and Japanese economic growth and productivity.

Saburo Okita is minister of foreign affairs in the Ohira cabinet, is also chairman and former president of The Japan Economic Research Center in Tokyo, and serves as a special adviser to the International Development Center of Japan.

Takeo Sasagawa is director of international projects and a member of the editorial board of the Tokyo newspaper *Sankei Shimbun*.

Robert A. Scalapino is director of the Institute of East Asian Studies at the University of California, Berkeley, and the author of ten books and countless articles on East Asian and international affairs.

Philip H. Trezise is a senior fellow at The Brookings Institution in Washington, D.C., and is the author or coauthor of five books on the national and international economy.

Introduction

This book is designed as a contribution to the current policy debate between the United States and Japan, which has increasingly assumed the attributes of an adversary proceeding. After the occupation of Japan following World War II, the erstwhile enemies were at pains to affirm their desire for "cooperation," "communication," and "partnership." As long as the United States remained the patron and Japan the client, their relations appeared to be harmonious. However, in both nations, discordant change has overcome continuity in recent years. In some respects, they have attained a reversal of roles. In particular, the student has become the teacher in the field of business management and in its role as an organizer of competitive economic power. (Paradoxically, the vicissitudes of Japan's domestic economy have been the source of supply-oriented exports, which on the external plane make its economic position look more powerful than it actually is.) Japan has also begun to assert an "independent" foreign policy, while the United States has become "reactive."

In the evolution of roles, the United States has sustained some erosion of its political, industrial, technological, and military preeminence. In becoming more dependent on external sources of raw material and in its deepening isolation as a democracy, the United States has begun to appear as an island rather than as a continent. In terms of economic policy, while Japan has become more liberal, the United States has become more protectionist. The speed with which these changes have crystallized is breathtaking. As recently as 1960, Peter B. Kenen wrote a book entitled *Giant Among Nations*. Two decades later, the identity of that nation may be less than self-evident.

In Japan, however, the climb to success has not been without pitfalls. Saying nothing of cyclical instability, its difficulties include structural problems, some of which are shared in common with the United States — such as a demographic transition and the need for reallocation of the productive resources of declining industries. Moreover, the motor force of some important growth-promoting factors in the Japanese economy (such as the expansionary mechanism of supply-leading investment) has dwindled.

As mentioned above, even prior to recent events, the relationship between the United States and Japan has been only apparently harmonious. Many divisive issues have simmered for years before flaring into the open. Some roots of the adversary relationship were planted during the occupation by inappropriate policies of General Douglas MacArthur. After the Korean war, an argument ensued concerning whether Japan was a "full and equal" partner, or only "equal" but not "full." There was controversy concerning U.S. military bases in Japan, the United States–Japan Security Treaty, Okinawa reversion, liberalization of trade and foreign exchange regulations, tariffs, quotas, foreign aid to Japan, foreign aid by Japan, "Buy American" policies, "Buy Japanese" policies, customs valuation, subsidies, countervailing duties, "orderly marketing," "voluntary" import and export restraints, the foreign exchange value of the yen, dumping, "safeguards," escape clause actions, ocean freight rates, import surcharges, "Nixon shocks," the "free ride" in military defense, and the development of nuclear fuel reprocessing plants in Japan. In recent years, U.S. officials have openly acknowledged the use of pressure in gaining acquiescence from Japan.

At the micro or individual industry level, the catalog of commodities about which the United States and Japan have had bitter arguments includes automobiles, beef, bicycles, ceramic tile, citrus fruit, computers, flatware, glass, leather goods, logs, petroleum, plywood, soybeans, steel, textiles, thermometers, tuna fish, and television sets. At the macroeconomic level, controversy between the United States and Japan has culminated in

Introduction xvii

a confrontation over the "locomotive" strategy with statements by U.S. officials to the effect that Japan's trade surplus in commerce with the United States is "unacceptable."

For purposes of balance, this book includes analysis by both Japanese and U.S. contributors. The diversity of their backgrounds is enhanced by the fact that they occupy posts in government and business as well as academia. A balanced approach is particularly appropriate at the present time inasmuch as the Japanese point of view has been poorly presented and insufficiently understood in the United States. Conversely, the Japanese have not been notably sympathetic to the problems of the United States, which they regard as largely of its own making. In Japanese terms, moreover, Japan has been "impolite" to the United States, which is "inside" (while it has been "polite" to the Soviet Union, which is "outside") the family. The United States has reciprocated in kind with its coldness to Japan. For example, Japan was excluded from the Guadeloupe summit meeting of January 1979, at which matters of vital concern to Japan were discussed. This sharpened Japan's already acute perception of itself as isolated in the world diplomatic community.

The increasing sense of isolation within the United States as well gives a new meaning to the term "convergence" as applied to the evolutionary paths of the United States and Japan. The extent to which this evolution will have an effect on their partnership remains to be seen.

The essays in this book are balanced in the further sense that some of the contributors differ with each other on major points. No attempt has been made to edit their views into artificial conformity.

Japanese names in this book have been rendered in Western order, with the surname last.

I would like to express grateful thanks to the Earhart Foundation for its support of my research, represented partly by my contributions to this book. Thanks are also due to the editors of *Pacific Affairs* and the *Journal of Contemporary Business* for permission to reprint as chapters 10 and 11 articles of mine originally published in those journals.

I would also like to express my appreciation to Mervyn W. Adams Seldon for her expert editorial assistance.

Leon Hollerman

Japan and the United States:
Economic and Political Adversaries

1
Interventionism and Foreign Trade Statistics in Occupied Japan

Leon Hollerman

The imprint of the Supreme Command for the Allied Powers (SCAP) was at least as indelible in the economic sphere as in the social and political institutions of Japan during the occupation that followed World War II. In particular, the postwar international policies of the shattered nation were profoundly conditioned by the comprehensive economic controls imposed (in the name of democracy) by SCAP. Thus the prospect for a free market economy in Japan was doomed for a generation by the occupation itself. Upon the departure of SCAP in 1952, given the tools placed in its hands by the occupation, the Japanese bureaucracy saw a historic opportunity for the restoration of its own status and power. It saw the system of controls as a cornucopia of splendid careers. SCAP's exercise in interventionism — a natural manifestation of military thinking — was the United States' contribution to the forces it professed to abhor. The result, in years to come, was a progressive deepening of adversary relations between the United States and Japan on the subject of economic liberalization.

SCAP's elaboration and implementation of economic controls provided an educational experience both for itself and for the Japanese. While learning its job, SCAP made many errors at Japan's expense. Whereas international economic controls as maintained by Japan after the occupation evoked the hostility of the United States, the errors committed by SCAP in the process of establishing the controls aroused the antagonism of the

Japanese at the very outset. It is with these errors that the present paper is primarily concerned.

One of the ways in which SCAP educated the Japanese was by demonstrating how economic controls could be implemented by means of statistical reporting requirements. (In applying this procedure after the occupation, the pupil revealed talent surpassing that of the teacher.) SCAP's attempts at economic control were particularly preemptive and authoritarian on the international plane. Moreover, while in the domestic sector of the economy its control was largely "indirect," being administered through the Japanese bureaucracy as surrogate, in the international sector SCAP assumed direct operating as well as policy jurisdiction. Many of its international economic controls, however, were poorly conceived and incoherently applied. This was revealed in the statistical procedures used by SCAP to monitor the international sector, to provide signals for its economic planning and to secure compliance with its economic regulations. It was also shown in SCAP's poor foreign trade results.

In organizing international controls, SCAP's approach was imbalanced, in some respects being excessively fussy in detail, while in other respects being egregiously careless. An example of the latter can be seen in the procedures by which it purported to maintain Japan's foreign trade accounts. Almost a year and a half after the inception of the occupation, the state of affairs prevailing under its exclusive management of the international sector was described in an internal SCAP memorandum as follows:

Fiscal Accounts:

Up to the present time no adequate or comprehensive fiscal records have been kept covering Foreign Trade transactions. Up to 31 December 1946, trade has been conducted largely on the basis of exchange of commodities, based on a future determination of dollar values.

An attempt to obtain an approximate evaluation of imports and exports has been carried on, based largely upon a pricing in estimating values of quantities. All import goods from the United States have largely been received without invoices or even landed cost figures. On imports from other countries, dollar values in many cases have not been arrived at prior to purchase.

The majority of all exports to the United States have been on a consignment basis to USCC [United States Commercial Company].

On exports to other countries, in most cases, the transaction has been made on the basis of a future determination of price.

No transactions have actually been billed to date.

Starting 1 January 1947, the Foreign Trade Division will, insofar as possible, enter into Sales Contracts with foreign countries with a definite price understanding as to the value of the commodity involved in the transaction. . . .

Many of the export transactions with the United States will have to be of a consignment nature.

Plans of the Foreign Trade Division for 1947:

During 1947, it will be necessary for the Foreign Trade Division to bill foreign buyers for all transactions entered into in the calendar years 1945 and 1946. This means that a quantitative statement of transactions by individual items will have to be made and these quantitative invoices as segregated by countries will then have to be priced. The pricing of the individual items will have to be largely on the basis of agreements reached with these countries inasmuch as previously stated the original transaction provided for a price agreement at a future date.

The Problem:

It is now necessary that an adequate fiscal accounting-recording system be established so that during the calendar year 1947, all transactions can be adequately billed, invoices checked against receipts of goods, and all transactions for the years 1945 and 1946 entered into a permanent record for each interested country. . . .[1]

This memorandum was issued as an agenda for a meeting "to determine: Firstly, the responsible agency which will set up an adequate bookkeeping and accounting system for SCAP operations, and secondly, to discuss some of the administrative details of such an organization." It aptly conveys the flavor of SCAP's autodidactic odyssey.

SCAP's complacency in developing foreign trade procedures was prompted partly by the fact that at the start of the occupation trade was practically nonexistent. The slow recovery of trade, moreover, was due in large part to SCAP's repressive intervention.[2] The latter began with SCAP's requirement that all foreign trade negotiations be conducted at the government-to-government level, the Japanese government being represented by SCAP. On this plane, the volume of transactions was relatively small. Thus, at first, the management of trade seemed a deceptively easy task. Accordingly, SCAP assumed its economic mission with informality. In addition to the casual record-keeping described above, it waited for almost a year before resorting to the use of written contracts in the conduct of trade. (Incidentally, SCAP did have a legal section.) Vital matters were thus left up in the air. These included the method of price determination for shipments, the type of foreign exchange to be used in settlement, the distribution of CIF charges, time limits for the fulfillment of orders, and the method of adjustment for loss, shortage or damage.[3] In trade with China and Korea, the net result during this period was a loss of $20.2 million in the form of uncollectible receivables.[4]

SCAP's procedures in the control and conduct of trade were reflected in its statistical accounts. The foreign trade statistical records were uncoordinated, overlapping, and inconsistent. In the first place, source documents were produced by various SCAP agencies that exercised operating control over trade, these being a by-product—if not an afterthought—of such operations. The documents were then processed and compiled in SCAP headquarters. Parallel accounts, based on different documentation, were maintained by the Ministry of Finance and Boeki Cho (Board of Trade), but these, ironically, were treated with scorn by SCAP, which regarded them as training exercises rather than as official records of Japanese foreign trade. Meanwhile, the flow of documents increased considerably as private parties were admitted into the negotiating process; also, the size of individual transactions became smaller as compared with those negotiated between governments.[5] SCAP agencies were thus progressively swamped with license applications and shipping documents to be compiled. Attempts to keep up with the flow fell into hopeless confusion. With ambivalence, SCAP at this stage "turned over" statistical compiling responsibilities to the Japanese.

Some of the difficulties that descended on SCAP in the preparation of its foreign trade statistics were self-inflicted while others were exogenous. Prior to January 1949, when the occupation had been functioning for almost three and a half years, SCAP had not yet arranged to have quantity and value figures for individual import and export transactions reported together on a single source document.[6] Moreover, a wide assortment of types of documents and sources of information having different degrees of coverage and reliability were used by the Economic and Scientific Section (ESS) in the process of compiling Japan's foreign trade statistics.

Compilation was not centralized and foreign trade documents were processed partly by the Eighth Army military government teams as well as by other SCAP organizations. As I found on field trips in behalf of SCAP headquarters, the Eighth Army's operations were inept due to lack of sufficient personnel to adequately process the documents it collected at the ports under its supervision. In the case of petroleum imports, consistent data were difficult to obtain because storage warehouses under Eighth Army control did not coordinate their procedures with those of SCAP's headquarter's sections. In particular, there was a lack of coordination between Eighth Army Headquarters and SCAP's General Accounting Section, as well as between the Eighth Army and the Foreign Trade Division of the Economic and Scientific Section.[7]

At the beginning of the occupation, American Aid supplies formed the bulk of Japanese imports, but commodities shipped to Japan by the U.S. government were not accompanied by documents stating the value of the goods transferred.[8] Thus, in many cases, when source documents arrived in SCAP headquarters where the statistics were compiled, values attached by the Economic and Scientific Section to imports (and to exports as well, as discussed below) were either wholly arbitrary or based on estimates, many of which were wide of the mark. United States Army supplies conveyed to the Japanese from stocks originally brought to Japan for military use (known as military transfers) were valued at prices quoted in the U.S. Army Quartermaster catalog plus a markup of 40 percent. The catalog price was distinctly inappropriate in those cases — commonly occurring — in which goods were received by the Japanese in spoiled, mildewed, or secondhand condition.[9]

SCAP had great difficulty not only in accounting for the value of American Aid goods received in Japan but also in reconciling the quantity of goods received as compared with the quantity shipped. American Aid supplies were shipped under various "program" designations. The program numbers, however, were not always specified on the shipping documents that accompanied the merchandise. Even when specified on the shipping documents, SCAP had trouble associating particular merchandise with particular programs because several programs might be included in a given shipment and the component packages of a shipment would lack identifying marks. Lack of identifying marks also caused confusion with regard to the intended "area destination" of American Aid shipments to particular regions of Japan.

During the period 1946-1949, moreover, according to the best information available to SCAP, "obligations" of U.S. government funds for American Aid to Japan exceeded congressional appropriations for that purpose — a technical impossibility.[10] After trips to Washington by SCAP officials concerned with the "reconciliation of civilian supply quantitative records" (as the inconsistency was known in official correspondence), the size of the unaccounted for discrepancy between the records in Washington and Tokyo for the period 1946-1949 was determined to be $50.1 million. This was a residual calculated after the discrepancy had first been reduced by attributing $105 million of the difference to "slippage." Slippage was defined as "the value of goods procured but not shipped and the value of goods shipped but not received in Japan as of 30 June 1949."[11]

Apart from the problem of collating quantity and value figures about particular shipments when the data were reported on separate documents, SCAP frequently received reports on the quantity of exports with no value information whatever. These reports came from Boeki Cho, which had been organized to handle the physical aspect of trade subject to SCAP's direct management. Boeki Cho was supposed to transmit shipping documents to SCAP as a basis for compilation of the foreign trade statistics. However, due to the chaotic state of affairs in that organization, bills of lading containing essential cost information were not available to SCAP at the time and place of preparation of the statistics.[12] Consequently, as mentioned above, SCAP relied upon a variety of sources for statistical purposes. Sometimes the reports of quantities exported were valued "provisionally" (in effect, permanently) according to price lists of official rather than actual prices. Sometimes they were valued according to a "schedule of price estimates" prepared by the Import-Export Division of ESS. The schedule was devised by ascertaining the prices of various commodities in 1936 and increasing these prices by arbitrary percentages. Exports on consignment to the United States (such as silk, consigned to the United States Commercial Corporation) were given arbitrary values in the statistics since their liquidated value was not known; even after consignment merchandise was sold, SCAP was not able to associate the sales value with the export documentation of particular shipments for the purpose of revising its statistics. In many cases, SCAP simply valued Japanese export products in accordance with the prices appearing in Sears Roebuck catalogs.[13]

In April 1950, plans were made for the transfer of official responsibility for compilation of Japanese foreign trade statistics from SCAP to the Ministry of Finance. The transfer was difficult, however, because of gaps in the information available to the ministry. Indeed, prior to April 1950, the "superiority" of SCAP's foreign trade statistics to those unofficially prepared by the Japanese government was attributable exclusively to the fact that information had been withheld from the Japanese. In particular, figures concerning the dollar value of American Aid import shipments into Japan, which by this time were being received by SCAP, were not recorded on documents furnished to the Japanese. Information concerning shipments arriving in Japan aboard U.S. military vessels or other vessels that used dock facilities reserved for the occupation forces was also incompletely available to the Japanese. It now became necessary to make all information available to the

Customs Bureau of the Ministry of Finance.[14]

Transfer of the foreign trade reporting function was not without difficulties within the Japanese government itself, however. The Japanese government's receipt for imports, an essential source document, was prepared by Boeki Cho prior to April 1950. Thereafter, the responsibility was assumed by the Ministry of International Trade and Industry (MITI), which became the trade control authority. Due to interministerial rivalry, however, MITI did not promptly transmit its import documents to the Customs Bureau of the Ministry of Finance, which was responsible for statistical reporting. In its guidance of the Japanese government toward resumption of the foreign trade statistical reporting function, and in presiding over the transfer of its responsibilities to agencies of the Japanese government, SCAP was partly the cause of this jurisdictional conflict.

In any event, the Japanese government's receipt for imports was soon superseded by the customs declaration as the basic statistical source document for both imports and exports. (Prior to resuming its prewar function as official compiler of Japan's foreign trade statistics, the Ministry of Finance had already been using customs declarations as the basic source for its "unofficial" version of the statistics.) Efforts of the Ministry of Finance to improve statistical coverage, however, brought further difficulties into the open. Foreign oil companies, such as Caltex, Standard, and Shell, were using U.S. Army port and storage facilities. Thus they filed no customs declarations and were able to avoid customs clearance on petroleum imported into Japan for commercial sale.[15] As late as January 1950, and as far as I know until the end of the occupation, the oil companies were exercising extraterritorial privileges in Japan in violation of both SCAP's published directives and Japanese law. My action in formally bringing this to the attention of SCAP authorities accomplished nothing whatever.[16]

Activities of the oil companies were so closely associated with those of the occupation that the two were not fully distinguishable to the Japanese. This was to the advantage of the oil companies as a means of avoiding payment of customs duties. During 1950, the Japanese were scheduled to commence the domestic refining of oil products, at which time duties would presumably be imposed on imports of refined products. The companies feared that if the refined products being imported by them were declared to customs, the Japanese would follow up by imposing customs duties. They also argued that customs "red tape" would interfere with shipments and delay the import process. However, another matter of importance was also at stake. By means of an informal arrangement between the oil companies and the U.S. Army, a few items such as navy special fuel were imported in large amounts by the companies and stored in U.S. Army facilities. A corresponding credit would be set up by the army to the companies' account. When the companies wanted to withdraw their oil, they were allowed to withdraw either what they had put in or any other product of equivalent value that the army might have available. Although they put only a few major types of oil into storage, the companies actually withdrew a wide variety of products from U.S. Army stocks for commercial distribution.[17]

According to a former member of General Douglas MacArthur's personal staff, the general "knew about the oil companies." However, "he did not want to interfere with U.S. business," especially big business. Also he believed that the privileged activities of the oil companies "would result in lower prices of petroleum products to the Japanese." MacArthur believed that "the economists didn't understand the real situation of Japan. He himself had a very simplistic view of the economy."[18]

As mentioned above, to a considerable extent SCAP's statistical procedures were linked to its economic controls. When trade was restored to private hands, SCAP's procedural requirements proliferated enormously. Specific authorization was required even for routine entrepreneurial initiatives. This was implemented by requirements for applications and the filing of reports. The revival of trade, however, created new contingencies for which procedures had not been provided. Traders, therefore, improvised their own procedures, which might or might not be approved ex post facto by SCAP. All this, of course, was quite inconsistent with SCAP's ostensible free market philosophy. (With few exceptions, chiefly that of the land reform, SCAP's democratic reforms were primarily political rather than economic.)

Both the international economic controls and the statistics by which they were monitored became a morass. Records maintained by SCAP and the Japanese government were subject to reorganization as new control systems were introduced. Likewise, personnel within SCAP and the Japanese government were periodically reorganized in attempts to keep up with the flood of paper. SCAP waged a losing battle in the effort to maintain continuity between records compiled under former systems and those prepared under successor systems. Much time was fruitlessly spent amending and adjusting old records rather than in advance planning of a realistic system for the control and statistical reporting of foreign trade.

In attempting to impose excessive international economic controls with inappropriate procedures, and then attempting to keep track of the results, SCAP achieved the worst of both worlds. The control system bogged down and became a drag on Japan's economic recovery, as seen by its poor performance prior to the Korean war. Moreover, as inherited by the Japanese government, these controls set the stage for mobilization of a large part of the nontariff barrier apparatus of which the United States has bitterly complained in recent years. Misconceived measures of economic control during the occupation thus constituted a legacy to the government of Japan, which fortified Japan's resistance to economic liberalization in the postwar period.

Notes

1. Memorandum from the Foreign Trade Division, Economic and Scientific Section (ESS/FT) to the Research and Statistics Division, Economic and Scientific Section (ESS/RS), January 8, 1947.

2. Formulation of foreign trade policy and the conduct of all trade negotiations with foreigners were initially placed under SCAP's exclusive jurisdiction: no Japanese participation was permitted. This was known as the period of "blind trade." Partial Japanese participation—"one-eyed trade"—was not allowed until the advent of "limited

private trade" in exports in September 1947. The recovery of trade was also discouraged by SCAP's requirement that exporters relinquish all foreign currency export proceeds for yen. (This was modified by a token foreign exchange retention scheme introduced late in the occupation — [SCAP instruction to the Japanese government] SCAPIN 2020, June 24, 1949.) Never rescinded during the occupation, moreover, was SCAP's order for the dissolution of the Mitsui and Mitsubishi trading companies (SCAPIN 1741, July 3, 1947).

3. In the case of imports from China, during the first six months of the occupation, Japan received 119,962 metric tons of salt according to weight reports at Japanese docks, whereas China's loading receipts indicated that 150,000 tons had been shipped. Further, on arrival, SCAP estimated that the salt was worth $14.20 a metric ton, but the Chinese were not willing to settle for that amount.

4. A U.S. government report makes an unexplained reference to a write-off of $20.2 million in Japan's foreign trade accounts as managed by SCAP. The write-off is accounted for by the facts given here. See *Report to the President on Foreign Economic Policies* (Gray Report) (Washington: U.S. Government Printing Office, November 10, 1950), p. 119.

5. In August 1948, the "buyer-supplier" contract system was introduced. This referred to exports only and permitted foreign buyers to negotiate with Japanese suppliers subject to "floor prices" specified by SCAP.

6. Following that date, the data were entered on a common document in most cases. Author's memorandum, "Source and Method of Tabulation of Japanese Foreign Trade Statistics," April 1950.

7. Author's memorandum, October 22, 1946.

8. Author's memorandum, June 27, 1946.

9. Presumably these facts were considered in the later negotiations between the U.S. and Japanese governments concerning the extent of Japan's indebtedness for American Aid supplies. According to SCAP statistics, their total value was $2.2 billion during the occupation as a whole. In a settlement reached in June 1961, this figure was reduced to $1.8 billion, of which amount it was agreed that Japan would pay 27 percent.

10. Author's memorandum, January 5, 1950.

11. "Memorandum for the Record," ESS/PS (Programs and Statistics), January 27, 1950.

12. Author's memorandum, June 27, 1946.

13. For a time, I was in charge of this procedure.

14. Author's memorandum, April 1950.

15. Imports for use by the occupation forces were legally not subject to customs clearance.

16. Author's memorandum, January 12, 1950.

17. Ibid.

18. Interview with Frank J. Sackton, lieutenant general, U.S. Army (retired), former chief of the Secretariat and secretary to the General Staff, Supreme Commander for the Allied Powers, Japan (1946-1948), April 15, 1978.

2
Technological Superiority: A Milestone in the Postwar Japanese Growth

Mieko Nishimizu

Only slightly more than a century ago, Japan stood at the northeast corridor of Asia almost completely secluded from the rest of the world. Several decades later (1904-1905) it was to win the Russo-Japanese War, and several decades subsequent to that it was to resurge out of its first defeat in World War II as one of the major economic powers of the world. Throughout the post–World War II period the United States has maintained its position as the world's largest economy and as the leader among industrialized countries in output per capita. During this period, Japan has risen to its current position as the world's third largest economy behind those of the United States and the Soviet Union. Although a substantial gap between U.S. and Japanese levels of output per capita still remains, Japan with its large trade surplus is considered a major constraint on the economic well-being of the United States today.

Nicholas Kaldor wrote in 1957 what seems now to be an exact diagnosis of the sources of Japan's successful growth perfor-

---

Part of this article summarizes the findings reported in my paper with Dale W. Jorgenson, "U.S. and Japanese Economic Growth, 1952-1974: An International Comparison," *The Economic Journal* 88, no. 352 (December 1978). Financial support by the National Bureau of Economic Research and the RANN Program of the National Science Foundation is gratefully acknowledged. The author wishes to thank Odette De Kezel for her able computational assistance.

mance. He wrote, in an article entitled "A Model of Economic Growth," that "the prime mover in the process of economic growth is the readiness to absorb technical changes combined with the willingness to invest capital in business ventures" (*Economic Journal,* December 1957, p. 599). Japan, like other latecomers, found itself in a position to import technology originating in the advanced countries of the West. Differences in the productive environment and in the availability and the quality of productive inputs set obstacles for the technology importers. Deficiencies in the social and political systems and institutions that supported the process of technological progress were also obstacles. Despite these, however, Japan effectively prepared its capacity to assimilate imported technology for economic growth. This chapter discusses how Japan continued to narrow its technological gap with the United States throughout the postwar period and even succeeded in eliminating the gap completely, attaining slight superiority over the United States by 1973.

In an economy, at any given time, many goods and services (*output*) are produced by combining the effort of the people (*labor input*) with tools, machinery, and equipment (*capital input*) and land. At the same time every output uses some technical knowledge. The store of technical knowledge employed in production takes a multitude of forms, from the information contained in a farmer's almanac to some specific chemical reaction formula, or from managerial skills and efficient organization of a large corporation to scientific advances in electronic engineering. We refer to this store of knowledge, collectively or individually, as *technology*, and we refer to the advancement of its frontier, collectively or individually, as *technological progress*.

In economic analysis, the concept of technology is captured in terms of observable units of factor inputs (capital and labor) and output, to represent the technical relationship that governs the process of production. With a level of technology given in the production of an output, there must be a maximum amount of the output that can be produced with a given amount of inputs (production of the output above that maximum being technologically infeasible for that given level of inputs). In fact,

Technological Superiority: Postwar Japanese Growth 15

a given level of technology must provide a series of such maximum output levels, each corresponding to a given level of inputs. Technology is therefore conceived as the technically feasible limits of production possibilities. A given level of technology implies that more output cannot be produced without more inputs and that inputs cannot be reduced without producing less output. A technology also describes how different inputs are combined and how each can substitute for another without altering the level of output produced. One can envisage in this manner any individual production process that provides an economy with its many goods and services at any given point in time. The economic concept of technology can also be applied to a group of production processes. A technology can describe how production of one output can substitute for production of another, using the same amount of inputs. In particular, it has been found convenient to aggregate the productive activities of an economy and to think of a technology for the economy as a whole. In this chapter, the process by which Japan has caught up with the United States technologically is discussed within the analytical framework of aggregate technology.

The economic concept of technology is expressed as the technically feasible limits of production. As the store of technical knowledge applied to production advances with time, so do these limits. The economic concept of technological change is simply the notion that greater output can be produced over time with given levels of labor and capital inputs. This implies that inputs employed in production become more productive over time; the term productivity change is frequently used synonymously with technological progress. Technological progress can take a variety of forms; and over time each affects the productive resources of machines or persons in different ways.

In the absence of technological change, expansion of the labor force and accumulation of various capital inputs can, in general, increase the output of goods and services. Technological progress extends further the capacity of these growing inputs to produce and hence is an important force in the process of economic growth.

Thus, the importance of technological progress to a country's economic growth cannot be disputed. And the advancement in the level of technology generates the economy's competitiveness in international trade. In light of the current state of economic and political relations between the United States and Japan, it is particularly important that the difference in the levels of technology between the two countries be measured. Hence the objective of this chapter is to measure and analyze the differences in U.S. and Japanese levels of aggregate technology for the period 1952-1974. The next section discusses the methodology for the measurement of technological gap in nontechnical terms. The following three sections present the measures of U.S. output, factor inputs, and technology relative to Japan. Technical discussion of the methodology is given in an appendix at the end of this chapter.

Methodology

The objective is to allocate the differences between levels of output for Japan and the United States into differences in factor input and differences in the level of technology. The methodology is based on the economic theory of production. The point of departure for this theory is a specific form of production function that expresses the technically feasible limits of production discussed earlier. The specific production function employed (the translog production function) states that the quantity of output produced depends on labor and capital input, as well as time, and a variable takes on the value of one for the United States and zero for Japan and is properly named a dummy variable. Production is considered to take place under the state of *constant return to scale*, that is, a proportional change in all inputs results in a proportional change in output. Production is also considered to take place under the state of *producer equilibrium*, that is, the producers have made a set of optimal decisions with respect to profits and costs in terms of quantities and prices of output produced and factor inputs employed given the technically feasible limits of production they face.

As noted above, technological progress, or technological change, for a given country over time can be expressed as that change in output produced over time when holding levels of capital and labor inputs constant. The difference in levels of technology between countries at each given point in time can be captured in an analogous manner. Conceptually, the technological gap is captured as that difference in levels of output produced between countries at a given point in time when holding all factor inputs constant. The model combines the producer equilibrium conditions for both countries and output and input differences between the countries to generate an index of the technological gap. This index (the translog index) depends only on the prices and quantities of inputs and outputs in the two countries.

The model dictates outputs and inputs for the two countries to be measured in terms of a specific form of quantity index (the translog quantity index), which aggregates over their respective components and sets out as ratios, outputs and inputs between the two countries. The corresponding price index represents the purchasing-power parity between the yen and the dollar in terms of aggregate output or inputs. If U.S. output is measured relative to Japanese output, the purchasing-power parity represents the amount of yen required to purchase goods and services equivalent to that which can be bought with one dollar. Based on work by I. B. Kravis and his associates, *A System of International Comparisons of Gross Product and Purchasing Power*, purchasing-power parities for output and input are developed according to the specification of the model.

The starting point for the construction of translog indexes of output and inputs for the United States and Japan for the period 1952-1974 is the measurement of the value of total product and the value of total factor outlay for each country in current prices. The fundamental accounting identity for the production account is that the value of total product is equal to the value of total factor outlay for each country. The product and factor outlay accounts are linked through capital formation and the compensation of property. To make this link explicit we divide total output between consumption and investment goods and total factor outlay between labor and property compensation. In analyzing productive activity we have limited the scope of our production account to the private domestic sector of each country.

The production account in a complete system of national

economic accounts includes the activities of the private sector, the government sector, and the rest of the world. Rest of the world production is excluded on the grounds that it can reflect a different physical and social environment for productive activity than the environment provided by the domestic sector. The government sector is also excluded on the grounds that the economic motive underlying the productive activities by the government sector is likely to differ from that of the private sector.

Output Gap and Its Anatomy

One unconventional aspect of the measure of output employed in this study is an imputation for the services of consumer durables. The objective is to attain consistency in the treatment of owner-occupied residential structures and owner-utilized consumer durables. Thus, the services derived from the ownership of consumer durables are recognized as consumption goods output while the purchases of consumer durables is a component of investment goods output.

The indexes of total output and its two components, consumption and investment output, for the United States and Japan are presented as ratios of U.S. over Japanese output in Table 2.1. Corresponding purchasing-power parities and shares of investment goods in output are also presented in Table 2.1.

First, a very rapid narrowing of the gap in total output produced between the two countries is observed (column 7). In 1952, total output in the United States was about 12 times that in Japan. By 1960 the ratio of U.S. to Japanese output had fallen to 7.4 and by 1969, down to 4.0. By the end of the period in 1974 this ratio had fallen still further to 3.4. A closer look at the results reveals one striking difference between the two countries. The narrowing of the output gap was accompanied by a rapid rise in the share of investment goods in total output in Japan, while no substantial change in investment share is observed for the United States (columns 1, 2). In fact, for the United States the share of investment goods output declined slightly from .321 to .292 over the period 1952-1974. For Japan the share rose dramatically from the level equal to or below that

TABLE 2.1
Output in the United States and Japan, 1952 to 1974

Year	1.	2.	3.	4.	5.	6.	7.	8.
1952	.321	.321	10.5	183.	16.3	272.	12.1	201.
1953	.317	.292	9.8	196.	17.0	282.	11.6	207.
1954	.305	.291	9.2	191.	15.1	280.	10.7	205.
1955	.337	.309	8.9	183.	15.0	271.	10.5	205.
1956	.334	.353	8.6	185.	12.5	282.	9.8	206.
1957	.326	.401	8.6	193.	10.1	291.	9.2	213.
1958	.297	.348	8.2	185.	10.1	277.	8.8	203.
1959	.318	.373	7.8	190.	9.4	275.	8.3	205.
1960	.300	.414	7.5	187.	7.1	281.	7.4	207.
1961	.294	.481	7.3	202.	5.3	298.	6.5	221.
1962	.305	.441	7.2	215.	5.7	295.	6.6	235.
1963	.309	.446	6.6	218.	5.2	297.	6.1	237.
1964	.310	.450	6.1	225.	4.7	301.	5.5	242.
1965	.317	.420	5.8	229.	5.0	300.	5.5	245.
1966	.317	.430	5.6	236.	4.7	304.	5.3	249.
1967	.304	.464	5.7	254.	3.7	308.	4.9	263.
1968	.306	.477	5.2	247.	3.2	302.	4.3	257.
1969	.303	.481	4.9	240.	2.9	296.	4.0	253.
1970	.291	.497	4.7	254.	2.4	296.	3.6	261.
1971	.296	.479	4.4	254.	2.3	285.	3.4	259.
1972	.303	.474	4.2	261.	2.3	285.	3.3	262.

(continued)

TABLE 2.1 (continued)

Year	1.	2.	3.	4.	5.	6.	7.	8.
1973	.306	.500	4.3	286.	2.2	310.	3.3	282.
1974	.292	.507	4.5	294.	2.2	356.	3.4	318.

Variables

1. Value share of investment goods output, United States.
2. Value share of investment goods output, Japan.
3. Ratio between United States and Japan's consumption goods output.
4. Purchasing power parity, consumption goods output, yen per dollar.
5. Ratio between United States and Japan investment goods output.
6. Purchasing-power parity, investment goods output, yen per dollar.
7. Ratio between United States and Japan's total output.
8. Purchasing-power parity, total output, yen per dollar.

Technological Superiority: Postwar Japanese Growth

in the United States in the years 1952-1955. The year 1956 marks a milestone in the transition of the relative growth of the two countries. The Japanese share of investment goods output overtook that of the United States and rose further to .507, almost 75 percent above the U.S. share, by the end of the period in 1974. At the beginning of the period, the quantity of investment goods output in the United States was more than 16 times that in Japan; this ratio fell all the way down to 2.2 by the end of the period (column 5). The year 1960 marks another milestone. The ratio of investment goods output between the two countries fell below that of consumption goods output (column 3), showing that the output gap had become narrower in investment goods production than in consumption.

Because Japan's productive resources were being directed into the production of investment goods, the closing of the difference in the level of consumption goods output was not as dramatic as that of investment goods; the consumption goods ratio fell from 10.5 to 4.5 during the period. Although purchasing-power parity for consumption goods remained below that of investment goods throughout the period, it increased by 75 percent while the parity for investment goods exhibited only a slight upward trend over 1952-1974 (columns 4, 6).

Input Gap and Its Anatomy

For each country, stock of capital is estimated by six asset components: consumer durables, residential structures, nonresidential structures, producer durable equipment, inventories, and land. The capital stock is estimated as the sum of past investments, each weighted by the relative efficiency of capital, which is assumed to decline geometrically with age. Thus, capital stock at the end of each period is equal to investment during that period less a proportion of beginning-of-the-period stock representing the loss of efficiency.

The price of acquisition of new capital goods (i.e., investment goods price) is not the price of capital input but represents the discounted value of the future prices of capital input, each weighted by relative efficiency as capital assets age over time. This implies that the price of capital input equals the sum of own return to capital (i.e., the after-tax nominal return adjusted for capital gain or loss) and the value of depreciation. Accordingly, the purchasing-power parities for capital input are developed from the corresponding parities of investment goods output. Differences in the two countries' tax structures as they affect the return to capital are fully taken into account.

The estimated capital stock and capital input prices are combined into the index of capital input for a United States–Japan comparison. Table 2.2 presents the index of capital input and corresponding purchasing-power parities, and the own rates of return to capital for each country. Value shares of capital for the United States and Japan are also given.

In the analysis of output differences above, we observed the dramatic role played by investment goods output. This leads us to expect a similar feat by capital input. The quantity of capital input in the United States was nearly 17 times that in Japan at the beginning of the period 1952-1974 (column 5). By the end of the period in 1974, this ratio had dropped to 6.0. The cyclical movement of the U.S. economy is reflected in the annual rates of growth of capital input in the United States for this period (column 7). Relatively high rates of growth characterize the beginning of the period, 1952-1954, the short-lived investment boom of 1956-1957, the more prolonged boom of 1964-1970, and the final years of the period, 1973-1974. Average annual growth rates of capital input rose modestly from 3.6 percent for the period 1952-1960 to 4.1 percent for the period 1960-1974. For Japan, the annual rates of growth of capital input are well below corresponding U.S. rates of growth of capital input 1952-1956 (column 8). Beginning in 1957 another milestone in the transition of relative growth performance of the two countries occurred when annual rates of growth of capital input in Japan rose above U.S. levels, running at more than three times the corresponding U.S. levels during most of the remarkable period 1957-1974. Annual growth rates of capital input increased dramatically from an average of 4.0 percent for the period 1952-1960 to 11.9 percent for 1960-1974.

In the United States the own rates of return to capital follow the business cycle over the period 1952-1974 (column 3). This rate of return reached a high of 7.6 percent in 1966 and a low of

TABLE 2.2
Factor Input in the United States and Japan, 1952 to 1974

Year	1.	2.	3.	4.	5.	6.	7.	8.	9.	10.	11.	12.	13.	14.
1952	.397	.355	.053	.043	16.7	241.	—	—	2.9	52.	.009	.031	5.7	96.
1953	.380	.295	.052	.019	18.2	255.	.036	-.061	2.8	58.	.017	.044	5.4	100.
1954	.399	.298	.052	.028	17.7	252.	.039	-.023	2.7	61.	-.033	.022	5.3	104.
1955	.402	.329	.060	.054	18.4	288.	.032	.016	2.6	59.	.035	.043	5.4	110.
1956	.388	.352	.029	.062	20.3	381.	.052	.024	2.5	58.	.021	.060	5.5	123.
1957	.384	.360	.047	.057	18.9	406.	.042	.072	2.4	59.	-.008	.054	5.2	128.
1958	.403	.334	.048	.036	17.1	323.	.033	.122	2.3	61.	-.026	.012	4.9	118.
1959	.398	.357	.051	.048	16.8	366.	.017	.069	2.3	62.	.040	.026	4.9	128.
1960	.401	.393	.046	.069	16.1	434.	.033	.086	2.2	66.	.013	.046	4.9	145.
1961	.406	.432	.048	.097	15.2	540.	.030	.120	2.2	73.	-.004	.019	4.9	176.
1962	.410	.404	.058	.073	12.4	423.	.022	.155	2.2	81.	.027	.009	4.5	164.
1963	.413	.404	.060	.078	11.3	427.	.034	.122	2.2	91.	.015	.008	4.4	176.
1964	.416	.434	.062	.106	10.5	476.	.038	.105	2.2	97.	.021	.025	4.3	194.
1965	.426	.417	.070	.091	9.7	418.	.043	.117	2.3	105.	.037	.018	4.2	191.
1966	.429	.431	.076	.107	9.5	448.	.053	.082	2.3	110.	.038	.032	4.2	204.
1967	.421	.444	.067	.129	9.0	510.	.057	.085	2.2	118.	.015	.037	4.1	226.
1968	.415	.449	.061	.139	8.0	515.	.044	.118	2.2	126.	.024	.038	3.9	234.
1969	.412	.448	.053	.130	7.5	509.	.046	.137	2.3	135.	.032	.016	3.8	241.
1970	.396	.443	.045	.128	6.7	543.	.045	.139	2.2	151.	-.011	.003	3.5	260.
1971	.406	.415	.047	.098	5.6	428.	.030	.149	2.2	168.	.005	.001	3.3	248.
1972	.415	.416	.054	.097	5.5	420.	.034	.120	2.3	182.	.038	-.000	3.3	259.

(continued)

TABLE 2.2 (continued)

Year	1.	2.	3.	4.	5.	6.	7.	8.	9.	10.	11.	12.	13.	14.
1973	.420	.402	.057	.086	5.9	465.	.045	.109	2.4	210.	.049	.029	3.5	322.
1974	.394	.368	.041	.044	6.0	514.	.049	.120	2.4	240.	.006	-.017	3.4	322.

Variables

1. Value share of capital input, United States.
2. Value share of capital input, Japan.
3. Own rate of return on business capital, United States.
4. Own rate of return on business capital, Japan.
5. Ratio between United States and Japan's capital input.
6. Purchasing-power parity, capital input, yen per dollar.
7. Annual rates of growth of capital input, United States.
8. Annual rates of growth of capital input, Japan.
9. Ratio between United States and Japan's labor input.
10. Purchasing-power parity, labor input, yen per dollar.
11. Annual rates of growth of labor input, United States.
12. Annual rates of growth of labor input, Japan.
13. Ratio between United States and Japan's total factor input.
14. Purchasing-power parity, total factor input, yen per dollar.

4.1 percent in 1974. For the period 1952-1959 the own rate of return to capital in the business sector for Japan was comparable to or slightly below that in the United States (column 4). The year 1956, however, marks yet another milestone when the own rate of return in Japan surpassed that of the United States. Beginning in 1960 and continuing toward the end of the period, Japan's own rate of return to capital was high, and at times approximately double that in the United States. This remarkable increase occurred with virtually no change in the share of property compensation in total factor outlay. In fact, the capital shares in the United States and Japan were remarkably similar, fluctuating around an average of two-fifths or 40 percent (columns 1, 2).

Reflecting the dramatic rise in own rates of return to capital in the business sector in Japan beginning in 1960, purchasing-power parities between the yen and the dollar in terms of capital input also rose sharply over the period 1952-1974, reaching a peak of 543 yen to the dollar in 1970 (column 6).

The relative quantity index of labor input for the United States and Japan is developed on the basis of wage and manhours by levels of educational attainment for each country. The quantity indexes of private domestic capital and labor input can be combined into the quantity index of private domestic total factor input. The indexes of labor input and total factor input in the two countries, together with purchasing-power parities between the yen and the dollar in terms of labor input and total factor input are also presented in Table 2.2. Annual rates of growth of labor input for the United States and Japan are given in Table 2.2 as well.

The quantity of labor input in the United States was only 2.9 times that in Japan in 1952 (column 9). This ratio fell to 2.2 in 1960, which resembles the population ratio between the two countries, and rose slightly toward the end of the period to a level of 2.4 in 1974. In a sharp contrast with capital input, we observe a substantial deceleration in Japan's growth of labor input. During the period 1952-1960, Japan's labor input grew on the average at approximately the same rate as its capital input of 4.2 percent. This implies that capital intensity in production, defined as capital input per unit of labor input, remained unchanged for Japan during this period. Average annual rates of growth of labor input in Japan fell to 1.5 percent in the next period 1960-1974 (column 12). On the other hand, corresponding averages for the United States increased from 0.8 percent for the period 1952-1960 to 2.0 percent for the period 1960-1974 (column 11). Purchasing-power parities between the yen and the dollar for labor input more than quadrupled over the period 1952-1974, rising from 52 to 240 yen to the dollar (column 10). And most of this dramatic rise took place during the period 1960-1974.

Combining the results of capital and labor inputs, we observe that the total factor input in the United States was 5.7 times that in Japan (column 13). By 1960 the ratio of U.S. to Japanese factor input had fallen to 4.9 and by 1969 this ratio had fallen to 3.8. By the end of the period in 1974 this ratio had fallen still further to 3.4, almost precisely the same level as the corresponding ratio of U.S. to Japanese output.

The anatomy of the factor input growth differs a great deal between the two countries. In Japan, the growth of factor input was accomplished, despite a substantial decline in the rate of growth of labor input, by a truly astonishing increase in the rate of growth of capital input, while the corresponding growth of U.S. factor input was associated with a substantial increase in the rate of growth of labor input and a much more modest increase in the rate of growth of capital input. A comparison of the labor input ratio and the capital input ratio between the United States and Japan gives the two countries' relative *capital intensity* in production, i.e., the amount of capital input employed per unit of labor input. In 1952, capital intensity of U.S. production was nearly 6 times that of Japan. Throughout the 1950s, the United States continued to increase the intensity of capital input, while Japan's intensity remained at about the same level; the relative capital intensity actually rose to 7.3 in 1960. Then the surging growth of capital in Japan began to narrow the difference. Although U.S. capital intensity was double that of Japan in 1973, the reduction from sevenfold to twofold in slightly over a decade is indeed an astounding accomplishment.

Technology Gap, the Anatomy of Technology Catch-up

As noted above, given the indexes of difference in output and factor input, we can construct the index of difference in technology. The index of difference in technology between the United States and Japan (in terms of the percent difference, United States less Japan) is given in Table 2.3. We also present the contribution of differences between U.S. and Japanese technology, U.S. and Japanese capital input, and U.S. and Japanese input in explaining differences between U.S. and Japanese output. Each of these contributions is defined as the ratio of the corresponding difference between the United States and Japan to the difference between U.S. and Japanese output.

The results presented in Table 2.3 describe a very remarkable closing of the gap in technology between the United States and Japan over the period 1952-1974. In 1952 the Japanese level of technology was merely one-fourth that of the United States (column 1). During the period 1952-1959 the difference between U.S. and Japanese technology was reduced from 75 percent to 51 percent. Beginning in 1960 the level of Japanese technology moved up sharply relative to that in the United States, reaching nearly 90 percent of the U.S. level by 1968. Between 1968 and 1973 the level of Japanese technology actually overtook that in the United States, so that by 1973 and also in 1974 the aggregate level of technology in Japan stood ahead of that in the United States.

By analyzing the contributions of differences in the level of technology, capital input, and labor input to differences between U.S. and Japanese levels of output (columns 2, 3, 4) we can obtain a different perspective on the disappearance of the gap in technology between the United States and Japan. For the period 1952-1959 all of the reduction in the difference between U.S. and Japanese total output was due to the increase in Japanese labor input relative to U.S. labor input and to the narrowing of the technology gap between the two countries. Relative levels of capital input in the two countries remained almost unchanged. During this period capital intensity increased

TABLE 2.3
Japan's Technology: Catching Up with the United States, 1952 to 1974

Year	1.	2.	3.	4.
1952	.757	.303	.426	.270
1953	.762	.311	.403	.285
1954	.702	.296	.429	.274
1955	.657	.278	.455	.266
1956	.565	.247	.489	.262
1957	.564	.254	.494	.251
1958	.585	.269	.484	.246
1959	.517	.243	.503	.252
1960	.399	.199	.551	.249
1961	.264	.140	.608	.250
1962	.384	.202	.540	.257
1963	.321	.177	.550	.271
1964	.240	.140	.582	.277
1965	.263	.153	.560	.285
1966	.214	.128	.580	.290
1967	.165	.104	.599	.296
1968	.108	.073	.612	.314
1969	.061	.043	.618	.337
1970	.015	.011	.619	.368
1971	.047	.038	.572	.389
1972	.009	.007	.580	.412
1973	-.047	-.039	.609	.429
1974	-.012	-.009	.557	.452

<u>Variables</u>

1. Difference between United States and Japanese technology.

2. Contribution of differences between United States and Japanese technology to differences between United States and Japanese output.

3. Contribution of differences between United States and Japanese capital input to differences between United States and Japanese output.

4. Contribution of differences between United States and Japanese labor input to differences between United States and Japanese output.

more rapidly in the United States than in Japan; capital intensity in Japan was almost unchanged during the period.

For the period 1960-1973 the dramatic reduction in the difference between U.S. and Japanese total output was due to the substantial increase in Japanese capital input relative to U.S. capital input and to the closing of the gap between Japanese and U.S. technology. Japanese and U.S. labor input grew at almost the same rate, whereas the average annual growth rate of capital in Japan was nearly three times that of the United States during this period. While the gap between U.S. and Japanese technology had closed by 1973, there still remains a substantial gap between U.S. and Japanese capital intensity of production. None of the remaining difference between U.S. and Japanese aggregate output in 1974 was due to a difference in levels of technology; all of the remaining difference between U.S. and Japanese output per unit of labor input is due to differences in the capital intensity of production in the two countries.

The thesis put forth in a recent paper by Moses Abramovitz (1977) highlights our analysis and adds further perspective in the evaluation of the results. Abramovitz argues that rapid postwar productivity growth resulted from the exploitation of the potential for such, provided not only by "advances in technological and organizational knowledge," but also by "enlarged initial gaps between actual and possible productivity." Given adequate political and economic institutional frameworks and productive endowments, the greater the "initial backwardness" with respect to own potential, the higher the probability for rapid productivity growth.

It is plausible, as Abramovitz suggests, that Japan's labor productivity level was particularly low with respect to its "potential" level at the beginning of the postwar period. Thus, according to this thesis, this study's results for 1952-1959 characterize these years as the period during which Japan exploited its potential for productivity advance in terms of labor, most likely through intersectoral reallocation of labor.

With respect to the turning point in 1960, after which capital input began to play a central role in Japanese growth, Abramovitz notes that the forces derived from the "initial backwardness" are "only potential, a permissive not sufficient condition for rapid growth." If they were a sufficient condition, a gradual productivity retardation would accompany the catch-up. This, he contends, "was avoided during the 1960's by conditions which favored capital investment and, therefore, supported the more rapid exploitation of opportunities for modernization." This chapter's finding for 1960-1974 is again supported by Abramovitz's thesis advanced for the industrialized market economies.

Japan is today one of the most important political and economic partners of the United States. Recent historical developments indicate that the economic health of Japan is a matter of great importance for U.S. trade and foreign policy. Since the early 1970s, the world economy has gone through yet another severe recession. The United States has recovered from the recession relatively faster than the rest of the world, but with a higher rate of inflation; thus it has been plagued with balance of payments deficits and the weakening of its currency. The rate of Japanese economic growth has declined from approximately 10 percent a year during the 1960s to approximately 5 percent since 1971. This decline has been one of the major factors in the emerging United States-Japan trade imbalance. As a consequence, the Carter administration has repeatedly pressed the Japanese government to engage in expansionary economic policies. The Japanese government, on the other hand, fearing inflation, has engaged in gradual economic stimulation and has not been able to return to its previous high growth rates. In view of these events, it is clear that the rate of Japanese growth has been a policy variable of considerable significance in United States-Japan relations. It is therefore important to understand the changing sources and patterns of Japanese economic growth. Although overshadowed by a series of political and other disturbances and related structural changes in the global economic system, it is extremely important to recognize that Japan has achieved economy-wide technological equivalence with the United States and has entered an entirely new era of economic growth.

Appendix:
Methodology of Measuring Differences in Levels of Aggregate Technology

The methodology is based on a specific form of production function:

$$Y = \exp[\alpha_0 + \alpha_K \ln K + \alpha_L \ln L + \alpha_D \cdot D + \alpha_T \cdot T$$

$$+ \frac{1}{2} \beta_{KK} (\ln K)^2 + \beta_{KL} \ln K \ln L + \beta_{KD} \ln K \cdot D$$

$$+ \beta_{KT} \ln K \cdot T + \frac{1}{2} \beta_{LL} (\ln L)^2 + \beta_{LD} \ln L \cdot D$$

$$+ \beta_{LT} \ln L \cdot T + \frac{1}{2} \beta_{DD} \cdot D^2 + \beta_{DT} \cdot D \cdot T$$

$$+ \frac{1}{2} \beta_{TT} \cdot T^2],$$

where Y is output, K is capital input, L is labor input D is a dummy variable equal to one for the United States and zero for Japan, and T is time. For this production function output is a transcendental or, more specifically, an exponential function of the logarithms of inputs. We refer to this form as the <u>transcendental logarithmic production function</u> or, more simply, the translog production function. The translog production function is characterized by constant returns to scale if and only if the parameters satisfy the conditions:

$$\alpha_K + \alpha_L = 1,$$

$$\beta_{KK} + \beta_{KL} = 0,$$

$$\beta_{KL} + \beta_{LL} = 0,$$

$$\beta_{KD} + \beta_{LD} = 0,$$

$$\beta_{KT} + \beta_{LT} = 0.$$

Denoting the price of output by q_Y, the price of capital input by p_K, and the price of labor input by p_L, we can define the shares of capital and labor input in the value of output, say v_K and v_L, by

$$v_K = \frac{p_K K}{q_Y Y}, \quad v_L = \frac{p_L L}{q_Y Y}.$$

Necessary conditions for producer equilibrium are given by equalities between each value share and the elasticity of output with respect to the corresponding input:

$$v_K = \frac{\partial \ln Y}{\partial \ln K} (K, L, D, T),$$

$$= \alpha_K + \beta_{KK} \ln K + \beta_{KL} \ln L + \beta_{KD} \cdot D + \beta_{KT} \cdot T;$$

$$v_L = \frac{\partial \ln Y}{\partial \ln L} (K, L, D, T),$$

$$= \alpha_L + \beta_{KL} \ln K + \beta_{LL} \ln L + \beta_{LD} \cdot D + \beta_{LT} \cdot T.$$

Under constant returns to scale the elasticities and the value shares sum to unity.

We can define the difference in technology between the two countries, say v_D, as the logarithmic difference between levels of output between the countries, holding capital input, labor input, and time constant:

$$v_D = \frac{\partial \ln Y}{\partial D} (K, L, D, T),$$

$$= \alpha_D + \beta_{KD} \ln K + \beta_{LD} \ln L + \beta_{DD} \cdot D + \beta_{DT} \cdot T.$$

We can also consider specific forms for the functions defining aggregate output Y, capital input K, and labor input L. For example, the translog form for aggregate output as a function of its components is:

$$Y = \exp[\alpha_1 \ln Y_1 + \alpha_2 \ln Y_2 + \cdots + \alpha_m \ln Y_m$$

$$+ \frac{1}{2} \beta_{11} (\ln Y_1)^2 + \beta_{12} \ln Y_1 \ln Y_2 + \cdots$$

$$+ \frac{1}{2} \beta_{mm} (\ln Y_m)^2].$$

The translog output aggregate is characterized by constant returns to scale if and only if:

$$\alpha_1 + \alpha_2 + \cdots + \alpha_m = 1,$$

$$\beta_{11} + \beta_{12} + \cdots + \beta_{\ell m} = 0,$$

$$\cdots \cdots$$

$$\beta_{1m} + \beta_{2m} + \cdots + \beta_{mm} = 0.$$

The value shares of individual outputs $\{w_{Yi}\}$ can be expressed as:

$$w_{Yi} = \alpha_i + \beta_{1i} \ln Y_1 + \cdots + \beta_{im} \ln Y_m, \quad (i = 1, 2 \cdots m).$$

Considering data for the United States and Japan at a

given point of time, the difference between logarithms of aggregate output for the two countries can be expressed as a weighted average of differences between logarithms of individual outputs with weights given by average value shares:

$$\ln Y(US) - \ln Y(JAPAN) = \Sigma \; \hat{w}_{Yi} [\ln Y_i(US) - \ln Y_i(JAPAN)],$$

where:

$$\hat{w}_{Yi} = \frac{1}{2} [w_{Yi}(US) + w_{Yi}(JAPAN)], \quad (i = 1, 2 \cdots m).$$

If aggregate capital and labor input are translog functions of their components, we can express the differences between logarithms of aggregate inputs for the two countries in the form:

$$\ln K(US) - \ln K(JAPAN) = \Sigma \; \hat{v}_{Kj} [\ln K_j(US) - \ln K_j(JAPAN)],$$

$$\ln L(US) - \ln L(JAPAN) = \Sigma \; \hat{v}_{Lk} [\ln L_k(US) - \ln L_k(JAPAN)],$$

where:

$$\hat{v}_{Kj} = \frac{1}{2} [v_{Kj}(US) + v_{Kj}(JAPAN)], \quad (j = 1, 2, \cdots n),$$

$$\hat{v}_{Lk} = \frac{1}{2} [v_{Lk}(US) + v_{Lk}(JAPAN)], \quad (k = 1, 2, \cdots p).$$

If we consider data for both countries at a given point of time, the average difference in technology can be expressed as the difference between logarithms of output for the two countries less a weighted average of the differences between logarithms of capital and labor input for the two countries with weights given by the average value shares:

$$\ln Y(US) - \ln Y(JAPAN) = \hat{v}_K [\ln K(US) - \ln K(JAPAN)]$$
$$+ \hat{v}_L [\ln L(US) - \ln L(JAPAN)]$$
$$+ \hat{v}_D,$$

where:

$$\hat{v}_K = \frac{1}{2} [v_K(US) + v_K(JAPAN)],$$

$$\hat{v}_L = \frac{1}{2} [v_L(US) + v_L(JAPAN)],$$

$$\hat{v}_D = \frac{1}{2} [v_D(US) + v_D(JAPAN)].$$

We refer to this expression for the average difference in technology as the translog index of difference in technology.

References

Christensen, L. R., Cummings, D., and Jorgenson, D. W. (1977). "Economic Growth, 1947-1973: An International Comparison," in J. W. Kendrick and B. Vaccara (eds.), *New Developments in Productivity Measurement*, Studies in Income and Wealth. Vol. 41. New York: Columbia University Press.

Christensen, L. R. and Jorgenson, D. W. (1969). "Measurement of U.S. Real Capital Input, 1929-1967," *Review of Income and Wealth* 15, no. 4 (December):293-320.

―――― (1970). "U.S. Real Product and Real Factor Input, 1929-1967," *Review of Income and Wealth* 16, no. 1 (March):19-50.

―――― (1973). "Measuring the Performance of the Private Sector of the U.S. Economy, 1929-1969," in M. Moss, ed., *Measuring Economic and Social Performance*, New York, National Bureau of Economic Research, pp. 233-338.

―――― (1973). "U.S. Income, Saving and Wealth, 1929-1969," *Review of Income and Wealth* 19, no. 4 (December):329-338.

Christensen, L. R., Jorgenson, D. W., and Lau, L. J. (1971). "Conjugate Duality and the Transcendental Logarithmic Production Function," *Econometrica* 39, no. 4 (July):255-256.

―――― (1973). "Transcendental Logarithmic Production Frontiers," *Review of Economics and Statistics* 55, no. 1 (February):28-45.

Diewert, W. E. (1976). "Exact and Superlative Index Numbers," *Journal of Econometrics* 4, no. 2 (May):115-146.

―――― (1977). "Aggregation Problems in the Measurement of Capital," Discussion Paper no. 77-09, Department of Economics, University of British Columbia.

Ezaki, M. (1977). *Nihon Keizai no Moderu Bunseki Kokumin Keizai Keisan Kara no Sekkin* [An analysis of Japanese economy: an approach from the system of national accounts]. Tokyo: Sobun-Sha.

Ezaki, M. and Jorgenson, D. W. (1973). "Measurement of Macroeconomic Performance in Japan, 1951-1968," in K. Ohkawa and Y. Hayami (eds.), *Economic Growth: The Japanese Experience Since the Meiji Era*. Vol. 1. Tokyo: Japan Economic Research Center, pp. 286-361.

Fisher, I. (1922). *The Making of Index Numbers*. Boston: Houghton Mifflin.

Goldsmith, R. W. (1955). *A Study of Saving in the United States*. Princeton, N.J.: Princeton University Press.

Gollop, F. and Jorgenson, D. W. (1977). "U.S. Productivity Growth by Industry, 1947-1973," in J. W. Kendrick and B. Vaccara (eds.), *New Developments in Productivity Measurement*. Studies in Income and Wealth, Vol. 41. New York: Columbia University Press.

Jorgenson, D. W. (1973). "The Economic Theory of Replacement and Depreciation," in W. Sellekaerts (ed.), *Econometrics and Economic Theory*. New York: Macmillan, pp. 189-221.

Jorgenson, D. W. and Griliches, Z. (1967). "The Explanation of Productivity Change," *Review of Economic Studies* 34, no. 99: 249-283.

Jorgenson, D. W. and Lau, L. J. (1977). *Duality and Technology*. Amsterdam: North Holland.

Jorgenson, D. W. and Nishimizu, M. (1978). "U.S. and Japanese Economic Growth, 1952-1974: An International Comparison," *The Economic Journal* (forthcoming).

Kaldor, N. (1957). "A Model of Economic Growth," *The Economic Journal* (December).

Kloek, T. (1966). *Indexcijfers: enige methodologisch aspecten*. The Hague: Pasmans.

Kravis, I. B., Kenessey, Z., Heston, A., and Summers, R. (1975). *A System of International Comparisons of Gross Product and Purchasing Power*. Baltimore: Johns Hopkins University.

Nishimizu, M. and Hulten, C. R. (1978). "The Sources of Japanese Economic Growth: 1955-1971," *The Review of Economics and Statistics* 60, no. 3 (August):351-361.

Ohkawa, K. and Rosovsky, H. (1973). *Japanese Economic Growth*. Stanford: Stanford University Press.

Ozawa, T. (1974). *Japan's Technological Challenge to the West, 1950-1974*. Cambridge: M.I.T. Press.

Patrick, H. (1977). "The Future of the Japanese Economy: Output and Labor Productivity," *The Journal of Japanese Studies* 3, no. 2 (Summer):219-249.

Patrick, H. and Rosovsky, H., eds. (1976). *Asia's New Giant*. Washington, D.C.: The Brookings Institution.

Peck, M. J. with the collaboration of Tamura, S. (1976). "Technology," Chapter 8 in H. Patrick and H. Rosovsky, eds., *Asia's New Giant*. Washington, D.C.: The Brookings Institution, pp. 525-586.

Theil, H. (1965). "The Information Approach to Demand Analysis," *Econometrica* 33, no. 1 (January):67-87.

Tornqvist, L. (1936). "The Bank of Finland's Consumption Price Index," *Bank of Finland Monthly Bulletin*, No. 10:1-8.

3
Japanese-U.S. Relations in Science and Technology

Takeo Sasagawa

Rivalry and cooperation have marked the postwar Japanese-U.S. relationship in science and technology as well as in commerce, currency, and other fields. After World War II, during the time when the United States was far stronger than Japan, relations between the two countries were hierarchical, like those of an elder with his immature younger brother. Both were friendly and cooperative, at least superficially so, but they were not equals. As the competitive strength of Japan and the United States began to approach an equilibrium, friction and confrontation arose and relations of mutual dependence and feelings of ambivalence deepened.

There is a characteristic of the field of science and technology, however, that sets it apart from other areas. That is, science transcends the relations between countries. "Science," it is said, "has no national frontiers," while technology, or "applied science," can sometimes be very specific and very national. However, science and technology are intertwined and interdependent. Indeed, the universality of science aided Japan in its efforts to mitigate the great gap between its technology and that of the United States in the post-World War II period, but that period is now behind us.

The new challenge lies in finding new sources of energy by which the world might be freed from dependence upon petroleum. In order to meet this challenge, meetings were held in the autumn of 1978 in Tokyo and in Washington, D.C., to plan joint Japanese-U.S. research projects in energy. To be sure, political and economic factors provided much of the impetus for these meetings. It was assumed, for example, that Japan's sharing of the costs for joint energy research and development would help to rectify the imbalance in the two countries' international balance of payments; it was understood that both countries would benefit from attaining stability in the supply of energy.

However, an even more important factor generated a strong motivation and sense of excitement, namely, the ideal and dream of the scientists of Japan and the United States—joint cooperation in the progress toward "big science" (as it was called in the Japanese press), the development of mankind's ultimate energy sources. Whether controlled-fusion energy, solar-energy conversion, or other futuristic resources discussed at the meetings, the "big science" that Japan and the United States are seeking to develop together is on a vast scale, with costs far beyond the capability of private enterprise to bear. Long-range investment of considerable sums of money will be required; true scientists will be needed, those whose search for basic truths and whose curiosity about natural phenomena are not bound by "national frontiers," any more than is science itself.

Japanese-U.S. cooperation must, of course, take into consideration their respective national interests. But, because both countries have become world powers deeply involved with international peace and prosperity, unless they are also prepared to work within a broader context of international interests, their cooperative efforts could prove fruitless. Thus, it is in regard to energy that the universality of science becomes painfully relevant: can the Japanese and U.S. governments devote national funds to programs whose results will not merely serve themselves but will ultimately become the common asset of all mankind, that is, will be for the benefit of world prosperity and the advancement of science?

Perhaps they can. In the words of the joint statement announced at the end of the meeting, Japan and the United States recognized that the energy problem was one of the major questions to be resolved for world prosperity in the twenty-first century, and that they would play a positive role in bringing about a better world through close cooperation.

The next section will briefly review Japanese-U.S. relations in the areas of technological innovation and basic scientific research in the years since the close of World War II, after which I would like to consider the new challenges facing Japan and the United States as they are seen to develop their cooperative relationships in science and technology.

The Postwar "Technology Gap"

One of the major causes for the Japanese Navy's defeat by the U.S. Navy in the Battle of Midway (regarded as the turning point of the Pacific War) lay in the difference in their ability to detect enemy warships. In addition to U.S. supremacy in decoding techniques, radar gave the U.S. Navy the decisive advantage. This is now common knowledge among the Japanese people.

Japan, isolated for nearly a decade from Western achievement and defeated in the Pacific War, was shocked to learn of the effect on overall fighting strength that resulted from the difference in the level of scientific and technological development (the Battle of Midway being but one example). To this discovery was added the startling realization that a similar gap existed between the two countries in the level of achievement of peacetime industries. In addition to those innovations that had been by-products of military science—such as radar and microwave communications technologies, jet planes, missiles, nuclear energy, and computers—the Japanese people marveled at the development of synthetic textiles, plastics, and penicillin.

Even more shocking for Japan, and a cause for despair among Japanese scientists, was the ban that the General Headquarters of the Occupation Forces imposed on scientific research relating to military affairs on the pretext of demilitarizing Japan. Aviation research and research concerning atomic isotopes were entirely prohibited. The Institute of Physical and Chemical Research was disbanded, and the cyclotrons at the University of Kyoto and the University of Osaka were destroyed. Television and radar research was also banned. Some people in the Occupation Forces seemed to wish to turn Japan into a peaceful agrarian society. Given its lack of natural resources and the paucity of land available for cultivation, Japan's future looked bleak without science and technology.

How did the Japanese people extricate themselves from this gloomy predicament? For one thing, there was a moderate level of achievement already: after all, Japan had possessed the technical ability during wartime to construct the 70,000-ton battleship, *Yamato*, and the highly efficient Zero fighter planes. Also, the high level of education that had been achieved during and after the Meiji Era (1868-1912) made it possible to learn and adapt technological innovations quickly.

Leadership was another factor. Japan was fortunate in having a well-formulated bureaucratic structure and a well-trained bureaucracy. Furthermore, the managerial level in private industry provided an invaluable resource. In his book, *Mohaya Gijutsu Nashi* (We Have Run Out of Technology), Yoshirō Hoshino, a noted commentator on science, noted that not all of Japan's management executives and technicians were despondent. Management executives, who had observed the course of events from the first stages of the war to the end, were not particularly shaken by the defeat, he said, or by the difference in technological development. In fact, men of ability in this field, while accurately gauging that difference, felt confident that they would be able to catch up. Because there were at least some technicians in various fields who were able to take the lead in adopting the new technologies developed by Europe and the United States, Japan's postwar technology made a new start.

Moreover, the postwar international environment was advantageous for Japan. Under the Cold War structure of the U.S.-Soviet confrontation, the West began to promote Japan's rebirth as a democratic industrial nation in Asia. Under the auspices of the Fulbright Exchange Program and through grants from the Ford and Rockefeller foundations, many outstanding young Japanese studied in the United States and learned of the advances that both the social and natural sciences had made. The argument that Japan owes its present prosperity solely to the advances of Western, and especially U.S., science and technology—analogous to the complaint that its growth was nurtured under the U.S. security "umbrella"—has some merit, but it ignores the factors of education, diligence, and bureaucratic and managerial leadership.

Japan, pushing on with the slogan of "catch up and go beyond" Europe and the United States, has made remarkable progress during the past thirty years. If Japan's final goal had merely been to achieve equivalence with the level of European and U.S. science and technology, the story would have had a happy ending.

Basic research was neglected, however; Japan was intent on filling the existing vacuum with imported technologies. With the exception of a few fields in which originality was shown (such as optics, including cameras), Japan—especially in the immediate postwar period—learned from the Western world and taught it very little in return.

The Science and Technology Agency addressed this problem in 1958 subtitling its 1958 white paper (the first issued after its establishment) "From Overseas Dependence to Independent Development":

> Japan's technology has already completed the stage of postwar rehabilitation. It stands at a qualitative turning point where plans must be made for the future. However, the habit persists of following the easy way of introducing foreign technologies and downgrading domestic research efforts. There is a basic need at this time to think about what should be done in the future.

Very few people were fully aware of this problem, either in government or in private industry. As a result, no real change in attitude took place until well into the 1970s.

In 1968, Japan became the third largest economy in the world. Having become a leader in international trade, it became subject to criticism by its trading partners. One of the causes of dissatisfaction, it seemed to the Japanese, was its technologically dependent position in contrast to its growing prosperity and growing dollar holdings, which Tokyo was doing little to reduce. *Fortune* magazine, for example, published an article in its February 27, 1978 issue entitled, "The Japanese Spies in

Silicon Valley." In this essay, the author maintained that Japanese companies were sending spies to ferret out industrial secrets from U.S. semiconductor companies located in Silicon Valley (along a part of the southwest corner of San Francisco Bay) and that Japan was using this stolen technology to export semiconductor goods to the United States. The Japanese consulate-general in San Francisco issued a statement flatly denying the allegation as "not true." It is possible that Japan's historical dependence might be at least partially to blame for creating the psychological atmosphere allowing the U.S. semiconductor industry to harbor such feelings of suspicion against Japanese business.

The fact remains, whatever the cause or causes for suspicion might be, that much of the science and technology that provided the motive power for Japan's great economic growth was indeed transferred into Japan from the United States. At the stage when they became commercially usable as industrial technologies, they were assimilated by Japanese manufacturers. There were many instances when, by using these technologies, Japan was able to export high-performance and high-quality products to the United States. At that time, Japan did not have vast sums to invest in research and development, nor was there any margin for risk. Faced with these circumstances, Japan felt that it was pursuing the only realistic policy. Today, however, when the United States is suffering from a staggering trade deficit and Japan is troubled by the problem of reducing its dollar reserves, a prolongation of the situation is neither desirable nor permissible by Japan or by the United States. The situation can more clearly be seen in the statistics, taking the year 1976 as an example. In that year, according to the 1977 *White Paper on Commerce*, Japan's trade balance showed an excess of exports over imports in trade with the United States amounting to $5,300 million. At the same time, according to the 1978 *White Paper on Science and Technology*, the amount paid by Japan for foreign technologies was $591 million (at the 1976 exchange rate of ¥300 to $1), and sales to other countries totaled $278 million. Of the $591 million, 64.6 percent represented imports from the United States and 24.3 percent came from three nations in Europe—West Germany (11 percent), Switzerland (7.1 percent), and England (6.2 percent). Of the $278 million representing exports of Japanese technologies to foreign countries, 38.3 percent of the payments came from Southeast Asia, 26.1 percent from Europe, and only 9.5 percent from the United States. In other words, while Japan showed a trade balance running into many billions of dollars, it was still recording a large excess of imports over exports of technologies. Foreign technology was imported primarily from the United States, (almost two-thirds), and Japanese technology was exported primarily (well over one-third) to Southeast Asia.

A brief analysis of research and development expenditures for that year further illuminates the problem. In 1976, according to the 1978 *White Paper on Science and Technology*, Japan spent a total of $9,800 million for research and development, as compared to the following totals for other industrialized nations: $36,930 million for the United States, $23,460 million for the Soviet Union, $10,230 million for West Germany, and $6,030 million for France. Of these expenditures, however, Japanese private companies provided a much higher proportion of the funding than did the Japanese government, presumably for research oriented toward the development of new products and new means of production or the improvement of existing techniques, which implies a longer range viewpoint and a greater margin for risk. The Japanese government's share of 1976 funding was 27.5 percent as compared with 54 percent for the United States, 51.7 percent for England, 54.3 percent for France, and 44.6 percent for West Germany. After subtracting the portion of government monies that went for defense-related research, the figures became: Japan, 27 percent; United States, 37.8 percent; England, 35 percent; France, 43.3 percent; and West Germany, 40.8 percent. While slightly closer, these adjusted figures still show that European countries and the United States have emphasized basic research more than Japan has and help to explain the success of these countries in developing independent capabilities for science and technology. As for the portion of funding that came from private enterprise, the value assigned to research by that sector can be determined by comparing research expenditures to total sales. As against Japan's 1.6 percent in fiscal year (FY) 1976, the figures for both the

United States and West Germany exceeded 3 percent. Even here, Japan has lagged behind the West. In its 1978 white paper, the Science and Technology Agency drew frankly self-critical conclusions from these statistics:

> Although Japan's technological capacity has caught up with the advanced countries in many fields, a difference still persists in the ability to develop independently new products and new techniques that will compete effectively internationally. In order for Japan to achieve a stable level of development, it is necessary to discard the past pattern of digesting and absorbing imported technology, and to devote greater efforts to the development of an independent technology with a high degree of originality.

International Cooperation Strengthened by the "Oil Shock"

The "oil shock" that followed the Arab-Israeli war in October 1973 deeply jolted the international economic and monetary system, exacerbating trade and currency imbalances and pinpointing oil dependence as a major cause of instability—political as well as economic. Governments of the principal oil-consuming nations, after cautious bilateral negotiations with OPEC countries, recognized that solutions must be found among themselves within the broader framework of multilateral energy policies. Conferences were called and meetings were held in Europe and in the United States, but efforts to formulate such a policy were aborted by differences in fuel priorities.

After a year of upwardly spiralling prices and faced with a gloomy projection of oil shortages, either naturally caused or politically inspired, sixteen industrialized nations sent delegates to Paris to make plans for possible emergency situations. On November 15, 1974, the International Energy Agency (IEA) was set up within the Organization for Economic Cooperation and Development. In this and subsequent meetings over the next few years members agreed to help one another in various ways. Among these were contingency plans to pool their energy resources in case of emergency, to conserve energy, to work toward stabilization of oil prices and supplies, and to promote international cooperation in the development of new and alternative energy sources, such as solar energy, controlled nuclear fusion, geothermal energy, and coal liquefaction. Members also agreed to reappraise the entire problem of energy supply in a broader perspective in hopes of decreasing their dangerous dependence upon oil and the oil-producing countries.

Japan was not among the charter members of IEA—not because its dependence upon oil was minimal but because it was too great. Ninety-nine percent of the oil consumed in Japan was derived from foreign imports. The IEA was viewed as a counterorganization to the OPEC. It was therefore clear that Japanese leaders' concern about protecting their oil supply delayed their joining the Agency. While the IEA itself did not at first attract Japan, planning for international research and development programs in basic energy science and technology aroused great interest from the beginning.

In the early 1960s, the Japanese and U.S. governments had encouraged scientific cooperation in a number of areas—ecological research of the Pacific Ocean environs; joint research on earthquakes, volcanoes, and tidal waves; and exchange of the results of research for the prevention of cancer. With the "oil shock" of 1973 as a turning point, scientific cooperation between the Japanese and U.S. governments expanded to the field of energy development. Until 1974 Japanese budgetary resources had been concentrated on nuclear energy programs, including nuclear fusion; indeed, with practically no domestic sources of oil, coal, or other fossil fuels, roughly 85 percent of the energy research and development budget had been allocated to such studies. In that year, however, Japan turned its attention to new energy sources other than atomic energy with, for example, the "Sunshine Project." This program, sponsored and funded by the Ministry of International Trade and Industry, was designed to develop solar and geothermal energy resources in Japan.

At the same time, talks with other nations—including Mexico, Canada, and Brazil—were initiated at the highest levels of the Japanese government, talks intended to promote international cooperation for basic scientific research in alternative energy sources. An agreement for cooperation in research and development of energy resources was signed by U.S. Secretary of State Henry Kissinger and Japanese Ambassador to the United States Yasushi Yasukawa in July 1974. With it, the concept of international cooperation for energy research was officially sanctioned as a policy of the Japanese government. There remained only the funding of specific programs to implement it, but there it rested for the next three years while other issues demanded the attention of the world.

In the summer of 1977, the fourth Japan–United States Shimoda conference for intellectual exchange was held. Delegates included members of the U.S. Congress and the Japanese Diet, leaders of the two nations' business communities, scholars, and journalists. Shimoda had been chosen as the site for the conferences because it was there that Commodore Perry had arrived in 1853 with his "black ships" of the U.S. Navy, demanding that the Tokugawa Shogunate open Japan to international diplomatic relations and commerce.

Many problems were frankly discussed. One of these, a matter bothering many members of the U.S. delegation, was voiced by Senator John Glenn (D-Ohio), chairman of the subcommittee on East Asian and Pacific Affairs of the Senate Committee on Foreign Relations (and also well known as a pioneer astronaut). During a discussion on the United States–Japan Security Pact, Senator Glenn asked how long Japan would continue to have a "free ride" on U.S. defense appropriations:

> What of the Japanese-U.S. military relationship? Critics in the United States habitually talk of the "free ride" or "free umbrella" provided Japan by the United States, and it is no small item. When the United States is running sizeable trade deficits and Japan has a current-account surplus, it is difficult to understand why Japan cannot increase its defense efforts in cooperation with the United States. Certainly the present U.S. administration and a majority in Congress recognize the domestic constraints on a major expansion of Japanese military forces. However, to ensure qualitative sufficiency for Japanese self-defense forces, improvements should be made in such areas as antisubmarine warfare equipment and fighter and patrol aircraft, all of which may require far less strict adherence to the ar-

tificially selected 1 percent GNP "barrier" now used as a limit for defense budgeting. By comparison, NATO countries average over 4.5 percent of GNP in defense expenditures. In time of need, less than an adequate defense force will be a poor bargain, whatever the percentage of GNP.[1]

Unquestionably, Japan's having in excess of a $20 billion reserve while enjoying a "free ride" on security preparations was a painful situation for both countries. The Japanese delegation undertook to explain to Senator Glenn their country's position, namely, that in its post-World War II Peace Constitution Japan had renounced the use of force in the settlement of international disputes (Article 9). Even should the government wish to change this, the opposition political parties had made it clear that they would obstruct any attempts at radically increasing Japan's military power. Having received the senator's assurances of understanding, the delegates went on to point out that one of the major causes of the United States' increasing deficit in its international accounts was the growth in its oil imports, and it was hoped that that problem would be addressed by cooperative efforts in alternative energy research.

In the official summary of the Shimoda Conference, the following concluding statement was made:

> In both countries, it was felt, the long-run energy problem was not being taken seriously enough by the public or the governments. To help meet these urgent needs, joint basic research on alternative energy sources and cooperative development of coal and other fuels were given strong support. The importance of the development of nuclear energy was stressed.

On the last day of the conference a discussion was held between Prime Minister Fukuda and the delegates. New York University President John Sawhill, former U.S. energy coordinator, suggested that hope for increasing energy supplies could be fostered by joint U.S.-Japanese research in the field of controlled nuclear-fusion energy. The prime minister had already come to the same conclusion and immediately accepted Sawhill's suggestion.

This proposal was in accordance with the prime minister's

thinking in a number of ways. He was an advocate of energy conservation, fully realizing the dampening effect this could have on economic growth. His philosophy, phrased as "limits to resources, limits to growth" (*Shigen Yūgen, siechō no genkai*), had indeed discouraged industry from investing capital for expansion. At the May 1977 London Summit Conference of the Industrialized Countries, however, on the basis of his political judgment, the prime minister had promised to promote continuous economic growth and to reduce Japan's dollar holdings. Another deep concern was the domestic financial impact of measures to reduce foreign currency accounts. For several years Japan had concentrated on accumulating foreign currency reserves while the national balance sheets were imbalanced by an overflow of red ink, over 30 percent of government expenditures being covered by the issuance of government bonds. If dollar holdings were reduced, then Japan might be forced to increase its deficit financing and thus could not by itself handle expenditures for nuclear fusion and solar energy research (which could involve many billions of dollars over a long period of time).

A joint international coordinated effort to develop these new resources seemed to offer the best chance for integrating all of these considerations into a coherent pattern. Optimistic predictions concerning energy sources would encourage the Japanese people to increase their investments and consumption, boosting economic growth. Advanced energy development technology would in itself constitute a resource and improve Japan's bargaining position vis-à-vis OPEC and other resource-rich countries. By working with the United States, the fiscal burden could be shared; and as a long-time Finance Ministry official, Fukuda found such an arrangement agreeably efficient and mutually beneficial. All of these practical reasons were augmented by Fukuda's naturally idealistic and optimistic character. Hence, he was determined to commit the necessary funds for the great purpose of solving the energy problems of the twenty-first century through a limitless energy resource: controlled nuclear fusion of hydrogen molecules found in seawater.

There was another inducement to his support, perhaps the most realistic of all. In the field of magnetic confinement for nuclear fusion, Japan was on the same level of achievement as the United States; two sides that can compete as equals can also cooperate as equals. Japan had already set as a goal the attainment of the so-called Lawson condition of energy breakeven by 1982-1983 and had decided to create a budget of ¥ 150 billion ($750 million at ¥ 200 per $1) for the design of the JT-60-TOKAMAK reactor. That Japanese scientists are able to achieve the requisite high intellectual achievement is demonstrated by Chihiro Okawa, vice-president of General Atomic in San Diego, whose "Doublet III" is a toroidal magnetic-fusion project designed to test the effectiveness of noncircular magnetic field configurations, and by Shoichi Yoshikawa, principal investigator of Princeton University Plasma Research Center's PLT TOKAMAK test reactor.

Thus, when Prime Minister Fukuda met with President Carter in the White House in May 1978 prior to the Bonn summit conference, the prime minister proposed that nuclear fusion be the central component in a program of joint research and development of new energy sources. The discussion was continued in July in a private conversation between the two leaders at the Bonn summit conference of advanced industrialized nations, paving the way for more specific plans to be formulated later in the year.

A New Challenge to Joint Energy Research

Some observers have characterized Japanese society as one based on consensus. Even a prime minister cannot get positive action on his decisions without first bringing about a consensus of opinion among his colleagues and subordinates, including officials in the government bureaucracy. For example, the epochal Japan-China Peace and Friendship Treaty, for which Fukuda received great acclaim, was brought to the Diet for formal approval only after two years of negotiations, during which the prime minister overcame the opposition within the Liberal-Democratic party of those of his colleagues who favored Taiwan. When it was finally brought to a vote, it passed immediately. Conversely, Fukuda was not successful in streamlining the government administration for cost savings, even though it was a prerequisite for financial stability. He was faced with the overwhelming resistance of the bureaucracy, which had learned of his plans prematurely by means of a "leak" to the press. Only a small group of senior advisers in the prime minister's office had known of the reorganization proposal, which they had been discussing prior to beginning the process of consensus-building.

Prime Minister Fukuda's initiative concerning joint research and development for new energy sources falls somewhere between these two extremes. Japanese scientists and some officials in the Ministry of Education and the Science and Technology Agency gave the proposal high marks. However, it would appear that the prime minister may not have given himself enough time to have the proposal thoroughly aired within the Ministry of Finance, which has the responsibility for providing the funds for such projects.

U.S. scientists and government officials assumed that the prime minister could commit himself to the large-scale funding requirements that would be needed, and they were deeply impressed with his idealistic proposal that some tangible contribution should be made to the energy needs of future generations. However, officials in the U.S. Department of Energy (DOE) gave higher priority to finding immediate alternatives to liquid fuels, believing that it would be too long a time before controlled nuclear fusion could become a viable alternative.

These differences in approach surfaced at the first meeting of the working group on Japanese-U.S. cooperation in science and technology held in Tokyo, September 4-6, 1978. Japanese representatives quoted Prime Minister Fukuda as saying that science and technology were a promising field for cooperation between the two countries, that there the two countries could collaborate in their efforts to build a better world in the twenty-first century, that cooperative research areas should be expanded to include new sources of energy, and that nuclear fusion was particularly promising for joint research and development projects. Dr. John Deutsch, the Department of Energy's director of energy research, spoke for the U.S. delegation. He agreed that controlled nuclear fusion research should receive high priority, but he also said that research into coal liquefaction should be given equal treatment.

Japanese delegates were aware that the practical application of controlled nuclear fusion as an energy source could not be achieved until some time in the twenty-first century and could not counter the U.S. position that coal liquefaction could be an extremely important source of energy for the near future, particularly in the 1990s, when oil resources are expected to be seriously depleted. The delegates arrived at an agreement in principle: collaboration would take place, with emphasis being given initially to both controlled nuclear fusion and coal conversion projects. The Japanese delegation was reluctant to make detailed plans for funding, however, knowing that each budgetary item would have to receive the approval of the powerful Ministry of Finance.

The group held its second meeting November 14-16, 1978, in Washington, D.C. Its purpose was to move the discussions that had begun in Tokyo two months earlier a few steps forward. Certain conclusions were reached.

First, all projects would be jointly financed by both governments. Approximately $1 billion would be devoted to them over a ten-year period.

Second, cooperative research projects would include nuclear fusion, coal conversion, solar energy conversion-photosynthesis, geothermal energy, and high energy physics.

Third, emphasis would be given to the following projects in the field of nuclear fusion: (a) a program of scientific exchange that would include an increased flow of technical information and of scientists; (b) joint research on noncircular cross section plasma by Doublet III to achieve "High Beta TOKAMAK" (the cost of this project was initially estimated at $120 million); (c) the creation of a joint research institute to conduct theoretical and computational research in advanced plasma physics; and (d) the joint planning of non-TOKAMAK magnetic confinement concepts.

Fourth, both countries agreed to participate in two projects in the field of coal conversion: (a) Japan will participate in the U.S. project "SRC II" by assuming 25 percent of the total cost, estimated to be $700 million; (b) the United States will participate in "direct hydrogenation," the tubular-type moving-bed reactor process that was developed in Japan, by assuming 25 percent of the total cost, estimated to be 4 billion yen (approximately $200 million) for Phase I, and 26 billion yen (approximately $2,300 million) for Phase II, over a period of nine years.

At this meeting agreement was also reached that the United States–Japan Joint Committee on cooperation in science and technology would examine additional projects in the near future. These were to include other proposals in the fields of controlled nuclear fusion and coal conversion, as well as in solar and geothermal energy and high energy physics.

Among these latter projects, it was reported that the U.S. delegates were especially enthusiastic in promoting joint research into high energy physics. They underlined their enthusiasm with a budget of between $13 and $19 million annually. Japanese scientists who participated in the meeting were profoundly impressed with this proposal, which reflected the "U.S. approach" emphasizing the importance of basic scientific research.

Conclusion

It is said that until the eighteenth century science and technology were considered separate fields. Building an irrigation system, constructing a clock, or casting a sword was "technology," whereas knowledge about nature and human beings or efforts to discover the principles of geometry were a part of "science." However, from the end of the nineteenth century into the twentieth century, the highest level of technology gave birth to the most advanced form of science. By means of atomic (nuclear) physics, it was possible to discover the nature and behavior of extremely basic matter (such as protons, electrons, and neutrons), which in turn led to the discovery of radioactive isotopes. This kind of scientific knowledge, when combined with advanced technology, led to the building of atomic bombs and nuclear power plants. Conversely, a profound knowledge of plasma physics and quantum mechanics is required to develop the kind of technology needed to create energy by means of controlled nuclear fusion. It is also probable that one must understand electronics in order to develop advanced computers.

Science and technology have provided the dynamic element in Japan's postwar economic growth, but most of this knowledge was imported from the United States. Moreover, according to the first white paper issued in 1958 by Japan's Science and Technology Agency, because Japan had separated science and technology, Japanese science was tied to international science and did not relate to domestic technology. Instead, Japanese technology imitated and assimilated foreign technology. Let us take nuclear reactors as an example. Japan imported light-water reactors from the United States; however, practically no attention was given to the basic scientific and engineering knowledge required to build them. All aspects of the reactors—their design, construction, and operation—were imported. The United States had devoted tens of billions of dollars over a period of thirty years to research on and development of light-water reactors.

Now Japan has agreed to participate with the United States in the research and development of controlled nuclear fusion as an energy source. If this is to be effective, it is essential that Japanese scientists and engineers engage in basic research in reactor engineering. Full collaboration with the United States on energy research and development means that Japan must not only commit funds, but must also contribute to basic research and research of its own systems. Without all of these elements, Japan will not be able to stand on an equal footing with the United States.

Because of its poverty of natural resources, Japan has no choice but to engage in research and development of new energy sources. It would have to do so independently if cooperation with the United States were impossible. Japan, and others (not just the United States) must achieve—in the shortest possible time frame—new, commercially usable sources of energy, whether the source be controlled by nuclear fusion, solar conversion-photosynthesis, or by any other alternative that is proved to be successful.

I should like to make one final point: one possible yardstick to measure the degree of Japan's fundamental commitment to conducting basic scientific research is its willingness to participate in high energy physics (HEP) research. HEP is an exploratory field at the frontier of basic research and is directed toward an understanding of the basic laws that determine the properties of energy, matter, and the forces of nature. Hence, this subject will be a salient aspect of the program to develop alternative sources of energy for the future, if it is effectively and jointly undertaken by both Japanese and U.S. scientists.

I would like to conclude with a summation by Professor Tetsuji Nishikawa, director of Japan's National Laboratory for High Energy Physics:

> In contemporary physics, there are still many unknowns concerning the forces inside elementary particles. I believe that these unknown forces, if they are explored, will become sources of energy for the next generation. That the smaller the element, the greater the energy that it can generate, is truly wonderful and mysterious. . . . European democracies are also extremely interested in HEP. Therefore, Japan–United States cooperation for basic research in this most advanced science would place Japanese-American relations in a world context, symbolizing its importance, and would be most highly esteemed.

Notes

1. John Glenn, Jr., "The Role of the United States in East Asia: A Legislative Perspective," in Herbert Passin and Akira Iriye, eds., *Encounter at Shimoda: Search for a New Pacific Partnership* (Boulder, Colo.: Westview Press, 1979), p. 41.

4
U.S. Trade Problems with Particular Reference to Japan

Eleanor M. Hadley

In 1977, the United States experienced a $27.7 billion trade deficit. Analysis of this deficit can best be performed in terms of the demand and supply factors that have contributed to it.

International Trade Demand

With extraordinary consistency—officially and unofficially—the deficit has been explained in the United States as due to the strong growth performance of the U.S. economy. It is said that our strong growth performance has attracted imports whereas, inasmuch as other strong economies have not shouldered their responsibility, our exports have not had comparable opportunity. (Formulated this way a neat political trick is performed—our trade problems are not our fault but the fault of others.) The argument is that the GNP is the major determinant of imports.[1] Parties inside and outside of the government take this position, and the press articulates it.

Failure of Our Trading Partners to Achieve Strong Growth

Item: Chase Manhattan Bank, *Business in Brief*, October 1977:

> If there is a single most important cause [of the worsening trade balance], it is probably the continued sluggish economic activity

in other industrialized nations, which is dampening demand for U.S. exports. . . . The outlook is . . . less promising largely because the U.S. economy is growing more rapidly than the economies of most other nations. In 1976 U.S. economic growth exceeded the average of the rest of the industrialized world by one-third, and the margin has risen to 60 percent in 1977.

Item: Council of Economic Advisors, *Report*, January 1978 (p. 110):

Although an increase in the deficit was widely expected, the magnitude of the shift proved to be much greater than anticipated, since growth abroad failed to develop as strongly as expected and U.S. oil imports were pushed up by a series of unforeseen developments.

Item: Frank A. Weil, assistant secretary of commerce, July 24, 1978, before the Senate Foreign Relations Subcommittee on Foreign Economic Policy:

Since 1975, the lagging growth rates in foreign economies have limited the growth of our export markets, while at the same time, our faster domestic growth has increased imports.

Item: Paul Lewis, the *New York Times*, July 26, 1978:

The change of emphasis reflects the failure of the OECD's so-called "locomotive" recovery strategy under which other economically strong countries, like West Germany and Japan, were urged to take some of the burden of sustaining world growth off the United States' shoulders by expanding their economies faster and taking in more imports.

Neither West Germany nor Japan followed the advice, with the result that America's relatively fast rate of economic growth led to overheating and an unsustainable balance-of-payments deficit with the rest of the world.

Item: Bank for International Settlements (BIS), Annual Report, June 1978 (p. 9):

The major expansionary stimulus last year came . . . from the

United States, which alone among the large developed countries expanded at a fairly rapid pace.... As a result, U.S. imports of goods and services increased in real terms from 1976 to 1977 by 10.5 per cent, while exports rose by less than 2 per cent.

However, the BIS is also candid enough to write (p. 69):

The poor performance of U.S. exports over the last three years, when world trade in manufactures expanded by 10 per cent, is difficult to explain.

The foregoing excerpts lead one to ask questions. First, is it true that U.S. growth has been distinctly above that of other economies, particularly that of Japan? Second, while admitting GNP performance to be a dominant factor shaping trade flows, can one proceed from the general to the particular and rest in comfortable assurance that it adequately explains current U.S. trade problems? The first question is factual, and the answer is "no." The second question is interpretative, and in my judgment the answer is also "no."

In real terms, the growth of the Japanese economy in recent years has equaled or exceeded that of the United States. During much of the 1960s, Japan's GNP grew at the rate of 10 percent per year, while that of the United States grew at around 4 percent per year.

When confronted with relative U.S. and Japanese GNP growth rates, some who subscribe to the currently popular version of determination of trade, namely that trade is determined by GNP, are likely to fall back on the argument that Japan's economy has grown less rapidly than pledged at various summits—as have all others—or that the Japanese performance is below its long-term trend line. Still others, including some prominent U.S. economists, opined in the early 1970s that the world would not further countenance such Japanese growth because we were moving into a new era of world demand pressing on world supplies in which such high growth put excessive pressure on world resources. Japan, with its paucity of resources, is the world's largest importer of raw materials.

Explanations for the imbalance in Japanese-U.S. trade relations have their faddish qualities. During the 1960s, when Japan's GNP was increasing at an average annual rate of 10 percent, there was no mention of GNP shaping trade. At that time, both official and unofficial commentators explained that we could not sell to Japan because of its innumerable trade barriers, both tariff and nontariff. The statistics do not support this claim. During the years 1964-1970, U.S. exports to Japan grew at essentially double the rate of U.S. exports to the world—at 16 percent rather than 8.5 percent. The only possible explanation for this seemed to be Japan's growth rate of 10.8 percent. The other half of the story, however, was that Japan's exports to the United States in the same time period were more buoyant still. While the U.S. economy was growing at 3.8 percent and its imports from the world were increasing 13 percent yearly, imports from Japan were growing at 22 percent. Thus, GNP was a powerful influence in shaping trade flows, but it was obviously not the sole influence.

Floating Exchange Rates and Price Competitiveness

The U.S. government's attitude toward the U.S. trade performance has inherent contradictions. While the administration basically blames sluggish foreign growth for the U.S. trade deficit, its remedy for the problem—floating exchange rates—implicitly concedes that U.S. products lack price competitiveness, a situation that the Council of Economic Advisors (CEA) simultaneously admits and denies. The January 1978 CEA report states:

> The weak U.S. export performance and the rise in the trade deficit in 1977 does not appear to stem from trends in relative domestic prices. U.S. and foreign prices measured in dollars held about the same relationship in early 1977 as in mid-1974, although there have been fluctuations in the interim. There has been some shift in relative export prices for manufactured goods, however, suggesting a greater willingness on the part of exporters in some foreign economies to compete on the basis of price. Nevertheless the depreciation of the dollar in late 1977 should result in a noticeable improvement in U.S. com-

U.S. Trade Problems with Particular Reference to Japan 61

petitiveness, with the trade volume response occurring after a lag of 1 or 2 years.[2]

Despite a U.S. trade deficit of $27 billion and rising industry and labor appeals to the government to erect barriers against imports, this appraisal of the U.S. situation focuses on total exports and only alludes to manufactured exports. In contrast, the June 1978 Report of the Bank for International Settlement (BIS) describes U.S. price competitiveness this way (p. 69):

> In world markets the U.S. position had deteriorated relative to those of its main competitors, namely Japan and Germany. Between the second halves of 1973 and 1976, for instance, the dollar prices of U.S. manufactured exports rose by nearly 50 per cent, roughly double the corresponding increases for German and Japanese exports. In addition, broad measures of competitiveness ignore the impact both of the growing volume of manufactured goods exported by developing countries and of the erosion of the technological lead formerly enjoyed by the United States.

As the value of the dollar continued to decline, a good many Japanese (not to mention other foreigners) saw the unconcern of the United States as verging on stark irresponsibility. Between the first quarter of 1977 and October 1978, the yen appreciated 36 percent against the dollar and 23 percent against the mark.[3] During most of 1978, the administration's approach to the enormous imbalance in trade between Japan and the United States seemed to be to tell Japan to grow faster, while bemusedly watching the appreciation of the yen against the dollar.

One consequence of the major realignment of the yen-dollar rates has been that petroleum, the price of which is denominated in dollars, has become 36 percent cheaper to the Japanese than to ourselves. The prices of Japanese imports have generally fallen. And so likewise have the yen prices of Japanese exports. For example, a comparison between April 1977 and April 1978 shows that the prices of Japanese imports declined 17.3 percent, while the prices of Japanese exports fell 5.2 percent. A comparison of the figures for October 1977 and October

1978 shows an even greater decline: 21.4 percent in import prices and 8.3 percent in export prices.⁴

The Depreciating Dollar

Between the early 1970s and November 1978, the United States has held sharply contrasting views on the depreciation of the dollar. Washington's official line in the period preceding the Smithsonian agreement of the spring of 1973 (when the world went on a floating system) was that, because the dollar was the world's reserve currency, the United States could not realign the dollar but had to wait for other governments to realign their currencies to the dollar. Our valid complaint then was that such realignments in certain conspicuous cases were not taking place, most especially in the case of the yen. For 1977 and much of 1978, the U.S. official position swung to the opposite extreme of allowing the dollar to fall. Since November 1978, however, the administration has begun to recognize the seriousness of the matter.

But so unreliable has the dollar become as a transaction currency and a store of value that the United States may have to forgo its unique position as provider of the world's reserve currency, a status that freed it, as Charles de Gaulle was so fond of pointing out, from having to operate within balance-of-payments constraints. The lack of another currency that can readily play this world role, as well as a perceived awkwardness in pricing in Special Drawing Rights (SDRs), may however extend the role of the dollar for some time to come.

Supply Factors Affecting International Trade

The foregoing examination of the relationship between GNP performance and trade and of U.S. reliance on a depreciating dollar as a solution to the lack of price competitiveness leads me to conclude that U.S. trade problems deserve far more careful attention than they have been given within the administration and the Congress. The conventional wisdom is to seek a solution on the demand side of the equation. While not in the least denying the power of the demand side to shape trade flows, I believe that the supply side of the equation also has governing qualities.⁵

Thus, in my judgment, we need to give critical attention to such items as relative rates of investment and savings, research and development expenditures, competition in the domestic market, labor-management relations, corporate financing, productivity, and so forth. Wassily Leontief in a 1974 interview in *Challenge* magazine commented:

> I'm rather skeptical about the usefulness of very aggregative, essentially symbolic descriptions of the state of the economic system. It can be effectively explained only in terms of rather deep-lying details. For example, you cannot deal with various aspects of technological development, trends in different industries, and the now very fashionable problems of resources and pollution in aggregative terms. As a matter of fact, the problem of inflation cannot be dealt with in aggregative terms either.[6]

Investment

Investment in plant and equipment inescapably has a profound effect upon a country's competitiveness. The ratio of gross fixed capital formation (excluding residential) to gross domestic product (GDP) will be seen in Table 4.1. This table shows that the United States has the weakest record of any major industrial country in that most vital of indicators, capital investment.

Although it is the rankest of heresies to raise the question, I have long wondered whether the scale of U.S. investment outside of the United States did not have a bearing on the scale of investment within the United States. For the years 1971-1975 inclusive, U.S. investment in manufacturing outside of the United States amounted to 28 percent of investment within the United States. If petroleum is added to manufacturing, the proportion is 41 percent.[7] Investment outside the United States may add to dividend flows to the United States but it does not add to the productivity and competitiveness of the U.S. economy or to U.S. employment. While the subject is highly contentious, I doubt that foreign investment strengthens the U.S. balance of payments.

Another way of comparing capital formation among economies is to compare the growth rate of gross fixed capital. An-

TABLE 4.1
Ratio of Gross Fixed Capital Formation to Gross Domestic Product[a], 1970 to 1977
(in percent)

Period	United States	Japan	Germany	France	United Kingdom	Italy	Canada
1970	13.7	27.7	20.0	16.7	15.2	14.3	16.8
1971	13.2	27.3	19.1	16.8	15.0	14.4	16.7
1972	13.3	26.9	17.9	16.8	16.0	14.0	16.2
1973	13.6	27.8	16.6	16.6	16.8	14.9	16.4
1974	14.1	26.2	15.4	16.9	16.0	16.1	17.1
1975	13.0	23.0	15.1	16.0	15.4	14.7	18.5
1976	12.3	21.7	15.1	15.9	14.5	14.5	16.7
1977	10.0	n.a.	n.a.	n.a.	n.a.	n.a.	17.0

[a]Gross fixed capital formation excludes residential construction. Gross domestic product is in terms of purchaser value.

Source: Organization for Economic Cooperation and Development, National Accounts Statistics, 1976, and Quarterly National Accounts Statistics, Third Quarter 1978.

drea Boltho, in *Japan, An Economic Survey*, has combined a number of sources to produce a comparison of seven countries, which is reproduced here as Table 4.2.[8] Again, the United States is the lowest among the countries shown.

Savings

Personal saving accounts for the major portion of net saving in many industrialized economies. In the United States, household savings are more than two or three times the size of corporate net savings. Yet, what do we find when comparing personal rates of saving among leading economies? Table 4.3 shows that the United States has far lower rates of saving than six other industrialized countries and that its saving ratio declined in 1976 and 1977.

The ratio of personal saving to personal disposable income in the U.S. economy is but one-third of its level in Japan, one-half that of Germany, and with the exception of 1970-1971 well below that of Great Britain. As is apparent from Table 4.3 the United States is alone in the meagerness of its personal savings. The implications are disturbing. A nation is competitive because of its investments in new plant and equipment. The wherewithal for new plant and equipment comes from corporate and personal savings.

Absence of Statistics on Age of Plant and Equipment

The age of plant and equipment indicates in an abbreviated manner the likely competitiveness of facilities. In most industries, technology is continuously changing so that 1975 equipment will have properties that 1965 equipment does not have. Besides the fact that the United States has proportionally far lower levels of investment and saving than Japan, Germany, and its other trading partners, it does not have any official statistics on the age of plant and equipment.

Gratifyingly enough, a 1976 conference of representatives of business, labor, and universities concluded that such data would be desirable. The report on the conference summarized the proceedings this way:

> While the many differences in approach and analysis among the participants led, inevitably, to differences in proposals

TABLE 4.2
Growth Rates of Gross Capital Stock During Selected Periods
(average annual percentage changes)

	Total	Agriculture	Industry	Services
Japan[1] (1954 to 1971)[2]	10.1	5.6	12.5	9.6
France[3] (1953 to 1970)	5.3	4.3	5.8	4.7
Germany[1] (1952 to 1971)[2]	6.4	3.4	} 6.9 {	
Italy[3] (1953 to 1971)	5.8	4.6	6.6	6.2
United Kingdom[4] (1954 to 1972)[2]	3.8	2.7	4.2	3.6
United States[5] (1953 to 1970)[2]	3.6	1.9	3.3	3.9
Soviet Union[6] (1950-2 to 1967-9)	8.8	7.4	10.8	8.3

Note: Figures are not strictly comparable.

1. Private, excluding dwellings.
2. End-year to end-year.
3. Excluding public administration and dwellings.
4. Total, excluding dwellings; industry excludes textiles which are incorporated in services.
5. Private, excluding dwellings; industry covers manufacturing only.
6. Excluding dwellings.

(continued)

TABLE 4.2 (continued)

Source: This table is reproduced from Andrea Boltho, Japan, An Economic Survey, Oxford University Press, 1975, p. 11. Its sources were as follows: Japan: E.P.A., "Gross Fixed Capital Stock of Private Enterprises," mimeo, 1973; France: J. Mairesse, L'Evolution du capital fixé productif, Collections de FINSEE, Serie C, 1972; Italy: G. Esposito, "Il capitale fisso in Italia per settori di attivita economica nel periodo 1951-71," Annali di Statistica, vol. 27, ISTAT 1973; Germany: Wirtschaft und Statistik, Oct. 1971 and Nov. 1972; United Kingdom: National Income and Expenditure, 1964 and 1973; United States: Survey of Current Business, March 1974; Soviet Union: U.N. (E.C.E.), Economic Survey of Europe in 1971, Pt. I.

TABLE 4.3
Ratio of Personal Savings to Disposable Personal Income, 1970 to 1977
(in percent)

Period	United States	Japan	Germany	France	United Kingdom	Italy	Canada
1970	7.4	20.0	14.8	12.6	8.8	16.0	5.3
1971	7.7	20.7	14.6	12.4	8.5	18.7	5.9
1972	6.2	21.9	15.8	12.1	10.4	19.7	7.4
1973	7.8	25.1	15.0	13.2	11.6	19.7	9.1
1974	7.3	25.7	16.2	12.6	14.0	n.a.	10.1
1975	7.4	25.1	16.9	n.a.	15.4	n.a.	11.0
1976	5.6	24.3	15.3	n.a.	14.9	n.a.	10.6
1977	5.1	n.a.	14.8	n.a.	14.5	n.a.	10.7

Source: U.S. Department of Commerce, *International Economic Indicators*, June, 1978, p. 44.

for action, the participants did agree on certain suggested measures. . . . An inquiry should be undertaken into the comparative age and quality of the stocks of capital goods, arranged by industrial sectors, within the United States and other countries. Such a study should emphasize comparison of U.S. industries with those in other countries of the OECD.[9]

Needless to say I heartily second this motion.

Research and Development

In recent years, the United States has been spending a smaller proportion of GNP on research and development (R and D) than was true earlier. Our relative expenditures have been falling at a time when the relative expenditures of Japan have been sharply rising. Not only is our proportion falling, but it is overstated for commercial purposes. Our R and D has centered heavily on space and the military.

Another way of looking at the productiveness of our R and D is to note the proportion of U.S. patents issued to foreigners—and to *which* foreigners. Foreigners have been accounting for a steadily rising proportion of patents. Moreover, Japan alone accounts for the rise. The proportion of U.S. patents issued to the Japanese has risen from 16 percent in 1961 to 29 percent in 1973. While the rising proportion of U.S. patents issued to foreigners is both unsurprising and welcome, it is also a cause for possible concern. We could not expect the highly artificial situation of the late 1940s and early 1950s to continue. The disparity between the U.S. and other economies was necessarily but a temporary circumstance. The rise is a welcome development inasmuch as foreign-held U.S. patents suggest a possible opportunity for U.S. licensing, and licensing is a far cheaper way of acquiring technology than developing it on one's own. In licensing one pays only for success; in R and D one pays for both success and failure. The rising proportion of U.S. patents issued to foreigners, however, could also imply a decline in U.S. R and D performance, and this is the worrisome aspect. The bare statistics do not give guidance in how to allocate causal factors.

Technology Transfer

I have long had profound doubts with respect to our conventional attitude toward technology transfer. Our conventional attitude is to take enormous pride in the "apparently" greater flow of technology out of rather than into the United States. Outflow has been "seemingly" some ten times inflow. I use "apparently" and "seemingly" advisedly for such statistics are based on receipts and payments on licensing fees. Inasmuch as licensing payments typically continue for many years, the data for any year include both payments on previously licensed technology and on new arrangements entered in that year. In *U.S. Statistics on International Technology Transfer—Need for Additional Measures,* the General Accounting Office (GAO) called attention to the importance of distinguishing between cumulative and current amounts for purposes of policy work. At the present time the United States has no information on the trend in new technology agreements. Japan does. Japanese statistics are presented two ways, cumulatively for purposes of balance of payments reporting to the International Monetary Fund (IMF) and on a current basis.[10]

But is it good public policy to favor a greater outflow than inflow of technology? I think not. I believe that the United States would be well advised to encourage a balance between outflow and inflow. Increasingly, there is technology "out there."[11] It is to be hoped that our corporations are not lulled by our earlier years of technological superiority into the "not invented here" syndrome, under which it is assumed that if the technology is not American it does not exist. A casual remark by a U.S. Information Agency (USIA) officer some two years ago that the USIA only publicized the export of U.S. technology and did not mention our technology imports is suggestive of our national attitudes.

From the point of view of the competitiveness of the economy, there is more to the R and D and technology transfer issue than invention and acquisition. There is diffusion—how widely the advanced technology gets adopted by the industry in question, not just by one or two firms. There is a real question as to whether the United States does as strong a job on diffusion as certain of our trading partners. Where saving and investment are high and where equipment is continuously being added, the diffusion of new developments is far more likely than where one is dealing with equipment in plants built ten, twenty, forty, sixty and even eighty years ago.

Relative Competitiveness of the Japanese and U.S. National Markets

Americans typically believe that the U.S. market is competitive and Japan's is cartelized and monopolistic, but the facts may be quite different. For many years I imagined that the competitiveness of an economy could be "read off" market structure in conjunction with antitrust statutes. I no longer believe so. I have not seen market structure statistics for the United States and Japan for the most recent years, but my guess, based on earlier statistics for the 1960s, is that market structure in Japan and in the United States in key industries is remarkably similar. While the Japanese antitrust statute is considerably more vigorous than most Americans imagine, I am quite prepared to admit that U.S. statutes are more "robust." Why do I then believe that the Japanese market may be more competitive than the U.S.? I so believe out of two considerations, one sociological and the other involving the respective role of international trade. There is intense rivalry in the Japanese market for market share. Workers define themselves in terms of their company, and in Japan's hierarchical world it is important to be in first place.[12] There is no equivalent rivalry in the U.S. market. The relationship among our oligopolists is more "cordial."

International trade fosters competitiveness both in exports and in imports, when imports are "independent." Regardless of the existence or nonexistence of "cordial oligopoly" among leading domestic producers, when competing in international markets, products have to be internationally competitive. Even in a world of multinational enterprises, there are very few international markets where dominance exists or is assured. Typically, price competition in international trade is far keener than in domestic markets. Similarly, when imports come in independently and not by a multinational corporation, they enhance competition. I have long speculated that part of the price competitiveness of Japanese imports in the U.S. market is due to the fact that they have been overwhelmingly independent imports. Out of a fear that outlived its reason, Japan was slow to open its economy to international investment.[13] Thus, in contrast to imports from Canada in particular, but also significantly to those from Europe, Korea, and Taiwan, Japanese products represent an injection of competition into the U.S. market.

The U.S. attitude toward exports contrasts sharply with the Japanese attitude. The United States, with its rich endowment of resources and continental-sized domestic market, has regarded exports as a luxury, as it were, something that could be taken or left. Thus, despite the enormous 1977 trade deficit of $27 billion and the prospects that it will approach $30 billion in 1978, the U.S. government did not announce any specific actions for bringing trade into balance until late September 1978. This casual attitude was accentuated by the fact that the dollar is the world's reserve currency, so that unlike the other economies of the world the United States has not felt the same sharpness of balance-of-payments constraints.

Because Japan has had to export in order to pay for vitally necessary industrial raw materials and food products, export markets have played a key role in Japanese economic policy, a totally different role than in the case of the well-endowed United States. For essentially a century, 1868-1968, exports were a restraining factor on Japanese economic development. Export performance determined the pace of development. Thus it has been of greatest importance to Japan to identify markets of export potential and to maximize opportunities. So basic have exports been to Japanese economic development that one finds the significance of international trade explained in elementary and junior or high school textbooks.

Labor-Management Relations

Because in Japan workers typically define themselves in terms of their employment group, labor-management relations rest on a quite different foundation than they do in the United States. In Japan, labor and management seek corporate success. Days lost by strike are a mere fraction of those lost in the United States.

And, because "success" in the Japanese context is conceived not only in terms of the domestic market but the export market as well, the price consequences of cordial relations are quite different than found in the United States where we typically think of the domestic market alone. When one thinks of the domestic market alone, one's only concern with international trade is with imports and here it is possible to appeal to the government to keep them out.

The U.S. steel industry is a good example of the consequences in the export market of cordial relations between management and labor. Wages in steel have risen 50 percent faster than wages in the rest of industry. Big labor has now been added to concentrated industry. For an industry that has given little attention to its international competitiveness, imports can be troublesome. The steel industry's method of meeting this problem has been to plead for government protection. The trigger-price mechanism, in the guise of preventing dumping—novelly defined—vastly minimizes foreign competition. Instead of a battering ram, there is but a gentle knock on the door. But a steel industry that has higher costs than our industrialized competitors not only affects international competitiveness in steel but in automobiles and in all the myriad products where this metal is important.

Other Factors Affecting International Competitiveness

Military industrial complex. Part of the lack of U.S. international competitive strength, particularly among consumer products, may result from the allocation of our most talented entrepreneurial talent to production for the military. Typically government contracting is a "lusher" field than the chase of the marketplace. When this sector attracts our most talented managerial persons, less talent is available for the civilian sector where most international trade takes place. Our weakest trade performance in manufactures is in consumer goods.

Bank financing versus capital market financing. I increasingly wonder whether Japan does not extract international competitive advantage by handling its corporate financing primarily through bank borrowing rather than through the capital market. When a company borrows from the capital market, it must be able to show fairly quick results on the loan in its annual report. Japanese banks do not require entrepreneurs to report such quick results and leave borrowers remarkably on their own so long as they are meeting obligations. Thus bank borrowing has advantages, except in situations of slow growth when it accentuates risks. An entrepreneur's ability to take the longer view can lead to long-run advantages.

Changing the mix of industries. Whether or not a nation perceives an advantage in changing its industrial mix over time probably greatly reflects deep-seated philosophical attitudes. One of the striking contrasts between the United States and Japan is Japan's willingness to believe that industries of tomorrow are not likely to be the industries of today or yesterday. Change seems normal to the Japanese. Most Americans do not perceive that changes in economic development elsewhere in the world are likely to predetermine change in the United States.

Productivity

When all of these factors are put together, there turns out to be a striking difference in the growth rates of labor productivity not only between the United States and Japan but also between the United States and its other trading partners. (Growth rates are, of course, to be distinguished from absolute levels of growth.) In the decade 1967-1977, Japanese labor productivity rose at a rate four times that of the United States. Over the decade, the U.S. improvement, like that of Britain, was 27 percent; West Germany's was 70 percent and Japan's was 107 percent. In the space of a decade, a Japanese worker on the average was able to turn out twice the amount of work turned out in years earlier; in the United States the gain was only a quarter more. The results in comparative annual changes are shown in Table 4.4.

These productivity statistics understate national changes in productivity because they are calculated from the domestic economy alone. No allowance is made for changes in terms of international trade. Although it is difficult to quantify the impact of such changes with any precision, clearly the United

TABLE 4.4
Output per Hour in Manufacturing in Selected Countries, 1960 to 1976

(average annual percent change)

Country	1960-76	1960-66	1966-76	1970-76
United States	2.9	4.0	2.2	2.9
Canada	3.8	4.3	3.5	3.0
Japan	8.9	8.8	8.9	5.8
Belgium[a]	6.8	5.0	8.1	7.8
Denmark	7.0	5.4	8.0	7.2
France	5.7	5.5	5.8	6.0
Germany	5.9	6.0	5.8	6.0
Italy	5.8	6.7	5.3	5.4
Netherlands[a]	6.7	5.6	7.4	5.8
Sweden	5.7	6.5	5.2	3.5
Switzerland	4.3	2.9	5.1	3.8
United Kingdom	3.3	3.7	3.1	2.9

[a] 1975 instead of 1976

Note: Data for 1976 are preliminary estimates. Percent changes are compound rates of change.

Source: Bureau of Labor Statistics, U.S. Department of Labor.

States is now obliged to export more goods for a given quantity of imports. While this is true of all of the oil-importing countries of the world, there are marked country-to-country differences in the relationship between import prices and export prices. As Penelope Hartland-Thunberg points out, "The fact that larger quantities of U.S. goods are now required in exchange for one barrel of oil means that on the world market the real productivity of U.S. labor and capital is lower."[14] Her article introduced me to the fact that standard productivity analysis, as discussed by Edward Denison and other analysts, ignores the impact on the domestic economy of the price relations of international trade.

Conclusion

For both the United States and Japan the present is a historical turning point. The overwhelming dominance of the United States in the postwar world could not have been expected to last. The U.S. economy was strengthened by World War II whereas all other major economies were grievously weakened. The U.S. economy will undoubtedly remain the strongest economy in the world, but the distance between it and other key economies will no longer be so great.

Through hard work, Japan has now attained a status of world, rather than merely regional, power and it must begin to conceive policy not only in terms of the consequences to its own domestic economy but also in terms of the consequences to others. Buddhist strictures against getting puffed up seem to inhibit the ability of many Japanese to see themselves as others see them. Also, of course, it is easier to design policy when one has only one's own nation to consider. But with the international stature that Japan has attained come international obligations.

Pressed by the United States and European countries to expand its economy and stimulate its weak private sector, the Japanese government has sharply increased public expenditures in the 1978-1979 budget even though such expenditures required a budget deficit of 37 percent or, expressed as a percentage of GNP, a deficit of 10 percent. To appreciate the magnitude of the risk involved one needs only to think of the scale of public debate in this country over a budget deficit of 10 percent or 4 percent of GNP. The Japanese administration is being pushed into taking an enormous gamble. Certainly the world can only hope that Japan will be able to carry through the effort without reigniting inflationary pressures. To date Japan and Germany have done an extraordinary job of bringing their inflation under control.

In longer-range terms, this historical turning point offers Japan the opportunity to meet basic needs that had taken second place for the past century while the nation concentrated first on protecting its national identity, then engaged in empire building, and since World War II concentrated on catching up with Europe. Japan now has the opportunity to put resources into badly needed housing, into greatly expanded sanitation systems, into more commodious school buildings, into better hospital facilities, and so forth. These sectors of the Japanese economy have long awaited their turn for official attention.

Notes

1. The argument takes various forms: (1) that GNP shapes *both* imports and exports; (2) that industrial production shapes imports more than GNP; and (3) that GNP in the cyclical, not secular, sense, shapes trade flows.

2. Council of Economic Advisors, Economic Reports, 1978, p. 110.

3. IMF, *International Financial Statistics*, December 1978.

4. Bank of Japan, *Export and Import Price Index, Monthly* (April 1978), p. 4; ibid., October 1978, p. 4. Only 1 percent of Japan's imports are denominated in yen (Masao Fujioka, "The Internationalization of the Yen," manuscript, p. 1).

5. In a presentation on productivity before the Technology Assessment Advisory Council of the Office of Technology Assessment on July 20, 1978, J. Fred Bucy, president of Texas Instruments, similarly emphasized the supply side of the equation.

6. *Challenge*, July-August 1974, p. 35.

7. National Academy of Engineering, National Research Council, *Technology, Trade and the U.S. Economy* (Washington, D.C.: National Academy of Sciences, 1978), p. 73. This publication cites various issues of the U.S. Department of Commerce, *Survey of Current Business*, as the source of these figures.

8. Andrea Boltho, *Japan, An Economic Survey* (London: Oxford University Press, 1975), p. 11.

9. The National Academy of Engineering, National Research Council, *Technology, Trade and the U.S. Economy*, p. 5.

10. Merton Peck and Shuji Tamura, "Technology," in Hugh Patrick and Henry Rosovsky, eds., *Asia's New Giant* (Washington, D.C.: Brookings, 1976), p. 541.

11. In reviewing "Location and Diffusion of Textile Machinery In-

novations," a paper given at the Southern Economic Conference, November 1978, William Davidson commented:

> As Dr. Benvignati notes, "Reverse technology gaps" have received insufficient attention from U.S. researchers. This phenomenon deserves far more study than it has been given. It is relevant not only in laggard industries such as textile machinery and steel, but in more advanced sectors as well.

12. See, for example, Chie Nakane, *Japanese Society* (Berkeley and Los Angeles: University of California Press, 1972), esp. pp. 3, 88-92.

13. Boltho, *Japan, An Economic Survey*, endorses Japan's reluctance. "Japan has been a good deal more successful than Western Europe in protecting itself from the onslaughts of multinational corporations" (p. 55).

14. "Prices and Crises," *Washington Review of Strategic and International Studies* (Washington, D.C.: Center for Strategic and International Studies, Georgetown University, July 1978), p. 44.

5
Japan's Foreign Trade Policy

Hiroshi Kato

In the modern world, no nation, regardless of its level of economic development and its political and economic systems, can hope to develop its economy without concern for the relationship of economic interdependence that ties all nations together to a greater or lesser degree. Even socialist states and those developing countries that have market or mixed economies are no exception, much less so the developed industrial states of Western Europe, North America, and Japan, which adhere to an open economic system. The increasing growth in the interdependence of nations in the world economy has two consequences. First, the management of one nation's economy never fails to affect the economic stability and development of other nations in one way or another. Second, domestic measures alone are not sufficient to ensure the stable development of a national economy. These days it is also necessary to stabilize the nation's external economic relations.

Since the end of World War II, external economic cooperation[1] by Japan has been subordinate to domestic considerations and colored by an atmosphere of economic nationalism; it therefore has been dependent to no small degree upon various internal political, economic, and social factors. There has been little room for policies conducive to the economic stability and growth of other nations and the development of the world economy as a whole. Under a foreign economic policy that has given top priority to the rapid growth of the Japanese economy, overseas economic cooperation has had only a secondary or tertiary significance in that it has been considered only when the nation could spare some of its economic resources. With the exception of World War II reparations, Japan has engaged in bilateral and multilateral economic cooperation only because it felt that its position in the world called for such action. Moreover, in the case of bilateral arrangements, Japan has always demanded direct economic benefits in return for any assistance, and the quality and quantity of such assistance has been directly proportional to the perceived size of the benefits. This has been the first and foremost characteristic of Japan's postwar economic aid agreements with other nations.

Another characteristic of Japan's economic assistance agreements is that Japan has no political or military designs upon recipients. The unfortunate but valuable experiences of the years before and during World War II and the benefits to be derived from economic cooperation with other states have led postwar Japan to elect to live as a peace-loving nation, as is manifest in its peace-oriented constitution. This peace-oriented policy is neither superficial nor fragile. Despite repeated outbreaks of local wars in Asia in the 1960s, not once did Japan entertain political or military ambitions or seek to wield political or military influence in the Asia-Pacific region in spite of the apparent expectations of some Western countries. In August 1978, Japanese Prime Minister Takeo Fukuda issued a statement declaring as one of Japan's three diplomatic principles that the nation would never depart from the path of peace or become a great military power, and that it would contribute to the peace of Asia and the world through this policy. In fact, Japan has pursued this basic foreign policy since the end of World War II. It is of great significance, however, that Prime Minister Fukuda chose the occasion of a summit conference of the Association of Southeast Asian Nations (ASEAN) to reaffirm this basic doctrine and belief of the Japanese people.

A third characteristic of Japan's postwar external economic policies is that, of all the available forms of economic cooperation, Japan has largely depended on official development assistance, direct private investment abroad, and export credits vis-à-vis developing nations, and on exports and international monetary and financial policies in its relations with developed countries. In either case, Japan's import policy, which was always of the utmost interest to other nations, has never taken on great importance in Japan's policies for external economic cooperation.

In these circumstances, Japan's economic relations with developed industrial states took on a dual character—the reform of Japan's export system, which had previously created a flood of Japanese products overseas, and the relaxation or abolition of import restrictions. As to the former, Japan has been curbing the sharp growth of exports by means of bilateral arrangements, known as "voluntary controls," since the latter half of the 1960s. This system of orderly exports is desirable for the reasons stated, but at the same time it also holds the danger of limiting market competition between the two countries involved. In particular, in most cases the products of oligopolistic industries are the ones most effectively regulated by voluntary export controls. It appears from this that there is a relationship of mutual reinforcement between the two countries involved in the agreement.

Liberalization of Imports

Japan's external economic cooperation policy should make it a cardinal and urgent task to ease or do away with the restrictive import measures that have been enforced since the latter half of the 1960s. Japan's traditional policy of curbing imports to protect and foster various domestic industries, such as agriculture, forestry, and small enterprises, needs to be subjected to constant review in the light of changes both within Japan and in the international economic setting. A long-term transformation of Japan's industrial structure must be smoothly carried out while minimizing the attendant social costs.

Even in regard to such products as foods, in which some measure of self-sufficiency is essential, it is possible to maintain a reasonable degree of self-sufficiency while liberalizing imports as well. If the problem is one of short-term adjustments necessitated by import liberalization, a prescription for that can be drawn from the experiences of other industries.

With respect to such commodities as industrial products in which self-sufficiency is not essential, there is no convincing reason for maintaining medium- and long-term import restrictions except in the case of new industries. The question of how to avoid adverse effects upon small businesses can be solved through a combination of short-term adjustment measures and the systematic introduction of measures for promoting the sophistication of the nation's industrial structure in the long term.

To neglect such long- and short-term measures and merely to continue with the present system of import restrictions would be the easiest policy to adopt in terms of domestic politics, but it would also be illogical for everyone concerned. The inefficient distribution of resources and the unfavorable effect on the economic welfare of consumers would be deplorable. If appropriate long- and short-term countermeasures were to be introduced, opposition to import liberalization from those engaged in agriculture, forestry, and small enterprises would largely disappear. Even if such opposition should persist, it would lose social acceptability and persuasiveness.

Foreign observers frequently complain that a major obstacle to expanding exports to Japan lies in the complexity and exclusivity of Japanese distribution channels. However, Japan's admittedly complex distribution system is not the result of any intention to discriminate against imports or to cause imported products to have high markups. It is the result of historical evolution. It is frequently assumed that Japan's imports will increase with trade liberalization. Yet, since most imported products must pass through traditional distribution channels in Japan before they reach consumers, relatively high price markups for such imports are inevitable.

Efforts obviously must be made to streamline Japan's distribution system in order to make it more efficient, both for domestic reasons and to facilitate importation. It should be remembered, however, that throughout its evolution and development, Japan's economy has been supported by precisely such a complex distribution system. Rationalization of distribution in Japan, if conducted too rapidly and too radically, could result in a sharp rise in unemployment, throwing Japan's economy into an even worse recession and making the expansion of domestic demand and imports still more difficult.

The complexity of distribution in Japan has given rise to claims that it constitutes a nontariff barrier against imports.

Japan's Foreign Trade Policy

Every country has its own established commercial traditions and practices, and while Japan's distribution system may be more complex than those of other countries, this alone is no justification for condemning the system as a nontariff barrier to imports. Foreign companies wishing to increase their sales in the Japanese market must find ways to deal satisfactorily with Japan's diverse and complex distribution system or they must take steps to develop their own distribution channels.

Nevertheless, the difficulties foreign companies face in adapting to Japan's distribution system cannot be ignored. Japanese distributors can and should show more initiative in marketing foreign products effectively. Also, Japan clearly does not need to maintain high import duties on products that Japanese manufacturers can produce and market competitively on an international scale. The government's recent decision to lift all import tariffs on automobiles is a welcome step in the right direction.

Another frequent target of foreign criticism concerns Japan's policies regarding agricultural imports. Some groups in Japan assert that Japanese residual import restrictions on agricultural products are no more extensive than those imposed by other countries. Yet such a view is difficult to support. Since a greater proportion of Japan's exports consists of manufactured goods than is the case in Western countries, if Japan's trade is in surplus, Japan must compensate by liberalizing agricultural imports sufficiently to help close the trade gap. Given the present large imbalance in Japan's trade, Japan should take positive steps to liberalize and expand agricultural imports.

Beef imports represent one example where liberalization is both possible and desirable. In view of the greater efficiency of beef industries overseas, it does not make much sense for Japan to continue to strive for self-sufficiency in beef production, especially when it must import most of the feed it requires to raise cattle.

Yet, if beef imports are to be liberalized, changes must be made in the structure of agricultural production in Japan. In particular, beef imports should be liberalized in stages in order to provide farmers sufficient time to shift from beef to other forms of production. Planned shifts in agricultural production of this sort have been carried out often in Europe and the

United States, so there is no reason why other countries would not show sympathetic understanding of Japan's needs.

Even with a liberalization of beef imports, however, the volume of beef imported by Japan will not increase much unless steps are taken to lower beef prices gradually. This can be done only if the channels for distributing beef in Japan are streamlined—a step that will require time. Japan must also move to liberalize beef imports gradually in order to avoid criticism that Japan, in seeking to reduce its trade surplus, is discriminating in favor of beef-exporting countries.

For all these reasons, Japan's liberalization of beef imports will not have much immediate effect on its overall trade balance. Nevertheless, liberalization is desirable and over the long run should result in a substantial increase in Japanese imports, particularly if appropriate measures are also taken to liberalize imports of citrus products, such as oranges. The adverse impact of greater orange imports on Japan's tangerine farmers could, in fact, be minimized by initial liberalization on a seasonal basis.

Western countries have used temporary import restrictions in the past to help domestic industries adjust to competition from Japanese and other imports. The U.S. and West German textile industries, for example, made a remarkable comeback following the mutual adjustments that resulted from the United States–Japan textile negotiations of 1970-1971. Therefore, in addition, Japan will require time to undergo adjustments in its industrial structure to reduce the nation's trade surplus.

If the United States and Western Europe demand orderly and controlled exports from Japan, they should develop plans showing how much time is required to restore the competitiveness of the protected industries. As long as these countries have the will to revitalize domestic industries that have declined in competitiveness, it is appropriate for Japan to make temporary concessions on their behalf. Yet such adjustments are possible only when both the importing and exporting countries demonstrate good faith. When the adjustments come as a result of unilateral demands, the consequences are likely to be chaotic.

Japan: A Trading Nation in a Dilemma

The Japanese economy's greatest weakness is the scarcity of raw materials, as is impressively demonstrated by the fact that Japan relies on overseas supplies to meet more than 80 percent of its energy needs as compared with less than 50 percent in 1960. The nation imports about 200 million tons of petroleum a year. Moreover, 85 percent of its oil imports come from the Middle East, and as much as 80 percent of the oil used in Japan is imported through the so-called "majors" — giant international oil companies. The ratio of dependence on overseas supplies is also high for other resources — for instance, 99 percent for iron ore, 86 percent for coke, 100 percent for bauxite, and 70 percent for copper ore.

A second weakness of the Japanese economy is its heavy reliance upon the U.S. economy. In 1977, about $22.8 billion of exports (a substantial 26.5 percent of Japan's total exports of about $85.7 billion) were destined for the United States. This has made bilateral economic ties very close, but at the same time it is one reason the two nations tend to clash over economic issues.

Japan has been widely criticized abroad for excessively relying on exports to support economic growth whenever domestic demand is too sluggish to absorb its normal share of domestic production. Critics argue that Japan should ease its dependence on exports by doing more to stimulate domestic demand, particularly by taking steps to improve social welfare and to increase the nation's standard of living.

To a certain extent this criticism is valid. A higher standard of living for the Japanese people should result in a greater domestic demand and a reduction of pressures to export. Yet, even if it is possible in theory, economic realities in Japan make it difficult to raise the living standard.

Japan's economic structure is classically one in which raw materials are imported from abroad and are processed into finished products, which are either consumed domestically or exported overseas. Since Japan lacks practically all natural resources and must, therefore, earn foreign credits to pay for the raw materials it imports, Japan cannot consume all its finished products in the domestic market but must also export some of these products overseas. In short, Japan must export in order to expand its domestic consumption.

There is nothing inherently wrong about an economic structure such as Japan's in which domestic prosperity is closely tied to export performance. The problem—and the source of Japan's current dilemma—is that exports can become so excessive as to cause disruption in the *importing* country. In turn, disruptions in Japan's foreign markets can result in protectionism, which has the effect of excluding Japanese products from those markets.

The critical task facing Japan, therefore, is to strive to expand domestic economic prosperity in relation to the expanding economic prosperity of its trading partners. What Japan must do to accomplish this task is to increase its imports from abroad while it continues to export. Historically Japan's imports have consisted primarily of imports of fuel and raw materials and imports have not necessarily been considered a direct means of enhancing the nation's standard of living. More imports of consumer and other manufactured goods, however, would help offset the impact of Japanese exports overseas while at the same time contributing to the improvement of Japan's standard of living.

Japan's Export Competitiveness:
An Economic Structure Well Adapted to World Trade

During the past two years, Japanese exports have grown at an unprecedented high rate, especially to the United States and the European Common Market. In fact, Japanese exports during 1977 registered a 44.4 percent increase over those of 1975.

Several factors account for this sudden surge in Japanese exports. The first, and perhaps most important, is that Japan's export products were highly elastic in relation to world trade—that is, Japan's exports corresponded well with the structure of world demand—at a time when the advanced industrial countries were beginning to recover from global recession and world trade in general had begun to expand. From the latter half of 1975 through 1976, moreover, the yen was undervalued relative to other currencies, giving Japanese dollar-denominated exports an added price advantage. In 1977, this advantage eroded considerably, because appreciation of the yen resulted in a series of export-price markups. However, the full effects of the yen's recent appreciation will not be felt for some time, since price elasticity for exports and imports does not fluctuate widely in the short run. In the long run, however, an appreciated yen should result in a reduction of Japanese exports.

Another important factor that should be considered in relation to the growth of Japan's exports is that economic conditions in the United States, a market accounting for about one-fourth of all Japanese exports, began to improve about 1975, accompanied by a rapidly increasing volume of imports. Since early 1976, in particular, recovery of the U.S. economy has resulted in a sharply increased flow of U.S.-bound exports from Japan. In 1976, the United States ran a $5.36 billion trade deficit with Japan, while during 1977 this trade deficit grew to $8.10 billion.

Although Japanese exports have increased dramatically, the nation's imports have lagged, in large part because of weak demand in the domestic economy. Japan chiefly imports industrial raw materials and fuel, and thus the primary variable affecting imports is the level of domestic production. Production, in turn, is affected by the level of domestic demand.

Reflecting the sluggishness of domestic demand, personal consumption in Japan in fiscal 1976 increased by only 3.9 percent, new housing by only 1.6 percent, private investment in plants and equipment by only 5.4 percent, and current government procurement expenditure by only 2.8 percent. Government-fixed capital formation, moreover, rose a mere 1.1 percent. Weak domestic demand in Japan became even more pronounced during the first half of fiscal 1977. Personal consumption grew by only 1.65 percent, while private investment in plants and equipment actually declined by 1.1 percent.

Given the sluggishness of domestic demand in Japan coupled with a high inventory-sales ratio for raw material imports, it is not surprising that during the past two years Japanese imports, especially imports of fuel and raw materials, grew at a greatly reduced rate. Yet, while lagging domestic demand in Japan has caused imports to decline and has created pressures for manufacturers to increase exports, the primary factor underlying the growth of Japanese exports and Japan's large trade and current-account surpluses is the strong competitiveness of Japanese products in international markets at a time of expanding world trade (see Table 5.1).

One often hears the contention in Western countries that the strong competitiveness of Japanese products abroad is largely due to cheap labor. Admittedly, Japanese wages were once considerably lower than those of the United States and Europe, but this is no longer the case. As Japan's economy has grown and as production has shifted toward more advanced products requiring higher worker skills, Japanese wages have steadily risen. In fact, a comparison of hourly manufacturing wages in 1976 (see Table 5.2) shows that Japanese wages are by no means low in relation to those of other advanced Western countries.

Another incorrect but widely held view abroad is that Japanese exports are highly competitive because Japan has concentrated investment in export industries, neglecting investment in social infrastructure and social welfare. A dozen or so years ago the level of investment in social welfare in Japan was inadequate, both institutionally and quantitatively. Since then, however, social welfare expenditures in Japan have greatly improved (see Table 5.3).

TABLE 5.1
Quarterly Trends in Manufacturing Productivity in Major Industrial Countries, 1976 to 1977

(1970 = 100)

Country	1976				1977	
	I	II	III	IV	I	II
Canada	128	130	142	143	145	130
United States	122	124	126	126	126	126
Japan	141	148	151	154	154	156
West Germany	135	136	134	136	143	142
France	133	133	135	136	141	139
United Kingdom	121	124	123	123	122	120

Source: Statistical Abstract of Japan, 1978, p. 279.

TABLE 5.2
Hourly Wage Rates in Major Industrial Countries, 1977[a]

Country	Hourly Wage Rate (in dollars)	Index
Japan	3.78	100.0
Canada	6.01	159.0
France	3.63	96.0
United Kingdom	2.80	74.1
United States	6.01	159.0
West Germany	5.51	145.8

[a] Hourly wage rate is defined as production worker's gross earnings divided by actual number of hours worked per month.

Source: Chingin: Rodo-Jikan no Kokusai Hikaku, [International Comparison of Wages and Working Hours], Special Committee on Labor and Economy, Japan Economic Association, Tokyo, December 7, 1978.

TABLE 5.3
Social Welfare Expenditures in Japan, 1966, 1971 and 1975

Year	Absolute Amount (in millions of yen)	Ratio to National Income (in percent)
1966	1,866,968	6.12
1971	3,966,408	6.02
1975	11,764,677	9.23

Source: Welfare White Paper, Ministry of Welfare, Tokyo, December 1977.

Avoiding Trade Friction Through Long-Term Cooperation

In light of the need for both the importing and exporting countries to make mutual adjustments, one may ask two questions in the present situation: (1) why has the United States refrained from taking steps to defend the value of the dollar amid growing currency unrest in the world's money markets; and (2) why does the United States, despite the clear need to develop a comprehensive energy policy, continue to import more and more foreign oil at the expense of its balance of payments? Surely, over the long run, the United States cannot hope to benefit from such economic policies.

To be sure, the recent lopsided increase in Japanese exports to the United States is a problem that must be resolved. But efforts to bring U.S.-Japanese trade into a closer balance will require time, and short-cut solutions—such as demands that Japan achieve a premature current-account deficit—will not contribute to harmonious trading relations. It will be extremely difficult for Japan to meet such demands, and even if Japan were to try to achieve a current-account deficit, the effort will require considerable time. Unrealistic U.S. demands might give rise to anti-U.S. sentiment in Japan in much the same way that protectionist sentiment is growing in the United States.

Japan's overseas economic assistance program is one of the weakest aspects of its present economic policy. The share of Japan's GNP allocated for foreign aid is one of the lowest among the Organization for Economic Cooperation and Development (OECD) countries—a fact that must puzzle the rest of the world. As noted earlier, however, Japan's social infrastructure is still inadequate in many respects due to the lack of social-capital accumulation and investment as compared with the United States and Europe. Thus Japan has found it necessary to concentrate on its own economic development, making it difficult to increase its overseas economic assistance despite a rising GNP.

However, a new start was recently made in Japan's overseas economic assistance program, with Prime Minister Fukuda's 1977 ASEAN trip and his pledge to cooperate in ASEAN development projects by increasing loan and grant aid up to a total of $5 billion over the next five years.

Another weak aspect of Japanese economic policy at present relates to Japan's share of its defense burden. Japan has been criticized in certain quarters in the United States for not spending enough on its own defense. Japan's military expenditures, however, are necessarily limited by its constitutional restriction against the maintenance of offensive forces, and by Japan's desire to contribute to world peace through economic rather than military means. Now that Japan's economy has become the second largest in the free world, however, the country can contribute more to its own defense.

Japan's Foreign Economic Policy

It is necessary, therefore, to consider how to develop Japan's exports in the years ahead. In recent decades, the character of Japan's exports has undergone an obvious change. The ratio of machinery and equipment in the export total, which stood at a mere 13.7 percent in 1955, soared to 35.2 percent just ten years later and to 61.8 percent in 1977. The total value of exports in this category was $49,734 million in 1977, accounting for nearly 60 percent of the nation's overall exports. The prospects are, moreover, for a further rise in the proportion of machinery and equipment to two thirds of total exports in 1985.

Japan's machinery and equipment exports consist for the most part of four major types of products: electrical appliances (such as radios, tape recorders, and television receivers); cameras; motor vehicles; and ships. In 1977 these four commodities together accounted for about $27.1 billion (or about 55 percent) of Japan's machinery and equipment exports.

Such Japanese products are subjected to import restrictions in France and Italy, however. For the European Economic Community (EEC), it has become a problem whether to seek voluntary export controls by Japan or to invoke a system of safeguards against Japanese products. As for exports to the United States, Japan has been obliged to exercise self-control on shipments of color TV sets and steel products. A similar fate seems to be in store for Japanese-made automobiles. In the world market for machinery and equipment, Japan faces intense competition from developing nations. For instance, the Republic of Korea has already caught up with Japan in the field of shipbuilding, while Japan has clearly fallen behind the Republic of Korea and Taiwan in the world textile market. The Republic of Korea has even started to export both monochrome and color television receivers to Japan, and similar exports of automobiles are generally expected to begin in the not-too-distant future.

In this situation, a major task (if Japan is to keep its relations with the world clear of friction) is to boost its plant exports to a level equal to that of the United States and the Federal Republic of Germany. The Ministry of International Trade and Industry (MITI) has already pointed out the need for efforts in the following areas.

1. In order to avoid any trouble on world export markets, Japan should seriously endeavor to diversify its export commodities and export outlets and to achieve a switchover from price-competitiveness to competitiveness in other aspects, including performance, brand names, and after-sales service. At the same time, Japan should expand imports by such means as reform of the domestic marketing structure.

2. More vigor must go into boosting exports of industrial plants and technological know-how, such as technical consultant services and engineering.

3. It is also important for Japan to develop its purely trade relationships with other countries into relationships of multifaceted interdependence by increasing the channels between itself and its trading partners. To this end, Japan should augment its overseas investments, encourage the expansion of private-level economic and technical cooperation with developing nations, promote joint international projects, and strengthen its ties with overseas importers and consumers.

Nevertheless, it is far from easy to carry out all these policies within a short time. If Japan had followed such policies in the past, the frictions that we witness today between Japan and the rest of the world would not have occurred. A quick look at Japan's economic relations with Southeast Asia will illustrate this point. Japan has striven to secure sources of supply for raw materials and bases for processing them in the non-Communist nations of Asia. The nations of Southeast Asia were best suited for this purpose because they were not yet afflicted with industrial pollution. Meanwhile, Japan's postwar trade with these countries centered on commodity exports. Since the Asian countries did not have enough money to pay for their purchases from abroad, Japan extended assistance in the form of war reparations. As a result, 90 percent of Japan's assistance had strings attached. Moreover, the terms and conditions of Japan's aid were far stricter than those of Western European nations. Meanwhile, government aid accounts for 60 percent of all Japanese assistance to developing countries.

This policy has provided some criticism among Southeast Asian nations, who tend to regard Japan as a good partner but not as one who is really helping them. They feel instead that Japan is making a normal profit from trade with them. Southeast Asia provides a large part of the raw materials that are essential to Japan. For instance, Japan is dependent on Southeast Asian nations for 40 percent of its copper (from the Philippines), about 50 percent of its bauxite (Malaysia), and 15 percent of its petroleum (Indonesia). The fact that Japan is benefiting from their natural resources signifies, from the Southeast Asian point of view, that Japan is making money from them. Therefore, should they want to use their resources themselves, they would naturally look upon Japan as their rival.

Using this aid policy as a tool of "economic diplomacy," Japan has advanced into Southeast Asia with giant strides since the latter half of the 1960s. One Japanese enterprise after another has invested in the region. This influx has led Southeast Asians to believe that Japanese enterprises were trying to find and secure new sources for the raw material supplies that they so badly needed, and that such efforts were actively backed up by the Japanese government.

The spread of such sentiment has given rise to anti-Japanese nationalism in the region, generating growing friction with Japan. In an effort to get around the resulting wave of protectionism, Japanese enterprises have set about building factories and assembly plants in Southeast Asia. These efforts have been singularly successful thanks to the low cost of labor in the region and the absence of strikes. Japanese enterprises eagerly invested in backward areas whenever they saw a chance of making money and went on to seize control of the principal industries of such areas. It was left to the Japanese government's economic diplomacy to deal with the frictions that resulted from this advance of private Japanese companies into Southeast Asia.

At first, the local people welcomed the expanded activities of Japanese enterprises in the hope that Japanese firms would conduct their business in such a way as to benefit Southeast Asian countries as well. In fact, these Japanese ventures did undoubtedly play a large part in providing much needed employment opportunities.

With raw materials from Southeast Asia as one of its major propellants, the Japanese economy continued to grow rapidly, and the gap in economic growth between Japan and the Southeast Asian nations continued to widen. Thus, the importance of the nations of Southeast Asia to Japan as trading partners rapidly waned. In 1955, Southeast Asia accounted for 26.3 percent of Japan's imports and 35.8 percent of its exports, but by 1977 the ratios had declined to 21.3 percent and 21.3 percent, respectively. Japan has now become so powerful vis-à-vis Southeast Asian nations that, in the case of a serious dispute, it can deal a heavy blow simply by halting or reducing its trade with them.[2] Raw materials account for 100 percent of Malaysia's exports to Japan, while the corresponding figure is 90 percent for Indonesia and 80 percent for the Philippines. Such heavy reliance upon Japan is likely to generate anti-Japanese feelings in the countries concerned.

The relationship as it stands is truly unfortunate. As Japan needs Southeast Asia, so does Southeast Asia need Japan. Japan is a suitable customer for Southeast Asian resources, while Southeast Asia is an ideal market for Japanese products. Southeast Asia needs capital and technology for the development of its vast natural resources, particularly for the manufacture of goods from these resources. Southeast Asian nations are short of funds, which Japan could supply through development assistance. However, there is a danger that the continued expansion of such development aid will further strengthen Japan's dominant position in that part of the world. Therefore, while boosting its aid to Southeast Asia, Japan should seek to alleviate the feeling among the local populace that the region is economically dominated by Japan.

Notes

1. "Economic cooperation" is the Japanese term for what in the West is described as "foreign aid." Its components are described on page 80.

2. This is similar to Japan's relations with the United States. Japan has greatly increased its dependence on the United States in trade, so that its economy is greatly affected by any move the United States takes. Import restrictions or reductions of agricultural exports on the part of the United States would now be a great blow to Japan.

6
ASEAN and Its Relations with Japan and the United States

Saburo Okita

It has been eleven years since ASEAN (Association of Southeast Asian Nations) was established as a regional organization composed of five major countries in Southeast Asia. Although ASEAN was inactive in its early stage and often described cynically as a place where foreign ministers got together to enjoy tea, it has become a definite and active entity both politically and economically. Its impact and influence are getting larger and larger, particularly in the context of changing international relationships in Asia.

ASEAN and Changing International Relations in Asia

As we witnessed just recently, ASEAN was approached by the big powers "making proposals of love" and was cast into the middle of the game of power politics. A few years ago, the word "flux" became a popular term to describe changing Asian situations. International relations around ASEAN today are indeed in a state of flux, yet it is obvious that all advanced Pacific countries can no longer be indifferent to the direction in which ASEAN may be heading.

I would like to describe briefly (1) the relationship between the growth of ASEAN and the changing international relations in Asia; (2) ASEAN's economic relations with advanced Pacific

This paper was originally presented at the Pacific Forum symposium in Kona, Hawaii, December 1978.

countries; and (3) ASEAN's economy in the context of the changing world economy.

As is well known, ASEAN is composed of five member countries that are divergent in many aspects. Although ASEAN was established in 1967 as a regional integration scheme, it was until recently a political rather than an economic entity. It has strengthened its political aspect particularly since the 1972 Kuala Lumpur Declaration on Peace, Freedom, and Neutrality. Since then, ASEAN has vigorously sought national resilience in its member countries, particularly in view of such developments affecting international relations in Asia as the Nixon Doctrine of 1969, President Nixon's visit to China in 1972, the collapse of the Saigon regime in 1975, and subsequent changes in the Indochinese region. In the post-Vietnam War era, it has been an urgent matter for ASEAN to pursue a policy of building an independent, resilient Southeast Asia.

The United States-ASEAN relationship has been friendly, although military considerations have been important in this relationship. Some time ago, according to the "domino" theory, it was believed that after Vietnam, Thailand, then Malaysia, and finally other states in the region would fall into the hands of the Communists. But ASEAN significantly increased its resilience and proved that the domino theory did not work. The United States was quite disillusioned with the outcome of the Vietnam War and is said to have demonstrated this by "departing from Asia." Recent developments, however, including Vice-President Mondale's visit to Southeast Asia in April-May 1978, seem to be signs of renewed U.S. interest in this part of the world.

In any event, it seems that the U.S. departure from Asia marked the extreme point of the U.S. foreign policy cycle, which swings between isolationism and foreign commitments (much as business cycles swing between recession and boom) and that a certain trend of revived interest in Southeast Asia is now seen. Needless to say, many factors, such as the Sino-Japanese relationship, Soviet moves in Asia, and the business activities of multinational corporations, are contributing to the renewed U.S. interest in Asia.

Japanese-ASEAN relations, on the other hand, are more or

less concentrated around economic matters. The likelihood that this tendency will persist in the future was suggested in the so-called "Fukuda Doctrine," which Prime Minister Fukuda announced in Manila in August 1977 on the occasion of his visit to Southeast Asian countries. In this doctrine he pronounced three principles of Japanese foreign policy toward Southeast Asia: (1) that Japan would reject the role of a military power; (2) that Japan would do its best to consolidate relationships with Southeast Asian countries based on "heart-to-heart" understandings; and (3) that Japan would be an equal partner of ASEAN countries and would cooperate positively with their efforts to strengthen their solidarity and resilience. Although this doctrine defines Japanese attitudes toward Southeast Asia as economic rather than military, Japan's economic relations with ASEAN have been somewhat problematic as the following analysis will show.

ASEAN's Economic Relations with Japan and the United States

During the 1960s and 1970s, when Japan was enjoying high economic growth, its trade with and investment in Southeast Asia increased significantly, and its economic presence in ASEAN countries in particular increased rapidly. For example, Japanese annual direct investment in ASEAN reached $950 million in 1976, compared to only about $70 million ten years earlier when ASEAN was established. Japan's exports to ASEAN have increased likewise from $1,106 million in 1967 to $6,892 million in 1977. Tables 6.1, 6.2, and 6.3 show in part the growth of Japan's relations with ASEAN.

The rapid increase of Japanese economic activities in Southeast Asia has created friction between Japan and ASEAN, and Japan's economic overpresence has become a sensitive issue in this part of the world. The problem of economic overpresence may be explained in relation to three elements, namely, speed, share, and balance. First of all, Japanese economic activities in Southeast Asia expanded rapidly during the early 1970s and ASEAN countries could not catch up with or adjust to such speed. For example, local businesses or overseas Chinese

TABLE 6.1
Japan's Direct Investment in ASEAN Countries, 1960 to 1976
(net basis, in thousands of United States dollars)

Nation	1970	1972	1974	1975	1976	Total (1960-76)
Indonesia	44,570	124,800	231,250	332,740	784,770	2,113,464
Malaysia	12,690	21,050	68,720	24,580	45,160	303,092
Philippines	28,770	12,920	71,640	94,680	56,290	323,445
Singapore	n.a.	n.a.	59,120	43,590	55,570	312,966
Thailand	13,790	25,060	40,550	5,230	7,710	190,499

Source: Foreign Ministry, Nanboku Mondai to Kaihatsu Enjo (North-south problems and development assistance), 1978.

TABLE 6.2
Trade Matrix, 1972

(millions of dollars)

Exports from	ASEAN	United States	Japan	Others	Total
Total	11,572	53,890	22,778	287,760	376,000
ASEAN	1,491	1,376	1,762	3,004	7,633
United States	1,358	–	4,965	43,472	49,795
Japan	2,567	8,981	–	17,109	28,657
Others	6,156	43,533	16,051	224,175	289,915

Source: I.M.F., Direction of Trade, September, December 1973; February, August 1974.

TABLE 6.3
Trade Matrix, 1977

(millions of dollars)

Exports from	Exports to				
	ASEAN	United States	Japan	Others	Total
Total	28,239	147,554	67,167	434,144	677,104
ASEAN	4,674	6,842	7,833	12,419	31,768
United States	3,882	–	10,522	105,760	120,164
Japan	6,892	20,077	–	54,157	81,126
Others	12,791	120,635	48,812	261,808	444,046

Source: I.M.F., Direction of Trade, June, July 1978.

business could not adapt to the sharp and almost simultaneous expansion of several Japanese textile companies into the region. Second, the share of Japanese exports in the total trade of ASEAN countries has increased. As Tables 6.4 and 6.5 show, Japan's share in ASEAN trade exceeds that of other states in both exports and imports. Moreover, Japan's share in ASEAN's imports, which is far larger than that of other partners, inevitably gives the impression of Japan's overpresence.

Third, there is a problem of balance about which the Thai government particularly complains. This problem is worsening and its seriousness is shown in a recent incident in which Thai delegates, headed by the Thai minister of commerce, shocked the Japanese government by unilaterally postponing the Thai-Japanese Joint Trade Conference. The reason for this action was reportedly the Thai government's impatience over Japan's tardiness in remedying its persistent trade surplus with Thailand.

The problem of Japanese overpresence reached a climax in January 1974 when Prime Minister Tanaka visited Southeast Asia and met violent demonstrations in Jakarta and elsewhere. Pressure and criticism against Japanese overpresence has been somewhat reduced as Japan's economic growth and rate of overseas investment have slowed down due to the oil crisis and the worldwide economic recession. In addition, the victory of the Hanoi regime in the Vietnam War and its increased influence over the ASEAN-Indochinese relationship have caused ASEAN to reduce its criticism against Japan and to look to Japan for economic cooperation. When I visited the five ASEAN countries and Laos at the request of Prime Minister Miki in the summer of 1975, I found scarcely any criticism of Japan but was eagerly asked to request the Japanese government to increase Japanese economic cooperation. The leaders of these ASEAN countries told me that Japanese cooperation in helping resolve the economic problems of ASEAN would contribute to increased political resilience in these countries.

Prime Minister Fukuda's visit to Southeast Asia in August 1977 was favorably received by ASEAN, and great expectations resulted from several promises he made in Kuala Lumpur. His commitments included the following: (1) to favorably consider

TABLE 6.4
Matrix of Export Share in 1972 and 1977

(in percent)

Exports from		ASEAN	Exports to United States	Japan	Others	Total
ASEAN	1972	20	18	23	40	100
	1977	15	22	25	39	100
United States	1972	3	–	10	87	100
	1977	3	–	9	88	100
Japan	1972	9	31	–	60	100
	1977	8	25	–	67	100
Others	1972	2	15	6	77	100
	1977	3	27	11	59	100

Source: See Tables 6.2 and 6.3.

TABLE 6.5
Matrix of Import Share in 1972 and 1977

(in percent)

Imports by		ASEAN	Imports from United States	Japan	Others	Total
ASEAN	1972	13	12	22	53	100
	1977	17	14	24	45	100
United States	1972	3	–	17	81	100
	1977	5	–	14	82	100
Japan	1972	8	22	–	70	100
	1977	12	16	–	73	100
Others	1972	1	15	6	78	100
	1977	3	24	12	60	100

Source: See Tables 6.2 and 6.3.

a financial contribution of $1 billion to five ASEAN industrial projects, (2) to cooperate with ASEAN's efforts to establish a STABEX scheme,[1] (3) to cooperate with ASEAN's efforts to increase its exports to Japan, and (4) to financially support the promotion of cultural exchange within ASEAN.

As shown in Table 6.3, ASEAN has the closest relationship with Japan. Its trade with Japan in 1977 was 24.5 percent of its total trade, but Japan's trade with ASEAN was 9.9 percent of its total trade. On the other hand, ASEAN's trade with the United States in 1977 was 17.9 percent of the former's total trade, whereas the United States' trade with ASEAN was only 4 percent of U.S. total trade. As these figures show, ASEAN's economic relationship with Japan is closer than that with the United States. ASEAN's trade structures vis-à-vis Japan and the United States are basically similar, however.

The ASEAN economy, except for Singapore, depends on the export of primary commodities, and therefore ASEAN is strongly interested in commodity agreements and in the common fund scheme, both of which were recommended at the fourth United Nations Conference on Trade and Development (UNCTAD) in Nairobi. When I was attending this UNCTAD meeting, I was invited by the representatives of the ASEAN countries to a dinner at which occasion they told me that if Japan wanted to seek friendship from ASEAN, it had better make efforts toward the realization of the UNCTAD proposals on commodities, including the establishment of a common fund. As this episode shows, Japan's relationship with ASEAN has implications bearing on the North-South problem. Anyway, the Japanese government in principle has been supporting the common fund scheme, and Prime Minister Fukuda proposed at the Bonn Summit to cooperate with the establishment of the common fund.

As is well known, Japan depends on imports for more than 60 percent of its consumption of major cereals, for 90 percent of its energy, and for many other primary materials. However, except for some items such as natural rubber and tin, ASEAN's share in Japan's imports of raw materials is relatively small, being around 15 percent in total and 16 percent for oil in 1977.

As a market, ASEAN absorbs about 8 percent of Japan's exports. Although the United States alone absorbs 25 percent of Japanese exports, Japan's exports are globally distributed. It is therefore not in Japan's interest to make special trade arrangements for ASEAN, such as the preferential trade system. Such special arrangements obviously conflict with Japan's global interests. In other words, Japan faces a dilemma between its worldwide ties and ASEAN's regionalism.

ASEAN and the World Economy

As an economic integration scheme, however immature it still may be, and with its growing economy, ASEAN cannot help but be affected by the trends and changes in the world economy. For example, ASEAN cannot escape the international currency problem and is experiencing various problems as a result of the recent rapid appreciation of the yen. Most ASEAN countries have linked their currencies to the U.S. dollar and are naturally annoyed by the change in the exchange rate between the yen and the dollar. A Thai high official complained to me recently that Japan's arrangements, such as its exports on a yen basis and imports on a dollar basis, are damaging Thai foreign reserve positions. But this is basically a problem of who bears exchange risks. I think that ASEAN central banks should increase their expertise in rightly judging changing currency values. Table 6.6 shows the linkage of ASEAN currencies to the dollar.

Another Thai businessman complained to me that because of the rapid appreciation of the yen, Thailand now has to pay 30 to 40 percent more for the ships that it had previously ordered from Japan. Another complaint I heard was that although Japan had promised to double its foreign aid, the developing countries' repayment in dollars to Japan had also increased. Even though Japan's interest rate is as low as 3.5 percent, debt repayment in a rapidly appreciating yen is a heavy burden. Therefore, some ASEAN countries are seeking to borrow from international agencies in dollars rather than from Japan in yen.

As these episodes indicate, the shift in the value of the yen will surely affect the Japan-ASEAN relationship in many ways. For example, the yen may have to increase its role as a financial

TABLE 6.6
Exchange Rates of ASEAN Currencies and the Yen, 1972 to 1978
(units of national currency per United States dollar at end of specified period)

Country	1972	1974	1976	1977	1978[a]
Indonesia (Rupiah)	415.00	415.00	415.00	415.00	415.00
Malaysia (Riggit)	2.8170	2.3128	2.5350	2.3655	2.3065
Philippines (Peso)	6.7894	7.0737	7.4383	7.3797	7.3702[b]
Singapore (S$)	2.8200	2.3120	2.4555	2.3385	2.2565
Thailand (Baht)	20.928	20.375	20.400	20.400	20.400
Japan (Yen)	302.00	300.95	292.80	240.00	190.20

[a] August figures
[b] July figure

Source: I.M.F., International Financial Statistics, October 1978.

currency as well as an asset or reserve currency. In any event, it is clear that both Japan and ASEAN have to deepen their mutual understanding regarding international financial and monetary problems.

Problems related to the changing industrial structure are another major issue with many implications for the ASEAN economy. Wage increases and the rise in the exchange value of the yen have deprived Japan of part of its competitiveness, particularly in labor-intensive industries. In addition, some countries of ASEAN and those around Japan are in turn gaining international competitiveness. It seems certain that this tendency will accelerate in the near future. Furthermore, some newly industrialized countries (such as South Korea, Taiwan, and some ASEAN countries) are becoming competitive even in some of the more sophisticated industrial goods and are expected to increase their exports of such industrial goods.

In the long run, it is possible and desirable to establish a horizontal division of labor among the concerned advanced countries and developing countries, including the ASEAN countries. In order to achieve this goal Japan will have to change its industrial structure in such a way as to strengthen its highly competitive industries while giving up the industries in which the developing countries have more competitiveness.

Finally, the recent development of the Sino-Japanese relationship is increasing concern in some ASEAN countries about Japan's overcommitment to China and about Sino-Japanese economic and political dominance in Asia. However, Chinese exports and competition with ASEAN exports will probably not become a serious threat to ASEAN because the development of the Chinese economy will be basically inward looking.

In conclusion, ASEAN's economic relations with Japan and the United States are diverse and closely related and relations with Japan are particularly important. However, an effort by Japan or the United States to seek excessively close relationships with ASEAN may invite an ASEAN reaction. We should now recognize that, as the ASEAN member countries increase their cohesiveness under a common ASEAN framework, their bargaining power, both political and economic, will also become stronger vis-à-vis the big powers. This increased bargaining power could become a stabilizing factor in Asian and Pacific international relations if it is successfully directed toward the economic and social development of the region. In this sense, it is important for Japan and the United States to cooperate with each other in promoting the economic progress of ASEAN countries.

Notes

1. STABEX is a stabilization fund negotiated between the EEC and African, Caribbean, and Pacific (ACP) countries in the Lomé Convention of 1975. The fund was designed to compensate ACP producers for losses on export earnings due to fluctuations in the prices of basic raw materials.

7
The Future of Japan–United States Trade Relations

Hisao Kanamori

The United States has been an important trade partner of Japan since 1868, when the Meiji rulers opened the country to trade with the West. As is shown in Table 7.1, Japan's exports to the United States accounted for 30 percent of its total exports until 1920. In the 1920s, when Japan increased raw silk exports, the proportion exceeded 40 percent. Japan's imports from the United States, on the other hand, were proportionately smaller in the 1800s and accounted for only around 10 percent of its total imports. As Japan's cotton industry made progress, however, the nation's imports of raw cotton grew; consequently, from 1910 to 1920 imports from the United States expanded to 30 percent of Japan's total. Until around World War I, Japan had a large export surplus in trade with the United States. Gradually, imports from the United States increased, bringing the trade into balance with both exports and imports in trade with the United States accounting for 30 percent of their respective totals by 1920.

After World War I, Japan's raw silk exports increased, raising the share of exports to the United States above 40 percent, thus opening an era in which exports to the United States exceeded imports from the United States. As raw silk exports subsequently declined, the share of exports to the United States decreased, restoring in the 1930s a situation in which imports from the United States exceeded Japanese exports to the United States. Generally speaking, the prewar pattern of Japan's trade

TABLE 7.1
The United States' Share of Japanese Trade, 1873 to 1977
(in percent)

Period	Exports	Imports
1873-1880	30.3	6.6
1881-1890	38.0	9.0
1891-1900	27.0	13.8
1901-1910	32.5	17.2
1911-1920	29.0	30.7
1921-1930	41.6	30.0
1931-1940	20.8	33.4
1951-1960	23.1	34.3
1961-1970	29.8	29.0
1971-1977	24.4	21.6

Sources: Toyokeizai Shimposha, Nihon Boeki Seiran [A Detailed View of Japan's Foreign Trade] for figures until 1940; Ministry of Finance, Clearance Statistics for postwar figures.

with the United States was marked by an alternation of export and import surpluses.

For a long time after World War II, Japan continued to import more from the United States than it exported to that country. In the period from the 1950s to the 1960s, the percentage of exports to the United States rose rapidly while that of imports from the United States fell, bringing exports and imports into balance in the first half of the 1960s. At this time, exports and imports in trade with the United States again constituted 30 percent of total Japanese exports and imports, respectively. Subsequently, however, the proportion of imports from the United States dropped sharply until the problem of excess exports to the United States came to the surface in the 1970s. Thus in the postwar period, in contrast to the prewar era, the pattern has been for Japan to export more to the United States than it imported. After 1973, however, the percentage of exports to the United States began to decline as well, with the result that in

The Future of Japan-United States Trade Relations

1977 Japan's imports from the United States accounted for 17.5 percent of total imports and its exports to the United States, 24.5 percent of total exports. In the past one-hundred-year history of Japan-United States trade, both in the prewar period (1910s) and the postwar period (1960s), exports and imports in Japan's trade with the United States constituted 30 percent of Japan's total exports and imports, respectively. It has been a rare phenomenon for both the proportions of imports and exports to decline and for a Japanese export excess to become a serious issue as in recent years. The following analysis of the causes of these developments will, I hope, shed some light on the future of Japan-United States trade relations.

Causes for the Proportionate Decline of Imports from the United States

The proportionate decline of Japan's imports from the United States by no means implies that Japan-United States trade has dwindled. Japan maintained rapid economic growth of around 10 percent annually until the oil crisis in 1973. Even after the oil crisis, though the rate of growth fell to zero in 1974, it was subsequently restored to a rate of 5 to 6 percent. Thus the rate of growth has dropped to half that of the period before the crisis. Japan has, nevertheless, sustained the highest growth rate among advanced countries. This resulted in a gradual rise in imports from the United States. As will be seen in Table 7.2, Japan's imports from the United States amounted to $1.6 billion in 1960, $5.6 billion in 1970, and $12.4 billion in 1977. This represents a large increase even when we take the depreciation of the dollar into consideration. Nevertheless, a decline in the U.S. share of Japan's total imports may be worthy of note. That share has been rapidly diminishing from about 35 percent in 1960 to 29 percent in 1970 and about 18 percent in 1977.[1] If the U.S. share of Japan's total imports during 1977 had been equal to the share in 1960, imports from the United States would have been nearly twice as large as the actual figure and the problem of excessive U.S. imports from Japan would not have existed. What has caused the fall in the U.S. share of Japan's total imports? There are three primary explanations for this decline.

TABLE 7.2
Japan's Imports During Selected Years, 1960 to 1977
(billions of dollars)

Year	Total (A)	From United States (B)	B/A (percent)
1960	4.5	1.6	34.6
1965	8.2	2.4	29.0
1970	18.9	5.6	29.4
1975	57.9	11.6	20.1
1977	70.8	12.4	17.5

Source: Ministry of Finance, Clearance Statistics.

Increased Oil Imports

The first and foremost cause of the shrinking U.S. share in recent years is Japan's increased oil imports. The commodity that occupies an overwhelmingly large proportion of Japanese imports is petroleum. Its price quadrupled in 1973. This resulted in a sharp rise in the share of Japan's total imports with the Middle and Near East (West Asia) and a decline in that of the United States. An examination of the regional distribution of Japanese imports (Table 7.3) reveals a reversal in the positions of the United States and West Asia in the years 1970-1977, with West Asia accounting for approximately 30 percent of Japan's total imports in 1977, about the same relative weight that the United States had had in 1965. The oil crisis of 1973 was a turning point marking a fairly important change in the relative importance of the U.S. position in the Japanese economy.

The Expansion of the Japanese Economy

The fall in the relative weight of the United States in Japan's trade, however, has not been caused by the oil crisis alone. It is also the result of a long-term tendency beginning around 1960 as seen in the figures given previously. (Even when mineral fuels are excluded, the U.S. share in Japan's imports has been gradually shrinking from 36.5 percent in 1960 to 32.0 percent in

TABLE 7.3
Regional Distribution of Japan's Imports, 1965, 1970 and 1977
(in percent)

Region	1965	1970	1977
Total	100.0	100.0	100.0
North America	33.3	34.4	21.6
United States	29.0	29.4	17.5
Western Europe	8.9	10.2	7.8
Southeast Asia	17.2	16.0	21.3
West Asia	13.1	12.0	28.6
Latin America	8.7	7.3	4.3
Africa	4.3	5.8	3.0
Oceania	8.0	9.6	8.7
Communist Bloc	6.4	4.7	4.7

Source Ministry of Finance, Clearance Statistics.

1970 and further to 27.8 percent in 1977.) As its economy has expanded, Japan has been compelled to rely, not only on the United States, but on the whole world for the supplies of raw materials, fuels, and food that are necessary to sustain its economy. Japan was a small country in 1960, became the world's second largest economic power in 1970, and almost ranked alongside the United States in per capita GNP in 1978. Japan has been forced to diversify its sources of food and raw materials globally in order to maintain such a large economy.[2] As Table 7.4 shows, in the period 1960-1970 there was a decline in the relative weight of imports from the United States of raw materials and mineral fuels. In the years 1970-1977 imports of food fell in relative importance. Among Japanese imports from the United States of raw materials and fuels, important commodities are lumber, soy beans, coking coal, raw cotton, petroleum products, scrap steel, and nonferrous ores. Table 7.5 gives the U.S. shares of Japanese imports of these commodities. A comparison between 1960 and 1977 shows that there have been declines in all commodities except lumber; while com-

TABLE 7.4
Japan's Imports from the United States, 1960, 1970 and 1977[a]

Commodity	Japan's imports from U.S. (millions of dollars)			U.S. shares in Japan's total imports (percent)		
	1960	1970	1977	1960	1970	1977
Total	1,545	5,560	12,396	34.4	29.4	17.5
Foods	122	812	2,733	22.3	31.5	27.1
Raw materials	732	1,649	3,602	33.7	24.7	25.1
Mineral fuels	178	761	1,351	24.0	19.5	4.3
Chemicals	148	401	1,166	55.8	42.1	48.5
Machinery and equipment	267	1,411	2,377	66.3	61.4	48.5
Other manufactures	101	491	1,090	27.7	20.2	24.3
Others	n.a.	34	77	n.a.	n.a.	13.5

[a]Details may not add to totals because of rounding.

Source: Ministry of Finance, Clearance Statistics.

TABLE 7.5
Japan's Imports of Principal Raw Materials from the United States, 1960, 1970 and 1977

Commodity	Japan's imports from U.S. (millions of dollars)			U.S. shares of Japan's total imports (percent)		
	1960	1970	1977	1960	1970	1977
Lumber	24	518	1,240	14.1	33.0	32.6
Soy beans	103	330	1,035	96.3	78.4	94.7
Coal	92	623	1,094	65.2	61.7	30.8
Raw cotton	215	80	347	51.2	17.0	30.7
Petroleum products	70	110	150	51.9	20.0	6.8
Scrap steel	155	270	79	67.4	79.2	63.7
Nonferrous netal ores	10	64	50	6.4	6.0	2.6
Iron ores	13	49	0	6.1	4.1	0

Source: Ministry of Finance, Clearance Statistics.

modities other than soy beans and raw cotton have registered falls when the figures for 1970 and 1977 are compared.

Among animal feed and food crops, overwhelmingly important are corn and sorghum for animals, followed by wheat, fruits, seafood, meat, and leaf-tobacco. As Japan increased imports of animal feed, the U.S. share in Japan's imports of food and animal feed expanded over the years 1960-1970 (see Table 7.6). In the subsequent period, however, the U.S. share of Japanese imports dropped as Japan increased imports of seafood (such as tuna and shrimp) and coffee, a small proportion of which Japan imports from the United States.

Declining U.S. Competitiveness in International Markets

A third explanation for the diminishing U.S. share of Japanese trade can be found in the relative decline in the competitiveness of the United States. This has been reflected in a decrease in the U.S. share of Japan's total machinery imports (Table 7.7). Japan's machinery imports from the United States amounted to $2.4 billion in 1977 and ranked next to its raw material and food imports. The U.S. share of total Japanese machinery imports, however, has been diminishing rapidly from 66 percent in 1960 to 61 percent in 1970, and further to 49 percent in 1977.

Declines in the U.S. shares are noticeable in many kinds of commodities, including metal-working machinery, telecommunications equipment, semiconductors, passenger cars, and precision instruments.

An analysis of the sources of Japanese machinery imports shows that the decline in the U.S. share has been caused by inroads made not only by advanced countries (such as West Germany and the United Kingdom) but also by the Republic of Korea and Taiwan (see Table 7.8). Especially significant is an increase in U.S. imports from the Republic of Korea of electrical machinery, such as semiconductors.

The decline in U.S. competitiveness in machinery may be attributed to many causes, including inflation in the United States, a deficiency in export-mindedness of U.S. enterprises, and the overvaluation of the dollar.

TABLE 7.6
Japan's Imports of Food and Animal Feed from the United States, 1960, 1970 and 1977[a]

Commodity	Japan's imports from U.S. (millions of dollars)			U.S. shares in Japan's total imports (percent)		
	1960	1970	1977	1960	1970	1977
Total food and animal feed	122	812	2,733	22.3	31.5	27.1
Meat	n.a.	15	201	n.a.	7.3	21.0
Wheat	63	174	375	35.6	54.7	64.0
Citrus fruits	n.a.	25	134	n.a.	100.0	95.7
Corn	11	218	706	13.6	74.1	89.5
Sorghum	n.a.	133	246	n.a.	57.8	47.6
Leaf tobacco	12	45	187	91.5	68.2	65.0

[a]Totals include items not separately specified.

Source: Ministry of Finance, Clearance Statistics.

TABLE 7.7
Japan's Machinery Imports from the United States, 1960, 1970 and 1977

Type of Machinery	Japan's imports from U.S. (millions of dollars)			U.S. shares in Japan's total imports (percent)		
	1960	1970	1977	1960	1970	1977
Total machinery	267	1,411	2,377	66.3	61.4	48.5
Aircraft internal combustion piston engines	11	63	133	77.2	81.8	86.4
Office machines	31	201	358	57.8	62.4	59.4
Metal working machinery	22	69	23	74.3	41.1	25.3
Nuclear reactor	n.a.	31	97	n.a.	91.2	93.3
Heavy electrical machinery	6	64	91	79.0	68.8	37.4
Telecommunications equipment	8	40	91	84.7	75.5	43.1
Electrical measuring instruments	n.a.	68	145	n.a.	78.2	72.1
Semi-conductor	n.a.	75	149	n.a.	81.5	51.9
Passenger cars	7	23	99	74.5	42.6	34.7
Aircraft	41	245	196	93.4	98.4	98.0
Precision instruments	20	78	237	62.5	51.7	37.4

Source: Ministry of Finance, Clearance Statistics.

TABLE 7.8
Japan's Imports of Machinery by Specified Country of Origin, 1970 and 1977

Country	1977		1970	
	(millions of dollars)	(percent of total)	(millions of dollars)	(percent of total)
Total	4,902	100.0	2,298	100.0
United States	2,377	48.5	1,411	61.4
West Germany	714	14.6	344	14.5
United Kingdom	344	7.0	128	5.6
Republic of Korea	256	5.2	6	0.3
Switzerland	160	3.3	87	3.8
Taiwan	134	2.7	20	0.9
France	127	2.6	60	2.6
Sweden	116	2.4	59	2.6
Netherlands	104	2.1	22	1.0
Italy	94	1.9	59	2.6

Source: Ministry of Finance, Clearance Statistics.

Causes for the Declining U.S. Share of Japanese Exports

Next, why has the U.S. share of Japanese exports, which had been growing proportionately larger after World War II, assumed a downward tendency recently (see Table 7.9)? As seen in Table 7.1, the U.S. share of Japan's exports reached its postwar peak in 1968 when it stood at 31.5 percent of total exports; the percentage remained unchanged for some time but then fell substantially after 1973. The decline may be attributed to three causes.

The Oil Crisis

The fall in the relative weight of Japanese exports to the United States after 1973 was partly caused by the oil crisis. The oil crisis caused a decline in the U.S. share of Japanese foreign trade with respect to both imports and exports. After the oil crisis, Japan deepened its economic relations with Middle Eastern and Near Eastern countries and boosted its exports (such as industrial plants) with a view to securing a stable supply of petroleum. An increase in the import capabilities of Middle and Near Eastern countries owing to their increased oil incomes has also enabled Japan to increase exports to these countries. As shown in Table 7.10, in the years 1970-1977 Japanese exports to

TABLE 7.9
Japan's Exports, Total and to the United States, During Selected Years, 1960 to 1977

(billions of dollars)

Year	Total (A)	To United States (B)	B/A (percent)
1960	4.1	1.1	27.2
1965	8.5	2.5	29.3
1970	19.3	5.9	30.7
1975	55.8	11.1	23.0
1977	80.5	19.7	24.5

Source: Ministry of Finance, Clearance Statistics.

the Middle and Near East (West Asia) grew from 3 percent to 10 percent of the nation's total exports; while the U.S. share declined by almost the same proportion.

Expansion of the Japanese Economy

Another important cause for the declining U.S. share of Japanese exports is that the Japanese economy has become so large that the nation is now compelled to diversify its export markets globally.

In the period from the 1960s to the early 1970s, sharp rises in Japanese exports often caused trouble in the U.S. market. These sharp increases were mostly of light-industry products, such as textiles or sundry goods. During the 1970s, however, the cause of the trouble has been the exportation of TV sets,[4] iron and steel, automobiles, or heavy-industry products. Table 7.11 gives the U.S. shares of Japanese total exports. It shows that exports to the United States of metal and machinery, which rose rapidly in relative weight over the years 1960-1970, declined sharply subsequently. These two items, which had accounted

TABLE 7.10
Regional Distribution of Japan's Exports, 1968, 1970 and 1977

(in percent)

Region	1968	1970	1977
Total	100.0	100.0	100.0
North America	31.9	33.7	26.6
United States	29.3	30.7	24.5
Western Europe	12.8	15.0	16.0
Southeast Asia	26.0	25.4	21.3
West Asia	3.4	2.8	10.2
Latin America	5.8	6.1	7.8
Africa	9.7	7.4	8.3
Oceania	4.7	4.2	3.8
Communist bloc	5.7	5.4	6.1

Source: Ministry of Finance, Clearance Statistics.

TABLE 7.11
Japan's Exports to the United States, 1960, 1970 and 1977[a]

Commodity Group	Japan's exports to U.S. (millions of dollars)			U.S. shares of Japan's total exports (percent)		
	1960	1970	1977	1960	1970	1977
Total	1,083	5,940	19,717	26.7	30.7	24.5
Food	73	135	199	27.2	20.8	22.9
Crude materials and fuels	22	31	50	37.3	15.6	7.4
Textile products	288	597	659	23.5	27.4	14.1
Non-metallic mineral manufactures	57	148	348	39.3	39.8	29.1
Other light-industry products	289	664	1,032	41.3	42.6	25.4
Chemical products	17	160	513	10.1	13.0	11.6
Metal manufactures	150	1,296	3,308	26.7	34.1	23.4
Machinery and equipment	187	2,840	13,351	20.1	31.8	26.8
Others	n.a.	73	257	n.a.	38.4	34.5

[a] Details may not add to totals because of rounding.

Source: Ministry of Finance, Clearance Statistics.

for an overwhelmingly large proportion of Japanese exports to the United States, reached a saturation point and began to decrease in relative weight. Their decrease is the most important cause for the proportional decline of Japanese exports to the United States.

The fact that Japanese per capita GNP has approached that of the United States, with a resultant reduction of Japan's comparative advantage in labor-intensive commodities, has also been responsible for a proportionate decrease of Japanese exports to the United States of textile goods and other light-industry products. As shown in Table 7.12, the Japanese share has been reduced significantly in the U.S. market due to the competition from less developed countries (LDCs) in light industrial goods.

An Enlarged Imbalance of Japan–United States Trade

An increase in the imbalance of Japan–United States trade

TABLE 7.12
Share of Japan and of Less Developed Countries in the United States Light Industry Product Market, 1965 and 1977

(in percent)

Product	Japan's share		LDCs' share	
	1965	1977	1965	1977
Gloves and mitts for baseball	98	5	2	94
European umbrellas & parasols	74	2	18	94
Rubber and plastic footwear	87	8	9	92
Rackets for badminton	95	7	3	86
Dolls and toy animals	68	9	24	85
Wooden table goods	56	6	21	85
Candles	60	16	13	67
Plastic table goods	42	14	33	56
Guitars	64	49	10	48

Source: Japan External Trade Organization, White Paper on Overseas Markets, 1978.

has constituted another factor inhibiting the growth of Japanese exports to the United States.

As shown in Tables 7.13 and 7.1, the postwar history of Japan–United States trade may be divided into three periods: a period of Japan's import excess until 1965, a period of equilibrium in the years 1965-1970, and a period of Japan's export excess from 1970 up to the present. The balance of trade was restored to equilibrium temporarily in the years 1973-1975 due in part to business fluctuations, but the general tendency has been for Japan to move from a position of import excess to one of export excess.

In 1971 and 1977, Japan's excess of exports to the United States caused a particularly serious problem. Japan was asked to increase imports from the United States in order to correct the imbalance and it promised to do so. The result, however, has tended to be a slowdown of Japanese exports to the United States, rather than an increase of Japanese imports. This leveling-off in the exports of Japanese textiles, TV sets, steel products, and so on is blamed on both direct and indirect import restrictions on the part of the United States. We cannot, however, overlook the huge imbalance of Japan–United States trade in the background. Had this huge imbalance not existed in Japan–United States trade as a whole, Japanese opposition would have been much stronger to the particular import restrictions imposed by the United States. In 1978 the Japanese government enforced "voluntary restraints" on exports of automobiles and other products through administrative guidance, with a view to keeping the nation's trade surplus from getting larger.

Factors Determining Future Japan–United States Trade

From the Japanese standpoint, Japan–United States trade relations have tended to become less close since 1973 with respect to both imports and exports. This has been the inevitable result of the expansion of the Japanese economy, which has become too large to depend excessively on the United States. How will Japan–United States trade relations develop in the future, then? To answer this question fully, one must con-

TABLE 7.13
The Balance of Japan's Trade with the United States, 1960 to 1977
(billions of dollars)

Year	Japan's exports to U.S.A.	Japan's imports from U.S.A.	Balance	Year	Japan's exports to U.S.A.	Japan's imports from U.S.A.	Balance
1960	n.a.	n.a.	n.a.	1970	5.9	5.6	0.3
1961	1.1	2.1	Δ1.0	1971	7.5	5.0	2.5
1962	1.4	1.8	Δ0.4	1972	8.8	5.9	2.9
1963	1.5	2.1	Δ0.6	1973	9.4	9.3	0.1
1964	1.8	2.3	Δ0.5	1974	12.8	12.7	0.1
1965	2.4	2.4	n.a.	1975	11.1	11.6	Δ0.5
1966	3.0	2.7	0.3	1976	15.7	11.8	3.9
1967	3.0	3.2	Δ0.2	1977	19.7	12.4	7.3
1968	4.1	3.5	0.6				
1969	5.0	4.1	0.9				

Source: Ministry of Finance, Clearance Statistics.

sider the matter with primary reference to Japan. It will focus on the following three points: (1) the growth potential of the Japanese economy; (2) changes in the industrial structure and the degree of dependence on foreign trade; and (3) the structure of trade markets.

Rate of Economic Growth

The average postwar growth rate of the Japanese economy (Table 7.14) reached a peak of 11.6 percent in the years 1965-1970 before dropping back to 8.8 percent in 1970-1973. The 1960s rate of growth was halved after the oil crisis, standing at 6 percent in 1976, 5.2 percent in 1977, 5.75 percent in 1978, and 4.75 percent in 1979.[5]

What will become of Japan's rate of economic growth in the future? Estimates are apt to be influenced by the present state of things. Before the oil crisis, the Japanese government anticipated a continuing growth rate of more than 10 percent annually. In contrast, its recent forecasts have become much more conservative. In August 1978, the Industrial Structure Council of the Ministry of International Trade and Industry (MITI) projected that the Japanese economy would grow at an annual rate of 6.25 percent over the period from fiscal 1977 through 1985. A new medium-term economic program (1979-1985) made public under the Ohira administration, formed in late 1978, was even more conservative and projected the rate of growth in the same period to be 5.5 to 6 percent.[6] This seems too low, however. The Japanese economy has overcome the oil shortage, the balance-of-payments uncertainty, and inflation, all of which were feared as a result of the oil crisis. In 1974, many economists anticipated that Japan, which imported a large quantity of petroleum, would suffer from deficits in its international balance of payments.[7] Instead, Japan expanded its exports to emerge as a country with a huge payments surplus. Economists predicted that the nation would suffer from inflation as a result of rising oil prices. In 1978, however, with consumer prices rising only 4 percent, Japan, like West Germany, saw prices remain highly stabilized. As shown in Table 7.15, Japan overcame in a very short time the unfavorable balance of international payments and inflation, which were problems in 1974. The Japanese

TABLE 7.14
Annual Rate of Growth of Japan's Gross National Product, 1961 to 1970, and Forecasts, 1978 to 1985

(in percent)

Actual				Forecast	
1961	14.6	1971	7.3	Japan Economic Research Center	
1962	7.1	1972	8.9	1978	6.0
1963	10.5	1973	9.8	1979	6.0
1964	13.2	1974	-1.0	1980	6.0
1965	5.1	1975	2.4	1981	6.5
1966	9.8	1976	6.0	1982	7.0
1967	12.9	1977*	5.2	Ministry of International Trade and Industry	
1968	13.5	1978*	5.75	1977-1985	6.25
1969	10.7	1979*	4.75	Economic Council	
1970	10.9			1979-1985	5.5 ~ 6

*O.E.C.D. forecast

Source: O.E.C.D., Economic Outlook, December 1978.

economy has been surprisingly adaptable to change. We may, therefore, safely expect that the growth of the Japanese economy will gradually accelerate, even if its growth rate does not reach pre-1973 levels. A medium-term forecast, which the Japan Economic Research Center made public in February 1978, predicts that the Japanese economy will realize a rate of 7 percent growth in fiscal 1982.

Industrial and Trade Structures

How will Japan's industrial structure change in response to a 6 to 7 percent growth rate of the aggregate economy? As anticipated by MITI's Industrial Structure Council, the size of the Japanese economy will expand 1.8 times in the years 1975-1985 assuming an annual growth rate of 6.25 percent (see Table 7.16). In that event, a decline in the relative weight of agriculture, forestry, and fishing would naturally be expected. The primary sector already suffered a decrease in its share of the nation's total output from 8.1 percent to 4.2 percent in the years 1965-1975. This tendency will be accentuated. Opinions differ as to which industry, secondary or tertiary (service), will grow at a higher rate. Will Japan make progress toward a postindustrial society with service industries growing in relative weight? The Industrial Structure Council maintains that there will be little change in the relative importance of tertiary industry in real output. (However, in the employment structure, the share of tertiary industry already exceeded 50 percent of the total in 1975 and the Council foresees a further expansion by 1985.) When the industrial structure is broken down, MITI forecasts that machinery industries, such as precision instruments and electrical and general machinery, will grow at a high rate and rise in relative importance; however, the textile, steel, and nonferrous metal industries will dwindle in contrast (Table 7.17).

The degree of dependence on foreign trade (Table 7.18) will remain almost unchanged in real terms from fiscal 1977 with respect to both exports and imports. The Industrial Structure Council foresees, however, that the nominal rate of dependence will decline substantially to an 8 percent level. This is because it judges that, since the exchange rate will rise, the nominal amounts of exports and imports expressed in yen prices will not

TABLE 7.15
Adaptation of the Japanese Economy to Changes after the Oil Crisis, 1970 to 1978

Indicator	1971	1972	1973	1974	1975	1976	1977	1978
Rate of growth (percent)	7.3	8.9	9.8	-1.0	2.4	6.0	5.2	5.75
Current balance of payments (billions of dollars)	5.8	6.6	-0.1	-4.7	-0.7	3.7	10.9	20.0
Rate of increase in consumer prices (percent)	6.1	4.5	11.7	24.5	11.8	9.3	6.5	4.0

Source: O.E.C.D., Economic Outlook, December 1978.

TABLE 7.16
Japan's Industrial Structure, 1965 to 1985 (Summary)
(percentage distribution of output based on 1975 prices)

Sector	Percentage distribution				Average annual growth (percent)			
	1965	1970	1975	1985	1970/1965	1975/1970	1975/1965	1985/1975
Primary industries, total	8.1	4.8	4.2	2.9	1.3	0.5	0.9	2.7
Secondary industries, total	54.5	60.5	56.9	58.5	14.7	2.2	8.2	6.6
(of which, manufacturing)	(41.7)	(47.0)	(45.3)	(46.0)	15.1	2.7	8.7	6.5
Tertiary industries, total	37.4	34.7	38.9	38.5	10.6	5.8	8.2	6.2

Source: Ministry of International Trade & Industry, A Long-Term Vision of the Industrial Structure, 1978.

TABLE 7.17
Japan's Industrial Structure, 1965 to 1985 (Breakdown)[a]
(percentage distribution of output based on 1975 prices)

Sector	Percentage distribution				Average annual growth (percent)			
	1965	1970	1975	1985	1970/1965	1975/1970	1975/1965	1985/1975
Total	100.0	100.0	100.0	100.0	12.3	3.4	7.8	6.3
Agriculture, forestry and fishing	8.1	4.8	4.2	2.9	1.3	0.5	0.9	2.7
Mining	0.6	0.6	0.5	0.4	10.6	0.6	4.9	3.4
Food and beverages	7.7	5.8	6.1	5.4	6.2	4.2	5.2	5.1
Textiles	3.3	2.6	2.3	1.5	7.1	0.5	3.7	1.9
Pulp and paper	1.7	1.7	1.5	1.4	12.7	0.4	6.4	6.0
Chemicals	2.6	3.1	3.2	3.3	16.8	3.8	10.1	6.8
Petroleum and coal products	2.4	3.0	3.0	2.7	17.0	3.7	10.2	5.2
Non-metallic mineral products	1.3	1.7	1.5	1.5	17.1	0.7	8.6	6.7
Iron and steel	4.9	6.3	5.6	4.5	18.2	1.1	9.3	4.0
Nonferrous metal	0.7	0.9	0.8	0.7	16.5	1.8	8.9	4.9
Metal products	1.5	1.9	1.7	2.2	17.6	1.7	9.4	8.6
Machinery except electrical machinery	2.2	3.5	3.7	4.7	22.9	4.8	13.5	8.9

(continued)

TABLE 7.17 (continued)

Sector	Percentage distribution				Average annual growth (percent)			
	1965	1970	1975	1985	1970/1965	1975/1970	1975/1965	1985/1975
Electrical machinery	2.2	3.6	3.1	4.5	24.1	0.3	11.6	10.3
Transport equipment	3.6	4.4	5.3	5.1	17.2	7.3	12.1	5.9
Precision instruments	0.5	0.6	0.5	0.8	13.7	2.3	7.8	10.3
Other manufacturing	6.1	6.4	5.6	5.7	13.3	0.7	6.8	6.5
Construction	11.9	12.5	10.7	11.7	13.4	0.4	6.7	7.2
Electricity, gas and water service	1.8	1.8	2.0	2.2	12.1	6.6	9.3	7.1
Wholesale and retail trade	7.5	8.6	9.6	9.6	15.6	5.7	10.6	6.2
Banking, insurance and real estate	6.2	5.5	7.5	6.9	9.7	10.0	9.9	5.4
Transportation & communications	4.3	4.1	4.3	4.4	11.2	4.6	7.8	6.5
Services	16.9	13.6	14.2	13.9	7.5	4.4	5.9	6.2

[a]Details may not add to totals because of rounding.

Source: Ministry of International Trade & Industry, A Long-Term Vision of the Industrial Structure, 1978.

TABLE 7.18
Economic Growth and Dependence on Foreign Trade, 1970 to 1985
(trillions of yen)

Indicator	1970	1975	1977	1985
Real (1975 prices)				
Gross national expenditure	114.0	147.7	164.0	268.0
Exports	12.4	20.9	26.6	38.0
Imports	14.7	20.4	22.4	35.25
Dependence on exports (percent)	10.9	14.1	16.2	14.25
Dependence on imports (percent)	12.9	13.8	13.7	13.25
Nominal (current prices)				
Gross national expenditure	73.1	149.6	188.3	487.0
Exports	8.7	20.8	25.7	41.0
Imports	7.7	20.6	22.0	39.0
Dependence on exports (percent)	11.9	13.9	13.6	8.25
Dependence on imports (percent)	10.6	13.8	11.7	8.0

Source: Ministry of International Trade & Industry, A Long-Term Vision of the Industrial Structure, 1978.

increase much even if the quantities may increase.

Table 7.19 gives a trade structure that would correspond to such an industrial structure. It shows that in exports the relative weight of machinery will grow further while in imports the relative importance of light-industry products, machinery, metal, and other heavy- and chemical-industry products will rise. In a country with an industrial structure like that of Japan the increasing relative weight of manufacturing-industry products may be a natural outcome. However, it would also be important for Japan to import agricultural and mineral products and petroleum, and there will be little likelihood of the imports of manufacturing-industry products accounting for more than 50 percent of total imports as they do in Western countries. The

TABLE 7.19
Japan's Trade Structure in 1985[a]

Industries	Exports						Imports					
	1975		1985		Average annual growth percent 1985/1975		1975		1985		Average annual growth percent 1985/1975
	(billions of dollars)	(percent of total)	(billions of dollars)	(percent of total)			(billions of dollars)	(percent of total)	(billions of dollars)	(percent of total)	
Total	53.6	100.0	100.0	100.0	6.5		60.3	100.0	103.5	100.0	5.6
Agriculture, forestry and fishing	0.8	1.6	1.7	1.6	6.8		15.1	25.1	25.2	24.3	5.2
Mining	n.a.	0.1	0.1	0.1	8.0		28.8	47.8	44.4	42.9	4.4
Light industrial goods	6.1	11.3	7.7	7.7	2.4		4.3	7.1	9.7	9.4	8.5
Metal	12.1	22.6	15.4	15.4	2.5		2.2	3.7	4.7	4.5	7.7
Machinery	29.1	54.2	65.4	65.1	8.4		5.0	8.4	10.9	10.5	8.0
Other heavy and chemical industry products	5.5	10.3	10.1	10.0	6.2		4.7	7.9	8.7	8.4	6.2

(continued)

TABLE 7.19 (continued)

Notes: a) in 1975 prices ($1=¥297)
b) Industrial classification:
Agriculture, forestry & fishing: Agriculture, forestry & fishing, and food & beverages
Light industrial goods: Textiles, paper and pulp, and other manufacturing
Metal: Iron & steel, nonferrous metal, and metal products
Machinery: Machinery except electrical machinery, electrical machinery, transport equipment, precision instruments
Other heavy & chemical industry products: Chemicals, petroleum & coal products, non-metallic mineral products.

Source: Ministry of International Trade & Industry, <u>A Long-Term Vision of the Industrial Structure</u>, 1978.

share that farm output occupies in gross national product will gradually decrease and the current restriction on imports of meat and fruits will be relaxed. The shift away from the present policy of protecting domestic agriculture, however, will progress slowly; with the result that the rate of dependence on imports for the supply of farm products will rise only slightly as well from the present 25 percent.

The Market Structure

An examination of the market structure of Japanese foreign trade reveals that, as stated already, the U.S. share has decreased considerably with respect to both imports and exports in the years 1970-1977. This is attributed to the emergence of important markets for Japan other than the United States. This tendency will likely continue into the future. A general view of such developments is given below, market by market.

The Middle and Near East. This region's share has increased in respect to both imports and exports as a result of Japan's increased oil imports. As Japanese exports of industrial plant grow hereafter, the region's relative importance in Japan's export market will rise further.

Southeast Asia. This area's share of Japanese trade has grown sharply (see Tables 7.20 and 7.21) because of a substantial increase in Japan's imports of industrial goods and Japan's increased oil imports from Indonesia. This region includes newly industrialized nations with the largest growth potential in the world, such as Hongkong and Singapore. Furthermore, Japan intends to achieve closer economic relations with ASEAN countries. It is expected, therefore, that trade between Japan and Southeast Asian countries will expand in the future.

Europe. There is a possibility that, as Japan raises its economic level, imports of industrial goods from this region will expand.

Australia. The nation is an important supplier to Japan of iron ores, coal, wool, beef, wheat, livestock feed, and seafood; Japan's exports to Australia are expected to expand in exchange.

Latin America. Brazil supplies Japan with iron ores, coffee, and other products; Japan reciprocates with steel products, machinery, and the like, with large possibilities that plant ex-

TABLE 7.20
Japan's Imports from Southeast Asia, 1970 and 1977

Commodity Group	Japan's imports from Southeast Asia (millions of dollars)		Southeast Asia's share of Japan's imports (in percent)	
	1970	1977	1970	1977
Total	3,013	15,077	16.0	21.3
Food and beverages	447	2,444	17.4	24.2
Raw materials	1,601	3,369	24.0	23.5
Mineral fuels	472	6,199	12.1	19.9
Chemicals	21	288	2.1	9.5
Machinery and equipment	37	540	1.6	11.0
Miscellaneous manufactures	406	2,129	16.7	47.5
Unclassified	28	109	n.a.	19.0

Source: Ministry of Finance, Clearance Statistics

TABLE 7.21
Japan's Exports to Southeast Asia, 1970 and 1977

Commodity Group	Japan's exports to Southeast Asia (millions of dollars)		Southeast Asia's share of Japan's exports (in percent)	
	1970	1977	1970	1977
Total	4,902	17,126	25.4	21.3
Food and beverages	277	222	42.7	25.5
Crude materials and fuels	90	298	45.2	43.8
Textiles	847	1,554	35.2	33.2
Non-metallic mineral products	85	248	22.8	20.8
Other light industry products	302	944	19.4	23.2
Chemicals	482	2,099	39.0	47.6
Metal products	837	3,392	22.0	24.0
Machinery and equipment	1,938	8,154	21.7	16.4
Unclassified	44	216	23.2	29.0

Source: Ministry of Finance, Clearance Statistics.

ports may grow. There is a possibility that Mexico may supply Japan with petroleum in the future.

Communist Bloc. As Siberian development progresses, Japanese exports to Russia of machinery and steel products will increase, while Japan's imports of coal, petroleum, and lumber from that country will also expand. Japanese trade with China is now expected to expand most rapidly. The 1978 shift of Chinese economic policy in a direction of rapid economic growth and conclusion of the Sino-Japanese peace treaty are expected to bring about an increase in Japan's exports to that country of steel products, industrial plants, and chemical fertilizers and an expansion of its imports from that country of petroleum and mineral products.

The Future of Japan–United States Trade Relations

The United States will remain Japan's most important trading partner. In 1977, the United States received 24.5 percent of Japan's total exports, although the Republic of Korea, which is its second largest trading partner, received only 5.1 percent, followed by West Germany with 3.5 percent (see Table 7.22). With respect to Japanese imports, on the other hand, the U.S. share was 17.5 percent of the total, followed by Saudi Arabia with 12.1 percent, and Australia with 7.5 percent. There is a wide gap between the share of the United States, which ranks first, and that of the Republic of Korea or Saudi Arabia, which stand second.[8] There is no likelihood that another of Japan's trading partners will replace the United States in first place. The scale of trade between Japan and the United States is the largest in the world, with the exception of United States–Canada trade. This is because the United States and Japan are, respectively, the world's largest and second largest economic powers, both economies enjoy comparatively high rates of growth, and both stand in a strongly complementary relationship. Table 7.23 shows the nature of the trade between the two countries. For example, Japan exports metal and machinery to the United States while the latter supplies the former with technology-intensive goods, such as aircraft, nuclear reactors and integrated circuits, as well as food and raw materials. In the past, as the two

TABLE 7.22
Principal Destinations of Japan's Exports, 1960, 1970 and 1977
(percentage share of total exports)

Country of Destination	1960	1970	1977
Total	100.0	100.0	100.0
United States	26.7	30.7	24.5
Republic of Korea	2.5	4.2	5.1
West Germany	1.6	2.8	3.5
Taiwan	2.5	3.6	3.2
Liberia	1.9	3.0	3.1
Saudi Arabia	0.4	0.4	2.9
Australia	3.6	3.0	2.9
Hong Kong	3.8	3.6	2.9
United Kingdom	3.0	2.5	2.4
China	n.a.	2.9	2.4
Soviet Russia	2.5	1.8	2.4
Iran	0.9	0.9	2.4
Other	50.6	40.6	42.3

Source: Ministry of Finance, Clearance Statistics.

economies grew, new kinds of trade goods appeared one after another to sustain the importance of trade relations between the two countries. Since the rate of increase in Japan's imports of food, animal feed and raw materials is expected to be low in the future, however, an increase in U.S. exports of technology-intensive industrial goods will be necessary if Japan–United States trade is to expand.[9]

Increasing Diversification of Japan's Foreign Trade Market

Though Japan–United States trade will remain as important as ever, for the reasons mentioned above, it is inevitable that Japan will move to expand its trade with the whole world. Japan has grown too large to remain dependent on the United States alone. The problems concerning Japan–United States trade will

TABLE 7.23
Principal Commodities Traded between Japan and
the United States, 1960, 1970 and 1977

(millions of dollars)

Commodity	1960	1970	1977
(1) Japan's Exports to the United States			
1. Motor cars	3	536	4,925
2. Iron and steel	75	899	2,311
3. Metal manufactures	69	324	854
4. Radios	71	397	821
5. Motorcycles	2	280	650
6. Tape recorders	6	256	532
7. Television receivers	1	265	506
8. Transceivers	n.a.	n.a.	368
9. Clothing	116	274	247
10. Pottery	38	89	234
11. Cameras	6	41	216
12. Electronic desk-top calculators	n.a.	77	167
13. Toys	54	78	145
14. Plywood	46	50	80
15. Footwear	49	81	23
16. Woolen fabrics	23	43	12
(2) Japan's Imports from the United States			
1. Lumber	26	518	1,240
2. Coal	92	623	1,094
3. Soy beans	103	330	1,035
4. Corn	11	218	706
5. Wheat	63	174	375
6. Cotton	221	80	347
7. Sorghum	2	134	246
8. Meat	n.a.	15	201
9. Aircraft	41	245	196
10. Pulp	24	64	182
11. Petroleum products	77	110	153
12. Semi conductors	n.a.	75	149
13. Citrus fruit	n.a.	25	134
14. Nuclear reactors	n.a.	31	97
15. Iron and steel scrap	156	270	79
16. Phosphate rock	21	36	68
17. Metal-working machines	41	69	23
18. Electronic computers	7	138	4
19. Iron ore	13	49	n.a.

Source: Ministry of Finance, Clearance Statistics.

The Future of Japan-United States Trade Relations 143

have to be dealt with in the context of world trade as a whole. It is of vital importance for Japan to develop multilateral relations for economic cooperation, to comply with common rules for currencies and trade, and to engage in the orderly pursuit of profits.

The Inevitable Imbalance of Japan-United States Trade

The imbalance of Japan-United States trade since 1976 is so excessive as to impede a smooth expansion of trade between the two countries. This imbalance is attributable in no small extent to the inappropriate foreign exchange rate, to economic depression in Japan, and to Japan's foreign trade restrictions and the noncompetitiveness of its distribution system. It is possible for Japan to reduce this imbalance by letting the foreign exchange rate fluctuate freely, by promoting the recovery of business conditions, and by liberalizing foreign trade. There was an indication late in 1978 that the imbalance was being reduced.

The restrictions on agricultural imports and the maintenance of a distribution system that obstructs imports of consumer goods not only impede the progress of Japan-United States trade but also cause great disadvantages to Japan itself. Protests and calls for their correction have been getting louder even within the country.

A policy to promote exports by keeping the yen's exchange rate artificially low now receives little support in Japan. Adjustment of this policy will help to reduce the imbalance of Japan-United States trade in the future.

In view of Japan's international balance of payments structure, however, it is inevitable that Japan's excess of exports in its trade with the United States will continue for some time to come. There are two reasons for this. First, since Japan will inevitably suffer an excess of imports from its trade with the Middle and Near East, it needs to offset this import excess by an export excess in its trade with the United States. Second, Japan's invisible trade balance will continue to register a substantial deficit. Japanese policy should, therefore, seek to attain not a bilateral equilibrium in Japan-United States trade but a global and overall equilibrium. Japan and the United States should not persist in efforts to achieve a bilateral balance of trade between them but need to consider an expansion of international transactions among all countries of the world.

The Growing Importance of Overseas Investment

In the future, not only foreign trade but also international movements of capital will become more important. In Japan, despite a high rate of domestic saving, demand for investment within the country has slackened. Japan, therefore, needs to become a capital exporter partly with a view to sustaining a balance between saving and investment. Japan's surplus in trade with the United States will be offset in part by movements of capital. Since the wage level has risen in Japan, industries have emerged there in which it would be more profitable to invest in the United States than within Japan, which involves the export of the products to the United States.

Japan will increase investment in Southeast Asia, Latin America, China, and the Soviet Union as well. There will be an increasing need for cooperation between Japan and the United States in such investment.

While economic relations between Japan and the United States will not become less important in the future, both countries will need to look beyond bilateral trade to the global dimensions of trade and will need to broaden their outlook to include invisible multilateral trade and capital transactions.

Notes

1. Japan's share of U.S. trade increased until 1970 but declined subsequently. In 1970, U.S. exports to Japan accounted for 10.7 percent of all U.S. exports and U.S. imports from Japan accounted for 14.7 percent of all U.S. imports. By 1977, these shares had dropped to 8.8 percent and 12.7 percent, respectively.

2. For a statement emphasizing this point, see S. Okita, "Natural Resources Dependency and Japanese Foreign Policy," *Foreign Affairs*, (July 1974).

3. J. C. Abegglen and T. M. Hunt state in their distinguished article, "The Trade Gap with Japan" (*Foreign Affairs*, Fall 1978), that the recent loss of share by the United States in nearly all the aggregate categories of trade in modern manufacturing must be laid to the com-

petitive behavior of U.S. companies. This might be said to be a right conclusion.

4. In May 1977, the Japanese government agreed that it would restrict exports of color TV sets to the United States in the three years beginning July 1977 to 1,750,000 sets of which 1,560,000 sets would be finished products and 190,000 sets unfinished in exchange for the U.S. government promise that it would take no restrictive measures against imports of color TV sets from Japan. As regards steel products, the U.S. government adopted in February 1978 a trigger price system in an attempt to restrict their imports below standard prices.

5. 1978 and 1979 figures are from OECD, *Economic Outlook* (1977, 1978).

6. E. R. Fried and P. H. Trezise predicted in 1974 that the rate of growth of the Japanese economy would drop to 6 percent in the years 1975-1985. This forecast preceded that of the Japanese government in foreseeing a slowdown in the rate of growth. *Japan's Future Position in the World Economy* (Washington, D.C.: The Brookings Institution, 1974).

7. Ibid. Fried and Trezise predicted that Japan would suffer a substantial deficit in the balance of trade for some time to come and thus failed to anticipate instead that a lopsided imbalance in Japan's favor of Japan-United States trade would cause a serious problem.

8. Ibid. Fried and Trezise ask if Japan could possibly enter into relations with any country that would be as close as Japan's relations with the United States and conclude that the answer is no.

9. George Ball, former U.S. under-secretary of state, stated in 1970 in Japan that as much as two-thirds of Japanese imports from the United States consisted of raw materials and farm products, a percentage that Americans "naturally consider almost insulting." He doubted that the industrial community in the United States could long refrain from retaliating against "such discriminatory treatment," and remarked that the world's most powerful industrial country was not satisfied with the large nonindustrial percentage of its exports to Japan. (*Jiji Hyoron*, September 1970.) According to Table 7.23, however, the proportion of industrial exports was lower in 1977 than in 1970.

8
The Evolution of United States–Japan Relations

Philip H. Trezise

> *We have here a relationship [between Japan and the United States] which . . . is unique as a test of the ability of both parties to handle themselves wisely and usefully in international affairs. If we cannot make a success of this, we are in a bad way.*
> —George Kennan, *The Cloud of Danger*

Kennan, whose acquaintance with Japan during his official career was quite limited, is impressed, like others, with the strategic importance of Japan because it is a great industrial power. But he has a more subtle point. He observes that Americans and Japanese, two very different peoples, were thrown into unexpected and unprecedented intimacy by war and defeat. The Americans took on the self-imposed task of teaching Japan to live "more safely and usefully in the modern age," while the Japanese in turn made their special relationship with their conquerors the overriding feature of the nation's foreign policy. In the process, as Kennan sees it, the two countries implicitly assumed unusual responsibilities for understanding one another and for working things out in common.

The close association between Japan and the United States has now endured for more than thirty years. That its parties have fully met the Kennan test is, one must suppose, implausible. But there is a case for the proposition that matters on the whole have gone well, that the relationship has been a success. Strains have appeared, to be sure, but they also have appeared in U.S. relations with closer and older allies in Western Europe and in North America. On questions considered to be of high importance, Tokyo and Washington generally have been able to make adjustments to one another's requirements. A mutuality of interests is a hackneyed phrase, but it does express the situation as it has been perceived in the two capitals much or most of the time.

Whether the past is a guide to the future is uncertain, of course. Some of the sources of potential or actual tension between Japan and the United States seem to have been much reduced in recent years. Specifically, the issues of China and the United States–Japan security treaty for the moment, anyway, have lost a great deal of their capacity for causing friction. Economic relations, on the other hand, have become increasingly troublesome, with few indications that mutual understanding has been reached in anything like an adequate measure. Most of this essay will be devoted to reflections on the state of the economic relationship. First, however, it is useful to consider how the China issue and the security or defense relationship have evolved.

The China Issue in United States–Japan Relations

As one of the conditions for the peace treaty in 1951, Prime Minister Yoshida's government was required to pledge itself not to recognize the Communist government in China. The pledge was given reluctantly[1] for Japanese opinion was anything but convinced that ostracism of Communist China would be in the national interest. Yoshida said, "Red or white, China remains our next door neighbor." Nonetheless, a peace treaty was duly negotiated with the Nationalist government on Taiwan, which was acting, it said, for all of China. This foreclosed for an indefinite period any official relationship with Peking and aligned Japan with the United States in two decades of diplomatic efforts to blink away the existence of a government in control of the China mainland.

Ironically, Japan's economic relationship with Taiwan turned out to be surprisingly rewarding, while Peking showed only limited and sporadic interest in trade and economic relations with Japan or other non-Communist states. Even so, the lure of the prospective mainland market and sentimental attachments to "historic" ties with China kept very much alive a Japanese vision of reconciliation with Peking. Divisions quickly appeared between pro-Taiwan and pro-Peking groups within the ruling Liberal Democratic party. And the leftist opposition naturally made Japan's China policies a major point of political contention.

It is probably right to say that few Japanese in or out of office ever considered the Chinese Communists to be the military menace in Asia that Washington saw. But doubts, and indeed worries, about being pulled into a renewed Sino-U.S. war were effectively stifled by the majority party in favor of the commitment to the security alliance with the United States. Thus the sudden change in the U.S. position on China in 1971 came as more than an ordinary shock. The absence of prior consultation, contrary to ordinary practice and repeated promise, was humiliating enough; but, in addition, the balance within the Liberal Democratic party was turned in favor of the pro-Peking faction. And, as it then seemed, Peking had been given a very strong hand for the negotiations that Japan now had no choice but to initiate.

Tokyo's worst fears certainly were not realized. Japan's politicians drew ranks promptly, whatever their inner feelings. Then, in a show of diplomatic virtuosity, Prime Minister Tanaka was able both to restore relations with Peking on easily acceptable terms and to make the inevitable break with Taiwan a relatively painless event. In one swoop, the substance of the China problem had been settled in a manner that appears to have been broadly favorable to Japan.

Some Japanese profess to find in modern history support for the proposition that United States–Japan relations can never be smooth when U.S.–Chinese relations are friendly. Although the future conceivably could bear out this reading of the past, it does seem to pass too facilely over the differences between then and now in the China–Japan United States triangular relationship. Equally, any U.S. fears of a developing Sino-Japanese concert aimed in some unspecified fashion at the United States or the West would seem to be wildly farfetched. Commercial rivalries over the China market doubtless are to be expected, but these can hardly become problems of great political import. Most compelling should be the evident common interest in finding ways to avoid being drawn unduly into the confrontation between Peking and Moscow. If this interest does not draw Japanese and U.S. diplomacy toward China together, then we are indeed lost.

Defense and Security Issues

For the largest part of two decades the United States–Japan security treaty was the single most contentious issue in Japanese political life. When it was negotiated (as a bilateral annex to the peace treaty), it did not even have the wholehearted support of the conservative coalition then in power.[2] When it was renegotiated in 1960 during a time of domestic tranquility and unexampled prosperity, Japan had its most severe postwar political crisis, ending Prime Minister Nobusuke Kishi's leadership career. During the 1950s and 1960s, the principal point in the Socialist opposition's program was not a domestic policy alternative to conservative rule but the treaty.

Aside from ideological objections to a defensive alliance with the main capitalist power, Japanese misgivings centered on the possibility that the country might find itself a partner in an unwanted, perhaps nuclear, war as long as U.S. forces could operate from bases in Japan. To many nonleftists and to nearly all Socialists, the security guarantees provided by the treaty did not outweigh the risks of being tied militarily to U.S. foreign policy. The treaty revisions of 1960, which occasioned so much controversy and violence, did give Tokyo a voice in decisions about the deployment of U.S. forces stationed in Japan and a veto on their nuclear armament, but vocal opposition to the treaty continued for years thereafter.

From one U.S. point of view, the security treaty was at best an incomplete bargain. When it was entered into, the hope was for a Japanese commitment to rearm and to join in a regional security system patterned on the North Atlantic Treaty Organization.[3] Rearmament, however, turned out to be a modest self-defense force. Participation in any form of regional security arrangement was simply not considered. Suggestions for a greater defense effort came periodically from Washington. These were regularly rejected or ignored.

Despite everything, the security relationship that began in 1951 has lasted and to all appearances is now firmly rooted. Japan remains a lightly armed power, as allergic as ever to military commitments going beyond its own territory. The United States continues to hold bases and to station air, naval, and ground forces in Japan. Concerns about nuclear arms have been carefully finessed; no nuclear weapons are placed in Japan, but the Seventh Fleet's nuclear capabilities are well advertised. The numbers of U.S. bases and personnel in Japan have been greatly reduced over the years, joint defense consultation has become routine, and Japan has made a substantial financial contribution to the upkeep of U.S. forces. Japanese uneasiness about the firmness of the U.S. commitment in the Far East crops up periodically, as when the Carter administration announced that it would be removing the army's Second Division from South Korea. But this is a far cry from opposition to the mutual defense system. And Washington has stopped suggesting increased Japanese armament some years ago in belated recognition that it could not effectively determine Japan's political choices.

Economic Relations

From the peace treaty in 1961 until the late 1960s, economic relations were generally easy. Initially, the United States saw Japan as a weak, vulnerable economy. This view, which persisted far longer than the facts warranted, made it possible to accept with little complaint Japan's extremely deliberate liberalization of the extensive array of trade and investment restrictions that had been instituted during the occupation. Japan's deficit in commercial exchanges with the United States was more or less balanced by receipts from transactions with the U.S. military forces in the Far East, a situation that both sides could find satisfactory. To be sure, product-specific trade problems of the "low-wage" variety appeared from time to time. These were customarily resolved by officially supported, nominally voluntary export restraints on such items as wood screws, umbrella frames, and thermometer blanks. Only in the case of cotton textiles, a major Japanese export, did serious controversy occur over U.S. demands for trade controls.

Change came rather abruptly. During the Kennedy round of multilateral trade negotiations, 1962-1967, Japan had been treated as a distinctly secondary participant, while the United States and the European Economic Community settled their differences in the center ring. After the negotiations had ended, however, attention turned to Japan, by then running a sizable trade surplus and still applying a host of quantitative import controls in contravention of the rules of the General Agreement on Tariffs and Trade (GATT). The notion of a small, import-dependent, trade-deficient Japan finally was seen to have lost its substance. Replacing it was the image of a frightening growth and export phenomenon, with no evident weaknesses. When the Nixon administration took over in 1969, the setting for confrontation on economic issues had already been established.

At that point, unfortunately, more fundamental questions were overshadowed by President Nixon's campaign promise to expand protection against textile imports beyond cotton textiles to articles made of wool and synthetic fibers. Almost by reflex, it was soon decided that the main target should be Japan, leaving the newer and actually more dynamic exporters—Taiwan, South Korea, and Hongkong—for a second stage. The approach to Japan went badly, partly because it was handled clumsily, partly because of lingering resentments in the Japanese textile industry over earlier disagreements, and partly because it struck an unexpected chord of hostility to bow to a U.S. demand. (A Diet resolution, sponsored by *all* political parties, was passed in opposition to further textile trade restrictions.) In any event, the "negotiation" took more than thirty months. It was concluded in 1971 only when the White House reportedly threatened to invoke the presidential import control powers residing in a World War I statute, infelicitously known as the Trading with the Enemy Act.

While textiles thus preempted the stage in economic relations with Japan, U.S. balance of payments difficulties were worsening steadily. The enumerated causes for this were various, but a prominent one was a rising Japanese current account surplus that reached an unprecedented $5.8 billion in 1971. President Nixon's second "shock"—the first, of course, being reconciliation with China—was to force Japan to raise the external value of the yen, an action that no Japanese politician of any party would have taken voluntarily at the time. That the Nixon measures were aimed at achieving a general revision of currency values, involving Europe and Canada as well as Japan, did not make the outcome less striking to the Japanese as a demonstration of U.S. unilateral power.

The 1971 shocks, as a White House foreign policy paper subsequently put it,[4] can be said to have registered forcibly the U.S. conclusion that Japan had become so consequential an economic power that the bilateral relationship had to be readjusted, however painful the process. Since 1971, many of the earlier points of friction have been moderated or eliminated. Japan's limitations on foreign direct investment have been substantially relaxed and its compliance with the GATT rules have been brought up at least to the international standard. Textiles are no longer a confrontational commodity; in fact, Japan helped the United States to establish the current multilateral arrangement that effectively puts international trade in textiles under tight controls. Product-specific trade problems have not vanished, although low wages have disappeared as a causal factor. Now it is steel and television sets, not cutlery and chinaware, that bring urgent calls for protection from imports. But none has aroused the high emotions that textiles did. The unfortunate U.S. soybean export embargo in 1973 has not been forgotten in food-importing Japan, nor has the Carter administration's 1977 effort to prevent the operation of a pilot nuclear reprocessing plant, but these are not issues of current moment.

Nonetheless, the state of the economic relationship in 1979 is certainly one of tension, perhaps dangerous tension. The proximate reason has been a rapidly growing Japanese surplus in trade and in current transactions. On current account, Japan's positive balance rose from $3.7 billion in 1976 to $11 billion in 1977 and to $16.6 billion in 1978. The global trade surplus in 1978 was $24.7 billion; with the United States alone it was $11.6 billion. This extraordinary development, which occurred in the face of an increase in the nominal value of the yen of 41 percent (between January 1976 and October 1978), has deeply disturbed official Washington. The Council of Economic Advisers' 1979 report speaks of the "one-sidedness" of Japan's import policies. In the Congress, the Ways and Means Committee has a special task force to monitor trade with Japan, the first of its kind. Congressional proposals to impose a discriminatory surcharge on imports from Japan apparently are seriously meant.

Felt grievances have not been entirely on the U.S. side. Japanese business and government alike made no secret of their dislike for U.S. exchange rate policies, which were interpreted as malignly intended when the yen was appreciating rapidly. The United States' conspicuous failure to curb its imports of petroleum has dismayed Tokyo. U.S. profligacy in oil consumption is considered to be a prime cause of the country's trade deficit and to give the OPEC cartel undue and unnecessary support.

Whatever may emerge from this situation, it has not been marked by a notable demonstration of mutual understanding. The U.S. reaction has been to point accusingly at Japanese protectionism, a term that sometimes extends to Japan's creaky private distribution system, and to suggest that Tokyo try harder to stimulate domestic demand. In answer, Japan has conceded in varying degree on particular import restrictions and has set official GNP growth targets that have proved to be beyond reach. There have been mildly critical comments, also, about the lethargy said to afflict U.S. exporters and about the Carter administration's failure to check domestic inflation. While none of the points raised by either side is clearly irrelevant, neither do they add up to a satisfactory basis for policymaking.

Among the explanations for the widening imbalance between the United States and Japan (and between the United States and the world), substantial weight must be given to the differential in GNP growth rates in relation to potential. During the period 1976-1978, U.S. growth was pushing close to the economy's limits, whereas in Japan (and in the other major industrial country with a trade surplus, West Germany) the actual GNP as a percentage of potential GNP was significantly lower than in the United States. The U.S. index of industrial production at the end of 1978 was 16 percent above that of the boom year, 1973. In Japan, it was not until 1978 that the index finally edged up (by 4.5 percent) above the 1973 peak. U.S. demand for imports has been strong, resources for exports relatively scarce while Japan's situation has been the reverse. Movements in the yen-dollar exchange rate were less of a corrective than the nominal rates would indicate. In 1976, the real effective yen rate (weighted for trade and adjusted for inflation differentials) actually depreciated. Not until 1978 did it rise enough to have an expected impact on trade volume in Japan.

At the present writing, the outlook is for a marked slowdown in the U.S. economy and a modest further strengthening of demand in Japan. These should be the conditions for a narrowing of current account positions and perhaps for some reduction in trans-Pacific tensions. It is difficult, however, to find grounds for believing that Japan will cease to run a sizable current external surplus, say over the next decade. This is the prospect to which both sides need to direct attention.

To make guesses about Japan's likely future, it is necessary to go back to the growth surge in the 1960s—and especially 1965-1970. Real GNP in those years rose at an annual average rate of 12.2 percent, strongly propelled by an astoundingly high level of gross domestic investment (peaking in 1970 at 39.5 percent of GNP), the bulk of it financed by voluntary savings. The current account, in real terms, was in modest surplus during this period, the high point being 1.4 percent of GNP in 1966.

From 1971 on, except for 1973, investment demand trailed off to a more modest share of total output—still high by international standards but plainly lower than would have been warranted by the society's savings habits. Personal consumption, which had been growing at a 9.7 percent annual rate, slackened as well. The real foreign balance, again with the exception of 1973, pushed up to above 2 percent of GNP, then to 4 percent in 1975, and to 7 percent in 1977. Table 8.1 compresses the key data.

Put briefly, we have in Japan the case of an economy that has been through an exceptional growth era, during which savings responded strongly to the requirements for heavy investment ex-

TABLE 8.1
Japan's Gross National Product, 1965 to 1978

(billions of 1970 yen)

	1965	1970	Annual Average Rate of growth 1965-1970 (in percent)
Gross National Product	41,184.0	73,365.0	12.2
Domestic demand of which:b	40,689.6	72,660.4	12.3
- Private consumption	24,272.9	38,616.4	9.7
- Private plant and equipment investment	5,650.8	15,430.0	22.3
- Private inventory investment	467.6	2,622.5	
- Private residential investment	2,460.9	4,748.4	14.0
- Government capital formation	3,510.7	5,870.6	10.8
- Government consumption	4,227.8	5,427.3	5.1
Foreign balance	494.4	698.6	7.2
Foreign balance as percent of Gross National Product	1.2	0.95	

(continued)

TABLE 8.1 (continued)

	1971	1973	1975	1977	1978[a]	Annual Average Rate of growth 1971-1978 (in percent)
Gross National Product	77,248.4	93,022.5	93,855.0	105,060.3	111,272.0	5.4
Domestic demand of which:[b]	75,271.4	92,346.4	90,132.0	97,832.2	104,486.7	4.8
- Private consumption	41,157.7	49,539.0	52,080.5	56,428.5	59,690.0	5.4
- Private plant and equipment investment	15,178.9	18,656.3	16,326.1	16,613.5	17,785.0	2.3
- Private inventory investment	1,621.4	1,927.2	106.3	797.1	395.7	—
- Private residential investment	4,977.7	6,876.4	6,148.5	6,821.3	7,421.0	5.9
- Government capital formation	6,987.4	9,006.8	8,168.4	9,306.4	11,055.5	6.8
- Government consumption	5,745.6	6,484.5	7,118.0	7,695.9	8,127.2	5.1
Foreign balance	1,977.0	676.1	3,723.0	7,228.1	6,785.2	19.3
Foreign balance as percent of Gross National Product	2.5	0.7	4.0	7.0	6.1	

[a] 1978 data are provisional.

[b] Government inventory investment, in most years a nominal amount, is not listed.

Source: Bank of Japan, Economic Statistics Annual 1977, March 1978; Nomura Research Institute, Quarterly Economic Review, October 1978; Japan Economic Journal, December 26, 1978.

penditures. As other sources of growth—a surplus of labor ready to be released from low productivity farming, for example—diminished in strength, growth potential and, relative to output, the demand for investment in the private sector also fell. Saving habits, however, are slower to change. In fact, the Organization for Economic Cooperation and Development (OECD) says that Japanese household savings (which account for more than half of total savings) as a share of disposable income rose from an average 19.6 percent in 1967-1971 to 23.6 percent in 1972-1978. The resulting excess of savings was absorbed by government deficits, by unemployment of labor and productive plants *and* by the surplus in foreign transactions.

In principle, government deficits could be increased until both unemployment and the foreign surplus would be reduced to any desired levels. Japan's fiscal deficits have been large, as tax revenues have stayed low and spending on public works has been expanded; the projected national accounts deficit for the fiscal year beginning April 1979 is $76 billion ($1 = 200 yen), or 7 percent of projected GNP. For comparison, a fiscal 1980 $29 billion federal deficit would be 1.1 percent of projected United States GNP. It is arguable, all the same, that the Japanese authorities have been excessively prudent and that much larger deficits could have been run without serious risks. But it is also true that marketing the government's rising volume of debt has encountered difficulties and that the Ministry of Finance bureaucracy's concern about managing the mounting deficit has not been without basis. In any case, official doubts about a more stimulative macroeconomic policy have been a political reality to which successive cabinets have had to give respectful attention.

Another answer would be to cut Japan's access to major foreign markets. That would mean, in effect, that the United States and the European Economic Community would allow protectionist sentiment to have its way. The political implications of such a step in Japan and internationally would be considerable and unpleasant. From an economic point of view, it would amount to a decision to forcibly reduce Japan's contribution to world output and productivity.

There remains the thought that a sizable Japanese current account surplus might after all be acceptable and even desirable. In a textbook model, the current account position that has developed since 1975 should have given rise to an outflow of long-term capital that would have offset the surplus. This has not happened in textbook fashion. The reasons are various but important among them has been Japan's legacy of exchange controls and of close bureaucratic management of domestic financial markets. While the application of exchange controls has been loosened in recent years, the Ministry of Finance's comprehensive legal powers over foreign financial transactions have remained a deterrent to the development of a more nearly free international capital market in Tokyo; so have the ministry's continuing tight controls over the hierarchy of domestic interest rates, from those applicable to postal savings to the rates on long-term bond issues.

Pressures exist inside Japan for liberalization of controls. The Japanese commercial banks, foreign banks, the security houses, and the Bank of Japan all favor movement to free up the financial markets. The current account surplus and the problems of marketing government debt have given impetus to these pressures. Matters of this kind move slowly in Japan, as they do everywhere when long-standing bureaucratic interests are involved. Nevertheless, a basic revision of the exchange control law already has been promised and a number of institutional steps have been taken toward greater flexibility of money market rates. Necessity is compelling enough to suggest that the process will go on, no doubt less rapidly than might be hoped but steadily in any event.

What should be the mix of capital outflows (as among direct investments, long-term loans, and concessional development aid) is perhaps a legitimate question. Japan has been niggardly in giving aid and as a latecomer to direct investment it has had to cope with a relatively unreceptive environment abroad. On the other hand, the burden on many debtors inherent in undue reliance on long-term borrowing at commercial rates may well argue for greater emphasis on concessional loans and equity financing. The market alone will not make all the necessary decisions on this score; politicians will have to face up to the need for budgetary allocations for concessional aid, and bureaucrats no doubt will wish to help direct investors to safe and rewarding projects. Even so, the development of an efficient capital market in Tokyo will go a long way toward making Japan the exporter of financial resources that it seems destined to be.

There is no question, in any case, about the world's need for capital flows; now that China has chosen to turn to the outside world for help with the modernization program, the requirements have jumped by some large amount. With large savings, highly productive Japan is an obvious source of capital. To serve as such a source Japan will require the current account surplus. And, as has been said, this will depend on the stripping down of a cumbersome set of controls that has become increasingly anomalous to the economic circumstances of today's Japan.

It does not follow that the longer run prospect sketched here should be taken as reason for passivity in Tokyo toward the outsized imbalance in Japan's current external accounts. There are import restrictions to be relaxed and the need for more venturesome fiscal-monetary policies to be reconsidered. But it is not out of order, either, for Washington to reflect on the kind of world economic relationships that ought to obtain over the next decade. In such a context, Japan's role looks to be that of a capital exporter on a scale commensurate with the economy's size and characteristics. It might just be worthwhile first to recognize and then to accept, if not to foster, that eventuality.

Notes

1. John M. Allison, *Ambassador from the Prairie* (Houghton Mifflin, 1973), pp. 165-66.
2. Prime Minister Yoshida, leader of the Liberal party, had to sign the treaty alone because his Democratic party colleague had so divided the constituency on the question. Shigeru Yoshida, *The Yoshida Memoirs* (Westport, Conn.: Greenwood Press, 1962), p. 191.
3. Allison, *Ambassador from the Prairie*, pp. 155-57.
4. *U.S. Foreign Policy for the 1970s*, February 9, 1972, pp. 52 ff.

9
The U.S.-Japanese Alliance — Cornerstone or Trouble Zone?

Robert A. Scalapino

Throughout the twentieth century, Japan has had a series of alliances with major Western powers, each fashioned to advance central Japanese goals of the era. This century had barely opened when the Anglo-Japanese alliance of 1901 was consummated, and for two decades Japan had moved toward modernization at home and expansion abroad under the aegis of close relations with the most powerful Western nation of those years.[1] On occasion, it should be noted, Great Britain served in the role of a restraining force as well as in the role of supporter. Despite the moral injunctions of the United States against Japan's Twenty-one Demands upon China during World War I, it was British disapproval that gave the Japanese government pause. On balance, however, the ties with England were conducive to advances on many fronts.

It is not surprising, therefore, that when a weak multilateralism was forced upon Japan in the form of the Washington Conference treaties of 1922, Tokyo was deeply unhappy, viewing the new efforts at an equilibrium in the Pacific–East Asian region as a wholly inadequate substitute for bilateral ties with Great Britain.[2] The next two decades were marked by a growing breach in domestic Japanese consensus over policies at home and abroad. Amid economic crisis, a significant urban-rural gap, and rising political instability, Japan drifted down an authoritarian-nationalist path that ultimately led to a new consensus, albeit one that required the silencing of some opponents.³ At once radical and conservative, the policies of the new era were dedicated to the exaltation of Japanese culture in its "pure" forms, purged of Western "excesses"; to the creation of a Greater East Asian Co-Prosperity Sphere, harnessing Japan's growing industrial might to the requirements of an underdeveloped Asia; and to the eradication of both Western and Soviet control or influence from the Pacific-Asian region.

Thus, the union with Germany and Italy in the Anti-Comintern Pact of 1937 was natural, even though once again Japan was aligned with two Western nations. If the Anglo-Japanese alliance was largely a formal, government-to-government tie having limited popular impact, the new alignment with Germany and Italy was also relatively distant and fragile, notwithstanding that all three nations shared a dislike of the status-quo, a growing concern over international Communism (and specifically over the emerging power of the Soviet Union), and a determination to challenge the global dominance of certain West European countries and the United States.

After the disastrous "Pacific War" (ending in 1945), Japan once again moved rapidly into a new Western-oriented alliance. The U.S.-Japanese alliance was initiated more by Washington than by Tokyo, but it served well the purposes of those who governed Japan and met with their full approval from the outset. At this point, moreover, it has remained intact for nearly three decades, longer than any alliance in the history of modern Japan. It has also resulted in more intimate cultural, economic, political and security ties than any previous external relationship in the whole of Japanese history. In most respects, this is equally true when the measurements are applied to U.S. foreign relations. Few if any alliances in U.S. history have had the breadth and depth of our alliance with Japan in the post-1945 period, despite the very significant cultural differences in our two societies and the reluctance with which both Americans and Japanese came to the concept of a permanent, in-depth foreign commitment.

The rhetoric of contemporary U.S. and Japanese leaders continues to testify to these facts. Carter and Ohira, like their predecessors, describe U.S.-Japanese ties as "the cornerstone" of the foreign policies of each nation, especially in the Pacific-Asian region.[4] Yet behind the flood of optimistic words from officialdom, various developments have promoted a growing sense of unease, even crisis, in various quarters. Is this a temporary phenomenon, connected with the movement of Japan from "client" to "partner" in its relation to the United States, and are the central economic and strategic problems en route to amelioration or solution? Or, are recent problems in the U.S.-Japanese relationship sending ever deeper roots, systemic in character, thus to be a part of the future? Rather than "cornerstone," is our mutual relation destined to become a "trouble-zone?"

Prior to attempting any answer (and an accurate answer at this point must be both complex and contingent), let us survey the current situation, commencing with cultural ties and the attitudes of our two peoples toward each other. In two democracies where public opinion can influence if not direct policies (and that is increasingly true in Japan as well as in the United States), cultural interactions and emotional attitudes are not unimportant to overall relations.

One of the remarkable aspects of the U.S. occupation of Japan (1945-1951) was the fact that two peoples who had fought so savagely against each other a few years earlier had come to have such a high degree of mutual respect in the course of the early postwar era. In considerable degree, this was because of certain personal attributes widely observed in a period when millions of Americans lived in Japan. Of the Japanese these attributes included a strong work ethic, cleanliness, honesty, and a sense of personal discipline combined with a commitment to social order; of the Americans these centered upon a comparable work ethic, friendliness, generosity, and a dedication to progress.

At the end of the occupation and for many years thereafter, the United States as a nation and the Americans as a people were rated more highly by Japanese than any other nation or people.[5] Correspondingly, the Japanese were evaluated much higher by Americans than many peoples who had been allies during World War II. In recent years, Japanese public opinion polls indicate three general trends. First, among countries "liked most," the rating of the United States has declined, although it remains close to the top—with such Western states as Switzerland and France often heading the list. Seemingly, the popularity of such countries reflects a Japanese ideal of "independence" and a nonthreatening international stance. Of at least equal importance, such polls have shown that a steadily rising percentage of the Japanese people prefer to indicate no country as most liked, suggesting an increased commitment to their own nation.

It is also significant, however, that China has shown a dramatic forward surge in esteem in recent years. At the time of the ratification of the Sino-Japanese treaty of friendship, an *Asahi Shimbun* national poll of October 1978 indicated that 29 percent of the people felt that China should be the country with which Japan should have most amiable relations in the future (only 26 percent in favor of the United States).[6] While the timing of this poll undoubtedly affected the percentages, it should be noted that in a similar poll precisely two years earlier, 20 percent answered "China" as against 45 percent responding "the United States." This would indicate a rather dramatic drop in U.S. prestige.

One must guard against placing too much emphasis upon such polls. The phrasing of a question, the timing of a poll, and the current international context can all affect the results. Cumulative data, however, taken over time, cannot be ignored. The United States is still relatively popular in Japan in comparison with other nations, but U.S. credibility has definitely been affected adversely by the events of recent years. Thus, while a rising percentage of the Japanese people believe that the United States–Japan Mutual Security Treaty is "useful" (49 percent as against 34 percent in May 1971—according to the *Asahi* poll of October 1978—with 13 percent regarding it as "not useful" and 22 percent "unable to say"), 55 percent of the respondents state that they do not believe that the United States would come to Japan's aid in case of an emergency (as against 45 percent in September 1969).

In the aftermath of the abandonment of Vietnam, the announcement of troop withdrawals from Korea, and other questions about the U.S. commitment in Asia, the Japanese along with other Asians remain skeptical about U.S. power and intentions. At first glance, the above poll results might seem contradictory—as is not infrequently the case with public opinion polls. If American credibility is down, why has support for the treaty increased? Perhaps this is the case because many Japanese feel that the chances of an Asian war involving the United States are remote today, and hence the risks to Japan via the treaty are low; it can therefore be regarded as useful in at least a limited degree without posing a threat. Also, the treaty is now implicitly endorsed by Peking. And for many, rising resentment against the Soviet Union gives the U.S. tie additional support. However, the security issue is a complex one, which will receive closer examination shortly.

Are Japanese doubts about U.S. credibility as a military ally warranted? Probably not. In the unlikely event of an attack upon Japan, the Carter administration—and any successor presently conceivable—would almost surely live up to the treaty provisions. But those provisions require actions in accordance with constitutional requirements, meaning ultimate congressional approval. And there is the additional uncertainty of U.S. public opinion, a critical factor in the Vietnam debacle. Recent polls have suggested that Americans would be deeply divided over military support in the defense of any nation except Canada, a border state, and although these polls are highly misleading, taken as they have been in the absence of a crisis, they are testimony to the current lack of a domestic consensus on U.S. foreign policy.[7]

In broader terms, U.S. opinions on Japan and the Japanese remain basically favorable,[8] but here too there has been some slippage and, more importantly, two important U.S. interest groups, business and labor, have shown increasing signs of resentment, even hostility, as a result of perceived Japanese economic policies. We shall deal with this issue later. Here, it is only important to note that as Japan has moved into the position of competitor, with economic conditions in the United States far from satisfactory, tension has increased, and with it demands for protectionism in various forms. Concerning U.S. opinion, therefore, distinctions must be made between government (still strongly supportive of close ties with Japan), selected elites (where mounting antagonism in certain economic sectors exists), and the U.S. public (which is still basically favorable to Japan and the Japanese).

Cultural exchange continues across many fields and takes a great diversity of forms but there are some lacunae. The Japanese have seen little need to send undergraduate students to U.S. colleges and universities, and indeed the flow of graduate students has been limited due to the tightly woven (and highly prestigious) Japanese educational system, with the sciences providing a partial exception. American students in Japanese institutions of higher learning are also few, due to language and curriculum problems. The Japanese higher educational system is one of the most conservative aspects of that nation's overall culture at present, especially in the humanities and social sciences. Sooner or later, it must undergo change if Japan's progress is to continue—but many would argue that the U.S. college-university system is also badly in need of renovation and cannot serve as a model for the future.

In any case, one of the weaknesses of the American-Japanese linkage lies in the relatively shallow intellectual interchange. Certain channels in the form of international conferences and exchanges exist, but these contacts are generally limited to the same small group of individuals. Language barriers combine with cultural differences to pose sizable obstacles to expanded contacts. As one result, Japanese intellectual conservatism flows first into Marxist, then nationalist channels—both of which have had a sizable impact upon the intellectual climate of modern Japan. And American intellectuals, however eclectic in ideological propensities, have a tendency to treat Japan either with indifference or to assume that, as a "modern" nation, it can be understood in Western (to be read American) terms.[9]

Interestingly, American intellectuals have very rarely developed that emotional attachment to Japan that has so often been the case with regard to China. The romanticism that sometimes surrounds interpretations of China has almost never dominated thinking about Japan or American-Japanese relations. Respect, not love, is the apt description if one must reduce it to a word. In part, this is because the Japanese are a very private, strongly introverted people—not easily given to intimacy and informality. They are not prone to invest casual relations with an extroverted heartiness.

Another lacuna—more understandable—exists in the very limited American-Japanese collaboration in research and development. Few societies have reached the level of technological-scientific capacity now achieved by the United States and Japan. A major development in this respect, moreover, is en route. Up to date, the United States has been the pioneer, Japan the adaptor. Now, the challenge is for Japan to initiate cooperation since in many fields it has come abreast of the innovator. The issue is whether future innovation in our two nations will be wholly exclusive and competitive in nature, or whether in such critical needs as energy, some collaborative work can take place.

Meanwhile, an intense cultural interaction continues in many fields. The influence of Japanese art, literature, motion pictures, ceramics, landscaping, and cuisine upon the United States—to mention only the most obvious influences—has been extraordinarily great in the past three decades, and there is no indication of a decline. Similarly, the American culture in both its "high" and "low" forms has struck Japan with a resounding impact. American music, literature, art, and architecture combine with American clothing, food (including the fast food innovation), and time-saving household implements to change the Japanese way of life, sometimes boldly, sometimes in more subtle ways. It is not an exaggeration to assert that no two societies in the world have had a greater cultural impact upon each other in recent decades than the United States and Japan.

Ironically, this is one reason for the heightening problems in the economic, political, and security arenas. Two-way trade between our two countries now surpasses $30 billion annually, indicative of our very great interdependence. Yet, as is well known, the very intensity of this economic relationship has produced serious controversies. The basic economic issues between the United States and Japan have been sufficiently explicated—and so well presented in this volume—that only a brief summary of the key points is required. The current issues as viewed by involved Americans relate to (1) the very high trade deficit with Japan incurred by the United States (over $13 billion in 1978); (2) the perceived tariff and nontariff barriers inhibiting U.S. trade and investment in Japan; (3) a government-business relationship that provides Japanese competitors with unfair advantages (exacerbated by Japanese overseas business practices that are regarded as not infrequently unethical); and (4) lower labor standards in terms of combined wages and fringe benefits, despite the substantial Japanese increases of recent years.

From a Japanese perspective, the issues would be phrased roughly as follows: (1) the inability of the U.S. government to construct viable domestic economic policies, especially with respect to the interrelated problems of inflation and energy (hence, the weakness of the dollar and the general unease surrounding economic relations among advanced industrial nations); (2) the absence of any leadership in developing a workable set of international economic policies; (3) the inability or unwillingness of U.S. enterprise to be truly competitive in the quest for overseas markets and its penchant for blaming others for its own deficiencies; (4) the lagging productivity of U.S. labor measured against that of certain other societies, including Japan; and (5) the failure to recognize the sizable reforms effected by Japan in the recent past and the tendency to ignore the higher degree of discrimination against Japan currently practiced by the European Economic Community.

There is some truth in both positions, hence the intractability of the problems. If one were to sum up the essential difficulties faced by each party, these might be summarized as follows: First, the United States must put its own economic house in order, devising policies that curb inflation by controlling government expenditures and adopting effective energy policies. At the same time, it must accept the need to construct a set of international economic policies consistent with its overall foreign policy goals and aimed at providing new impetus to U.S. overseas activity while also helping to build greater stability in the international economic arena. Otherwise, problems with the advanced industrial world will persist. Because economic relations with Japan are so intense, moreover, and because the Japanese system has long been geared to the maximum exploitation of overseas opportunities, the problems here are likely to be the most acute. In addition, U.S. industry and labor must see the importance of expanding international markets and be willing to make the necessary commitment and to apply rigor and efficiency to this end. Given the present lethargy and noncompetitiveness, U.S. international advances will be insufficient for a healthy economic interaction with societies like Japan.

On the Japanese side, a coordinated economic system involving a broad consensus on goals and methods, which has worked beautifully for Japan over many years, has recently shown itself slow to adjust to the changing requirements and demands of the international community. Japan must lessen its dependence upon export-oriented economic growth and accept greater social responsibilities with regard to both its own people and the larger community of late-developing countries. It must also show a greater commitment to adjusting its own internal system to accommodate increased imports and foreign investment. Finally, its extensive dependence upon heavy industry must shift rapidly toward a greater reliance on high technology production, and the banking practices of the past, which have enabled very heavy corporate indebtedness, must be revised.[10]

The types of changes outlined above not only represent very basic policy shifts for both societies but they require systemic and ideological adjustments. Hence, they will not come quickly or easily. The problem is the more complex because major changes are required on the part of both the public and the private sectors and in a political setting where powerful interest groups operate freely and must frequently be accommodated. Unfortunately, there is very little short-run political payoff for anticipating crisis, and in a democracy it is the short-run political payoff that is usually most crucial to the political leadership.

What may we anticipate, then, in the realm of future U.S.-Japanese economic relations? On the positive side, there is growing awareness of the dimensions and nature of the problems of both parties, a thorough airing of the issues having taken place. Circumstances, moreover, are forcing the U.S. government to take the issue of inflation seriously, albeit with policies of dubious effect thus far. And for the first time, the U.S. government is showing an interest in stimulating U.S.

business activity abroad, although concrete policies to this end remain to be drafted. It is possible that we are seeing the first tentative steps in the direction of a more viable U.S. economy at home and a more competitive one abroad, despite the formidable obstacles that remain. Whether this proves to be the case will depend upon the private as much as the public sector.

Japan has also been half-persuaded, half-forced into a reconsideration of certain basic policies of many years' duration. Tariff reductions have actually been quite dramatic and, with respect to nontariff barriers, the top political leadership has evidenced a growing willingness to cooperate, but it remains to change the attitudes and policies of the lower bureaucratic-industrial structure, which must implement such policies.[11] Meanwhile, a rising commitment to social programming will be enforced by the aging of the Japanese population and the slowly diminishing role of private welfare, long the hallmark of Japan's uniqueness. In overseas economic policies also, Japan has signalled an interest in less exclusively market-oriented assistance programs but implementation remains scanty. Once again, the beginnings of change can be discerned, but with issues of timing and depth unresolved. In more immediate terms, the radical appreciation of the yen should reduce the U.S. trade deficit with Japan substantially in the next few years, barring some major unforeseen events.

Unfortunately, the negative side of the ledger remains ominous. Whatever the future may hold, the problem of inflation continues to be very serious in the United States; no coherent international economic policies, either with respect to the United States itself or to the broader community of nations, have been formulated; oil prices continue to rise; the arc from Iran to Turkey—together with the Middle East heartland—seems to promise recurrent instability; a domestic recession, at least modest in proportions, is forecast; and there are no signs of bold, new innovative steps on the part of the U.S. private sector to seek a global market—most hope being placed upon an accelerated technological revolution in which the United States will continue to hold the lead.

In Japan, one may discount as a historically ingrained habit of the Japanese the persistent pessimistic notes sounded from various quarters, but those notes have once again become strong. The reasons most frequently cited for the pessimism are the threat of protectionism by both the advanced and developing nations; the rising costs of and increasing competition for raw materials; changes in the Japanese population structure leading to a decreased working force and increased social costs; political instability combined with the inhibiting "statist" character of government in many developing societies; and the advent of political uncertainty at home.

Some of this gloom seems unwarranted. Japan continues to make gains at home and to capture sizable markets abroad. Even if it has to settle for 5 to 6 percent GNP gains in the future, this will still make it the fastest growing advanced economy in the world. But Japan's very successes may retard the type of changes earlier described as necessary for a healthy U.S.-Japanese economic relationship. Every current sign suggests that Japan will continue to pursue an aggressive export and overseas investment policy. In 1977, for example, Japanese concerns expended nearly $640 million in direct investment in the ASEAN countries of Southeast Asia alone, almost twice as much as U.S. investment in all of Asia except Japan. As is well known, Japan hopes for investment as well as trade in China, although one prominent Japanese economist predicts that such trade will not rise much above 5 percent of total Japanese trade. Eventually, the development of Siberia also beckons, despite current political and economic obstacles. Already, Japanese investment in the United States has assumed sizable proportions with greater advances likely ahead.

While these developments are natural, they are not necessarily conducive to cordial relations between the United States and Japan. Indeed, they promise an aggressively competitive Japan that the United States will find hard to match. Japanese investment here has already produced political repercussions in some areas, stimulated by such sensational phrases as "the selling of America." Meanwhile, the current obstacles to mounting U.S. investment — or even imports — in Japan seem destined to recede slowly. At the same time, as the two largest consumers of the world's raw materials and resources, the United States and Japan are likely to be pushed toward an ever more intense competitive position.

In this setting, can protectionism in various forms be avoided? While scholars have been busily chronicling the rise of nationalism in various emerging societies (and generally praising it), they have tended to overlook the rise of nationalism in the "advanced" world, but that is surely an important component of recent developments in both the United States and Japan. The growing insistence within the U.S. business community upon control over Japanese "saturation" tactics, and the new slogan of the AFL-CIO, "fair trade, not free trade," are symptomatic of this era—paralleled in Japan by the stubborn resistance to foreign imports and the reluctance to see foreign investment grow.

One can devise both an optimistic and pessimistic scenario, with much hinging upon decisions and capacities within the domestic context of each society. An optimistic scenario would envisage a situation wherein the United States had its domestic and international economic policies in order, where the private sector demonstrated a heightened vigor in international competition and where technological developments proved sufficiently dramatic and timely to cut through current resource and energy difficulties. It would also assume that Japan was able to undertake successfully the transition from a largely export-oriented economy to one increasingly playing to domestic needs and, at the same time, that Japan admitted the United States more fully into its domestic economy. The pessimistic scenario envisages a "too little, too late" approach to the problems that have been sketched, resulting in recurrent crises and a rising nationalist-exclusivist tide, with Japan once again turning toward Asia as in the 1930s, striking a Gaullist posture, but with a global economic thrust, and the United States playing a less important role than in the past.

The fact that much hinges upon domestic policies illustrates the close interrelation today between internal politics and external relations. How shall we describe the political currents in the United States and Japan? How well do they mesh and are they conducive to close ties in handling bilateral as well as multilateral issues? Political projections are fraught with danger in this transitional, complex era. Up to date, our political compatibility has been of major assistance in strengthening the ties between the United States and Japan. In a period of great fluidity, the U.S.-derived constitution has survived intact in Japan and that nation remains one of the most politically open societies in the world. Together with India and Sri Lanka, Japan represents the last of the Western-style democracies in this part of the globe. Even more significant, Japan has been a stable democracy; indeed, in free elections, the Japanese voters have returned moderates to national power continuously for three decades.[12]

While factionalized like most other Japanese parties, the dominant Liberal Democratic party (LDP) has hewed to a relatively consistent set of policies, domestic and foreign.[13] Together with the Ministry of Finance and the Ministry of International Trade and Industry, it has fashioned Japan's export-oriented economy and the decision to separate economics from politics in pursuing economic outlets everywhere. Critics have charged that Japan has had no foreign policy, only a market policy, and one directed wholly toward Japanese self-interest. It has been a policy pleasing to the Japanese electorate, however. In general terms, moreover, the LDP has been regarded at home and abroad as a party generally sympathetic to the United States and to U.S. foreign policies.

Will democracy and stability continue in Japan? An affirmative answer, put cautiously, seems warranted, at least for the period immediately ahead. Democracy clearly has its greatest chances of survival in an advanced, affluent society, and despite the hazards Japan seems likely to retain that status. Japanese culture, moreover, notwithstanding the assaults upon its traditional forms, clings to a type of conservatism that resists violent upheaval and supports incrementalism. Nevertheless, within the democratic framework, a transition of considerable importance seems likely. The older generation will be different both in background and political style. Many leaders will be "pure politicians" rather than bureaucrats transferring to politics in midcareer. They are likely to be more amenable to the media and a wider variety of interest groups. Indeed, this trend is already underway. More broadly speaking, the Liberal Democratic party itself may undergo a series of renovations, and the communication between the LDP and certain other parties will grow.[14] In one form or another, Japan will move toward coalition politics, whether or not a formal coalition is necessitated. Despite its majorities in the Diet, the LDP has polled below 50 percent of the total vote for some years, and this is not apt to be reversed.

As these developments materialize, some increase in political instability is likely. Only a prolonged economic or international crisis, however, would produce dramatic political oscillations. Would these be toward the "left" or the "right"? Unfortunately, these terms have always been misleading and never more so than today. The initial bent would in all probability be "right" as that word is conventionally used. A more strongly nationalist tide would flow, protective of "Japanese values and interests," pursuing Gaullist type policies, and with a pronounced bias toward pan-Asianism despite global economic interests. This trend, however, would not preclude a more direct appeal by political leaders to the citizenry at large, a quasi-mobilization politics, and greater attention to social services of many types.

Even if no major crisis affecting Japan emerges, the above trend—in moderate form—seems destined to grow. It is already in evidence, albeit as a contrapuntal theme. The decline of U.S. credibility in Asia, the uncertainties surrounding economic relations with the "advanced" West, and the seeming vitality of the new East Asian Co-Prosperity Sphere—these and other factors figure into present reality.

Only a few years ago, it would have seemed ridiculous to ask whether democracy is in jeopardy in the United States but few Americans are unaware of the serious problems that have confronted their political system in recent years. The Vietnam defeat, Watergate, "stagflation," and the general problems of urban life have served to divide the American people as deeply as during any period since the Civil War. Today, no consensus exists, either with respect to domestic or foreign policies, and elements of contradiction and indecision abound, both at the public and leadership levels.

Unlike the era of the Great Depression, however, there has been no pronounced shift of voter sentiment toward the political extremities. Apathy has been a more prominent feature, suggesting that alienation is widespread but does not (yet) run deeply. Public opinion polls, moreover, indicate that the overwhelming majority of the American people, including all generations, still support democratic institutions, and many more failures and crises would have to ensue before the system was in peril.

As in Japan, the current political trends in the United States are largely conservative. Concern over inflation, heavy taxes, crime, "big government," and a perceived lack of stature in political leaders dominate political thinking on domestic issues. On the foreign policy front, nationalism is achieving a new respectability in various areas: increased, though tentative, support for a strong defense in a position of at least "parity" with the Soviet Union; greater concern about "American interests" rather than "global welfare," and hence demands for burden-sharing, a reduction in international aid in unilateral form; and a strong desire to keep out of foreign conflicts. As noted earlier, some trends seem contradictory; others might well be subject to dramatic changes were circumstances suddenly to be altered. But in any case, there is little likelihood that the current political mood in the United States will produce drastic alterations in the political structure. More probable is the continuing adjustment of the two major parties to public opinion, a development that is well under way at this point.

The political issues in U.S.-Japanese relations, therefore, are not apt to focus upon the problem of radically diverging political systems, at least in the near term. The problem that suggests itself is rather that of a growing conflict over certain issues related to the rising nationalist tides in both nations. As has been suggested, this conflict could affect all aspects of U.S.-Japanese relations, from the cultural to the strategic. Pride in "Japanism" or "Americanism" is not in itself unhealthy; on the contrary, it is essential to a self-respecting, progressive society. But it can lead to cultural chauvinism and indiscriminate antiforeignism. When nationalism takes an economic form, as is natural in some degree, will it lead under present circumstances to protectionism? Burden-sharing and interdependence, translated into U.S.-Japanese security issues, have already produced complex cross-currents. In both the United States and Japan, fissures have been opened over the extent and nature of Japan's military responsibilities, as we shall shortly discuss.

How does one best capture the nationalist trends and relate them to the broadest aspects of U.S.-Japanese relations? At a minimum, the United States intends to cast off certain foreign policies of the past considered at home to be lacking in any reciprocity or accountability; "American interests," as defined by a combination of administrative and interest group spokesmen, will receive heightened attention, and while there will be no complete agreement on the implication of this phrase, policies in general will take on a stronger nationalist hue. Japan will also manifest its nationalism in a variety of ways, not the least by electing to follow a separate path on certain international issues without abandoning its efforts to retain close ties with the United States. Policies toward the Middle East during the oil crisis provide an example. The potential for some rise in the degree of conflict between our two countries in these connections is not insubstantial.[15]

Let us turn finally to security issues.[16] Present Japanese policy with respect to national defense is still based fundamentally upon the "MacArthur Constitution," which provides in Article 9 for the outlawing of war as an instrument of Japanese national policy. Under a strict interpretation of this article — once staunchly demanded by the Left — it might be considered illegal to possess any armed forces, but that issue was first sidestepped and then eliminated via various court decisions. Today, Japan has a Self-Defense Force of 260,000 men, and in 1978 it expended $8.6 billion on defense, just slightly less than 1 percent (.9 percent) of its gross national product.

Those who want to emphasize Japan's military strength point to the fact that it now spends more on defense than any other Asian nation except China, that using certain measurements it can be considered the seventh most powerful nation in the world militarily, and that with its recent purchases it has moved toward a highly advanced military technology that compensates in some degree for its relatively small size.

Those who regard Japan's defense commitments as inadequate — both Americans and Japanese — emphasize other factors: that among its neighbors in Northeast Asia — Russia, China, South and North Korea, and Taiwan — Japan has the smallest armed forces numerically and is inhibited by its constitution from playing any direct role in regional security; that the present narrow definition of the term "defensive weaponry" precludes any meaningful defense—rather, Japan confronted with a Soviet attack, for example, could hold out for only hours—or days at most—and is therefore totally dependent upon an uncertain U.S. commitment; and, for some Americans, that Japan has for too long obtained a "free ride," with U.S. expenditures on behalf of Japanese and Northeast Asian security going unreciprocated.

What is the status of this debate? Let us turn first to its strictly Japanese dimensions. Recently, a prominent Japanese "think-tank" expert long associated with defense issues asserted:

> The perimeter of the defense discussion has been greatly expanded. There are no longer subjects that are taboo, including that of nuclear weaponry. But there is no indication at present that the government is going to allocate the funds that would be necessary if Japan were to make a dramatic change in its security policies, or that it is prepared to launch the type of sustained, long-term educational campaign among the Japanese people that would be essential if support were to be obtained. Changes will be gradual and incremental.[17]

Yasuhiro Nakasone is one of the possible leaders of the future who has called for major changes in Japan's security policies. He advocates amending the constitution to permit an expanded security role and greater independence from the U.S. defense umbrella, including a consideration of a wide range of new weapons, some of which could not be denominated as strictly defensive. Japanese public opinion, however, remains firmly committed to the status quo. According to the October 1978 *Asahi* poll cited earlier, 57 percent of the people would keep the Self-Defense Force as it is, while 19 percent would strengthen it, 11 percent would decrease it, and 5 percent would abolish it (figures from an identical December 1968 poll were 55 percent, 19 percent, 4 percent, and 9 percent, respectively). This represents some decrease on the "dovish" side as uncertain respondents moved to establish their position, but no real change on the "hawkish" side, and a very strong sentiment for continuing the present level of commitment.

Nevertheless, some U.S. observers believe that Japan will make a quantum leap in the near future with respect to security issues, supported by both China and the United States.[18] Certain new developments lend some credence to that belief. In the recent past, the United States and Japan have agreed to set up a joint defense planning body and joint military exercises have already taken place. Japan has indicated its interest in purchases of U.S. air defense missiles, sophisticated computer and communications equipment, and other items not previously in the Japanese military arsenal. At the same time, Japanese authorities have agreed to contribute additional funds to the cost of U.S. troops in Japan.

It remains very doubtful, however, that any massive shift in the character of Japanese security commitments will take place in the foreseeable future. A draft of a seven-year medium-term plan carrying through the fiscal year 1984 is presently under review by the Japanese Defense Agency. That plan calls for the strengthening of antiaircraft and antitank forces; the deployment of new weapons systems including various SAM missiles; the strengthening of antisubmarine warfare capabilities; and the addition of F-15 fighter interceptors. Its thrust, however, is wholly defensive. Nor is there any indication that the Japanese government intends to make any move toward constitutional amendment, notwithstanding the views of Nakasone and some others. In sum, the sensationalist accounts of Japanese military expansion are not supported by current data. This does not preclude the possibility of a change under certain circumstances. If the perceived threat from a major power like the Soviet Union were to increase greatly and U.S. credibility were to continue to decline, rapid shifts in Japanese public opinion and in national policies could occur.

Meanwhile, the security issue produces certain differences in Japanese and U.S. positions that produce tension despite recent cooperative measures. In truth, the U.S. position with respect to Japanese rearmament has been ambivalent and hence confusing to Japanese authorities. Washington has frequently emphasized its strong opposition to any Japanese move toward the acquisition of nuclear weapons. Indeed, few official U.S. spokesmen have indicated an interest in seeing Japan become a major military power in Asia. At the same time, both in the Congress and among the U.S. public at large, the feeling that the United States bears an undue share of the security burden in Northeast Asia has grown, and criticism of the fact that Japan spends less than 1 percent of its gross national product upon defense is widespread. Such complaints easily meld into the broader unhappiness over economic relations.

The Japanese concern is of a different nature. The Japanese government has become increasingly aware of pressures emanating both from China and the United States to move into a united front against the Soviet Union. The protracted struggle conducted by Tokyo to soften the "antihegemony" clause in the Sino-Japanese friendship treaty was illustrative of the problem as it involved China. While Japan has serious differences with the Soviet Union, ranging from issues of maritime jurisdiction to the northern islands controversy, and esteem for the Russians is low both among the public and in political circles, no Japanese government wants to be placed in a highly exposed position as the spearhead of a united front against the USSR. Tokyo has not given up hope of eventually playing a major role in the development of Siberia, supplementing—and balancing—its role in fueling the Chinese industrial revolution. In any case, to deliberately cultivate a cold and possibly a hot war with the Soviet Union is a most unattractive alternative to Japan's low-risk policies of the past.

Thus, recent trends in U.S. policy toward the Sino-Soviet issue have been no less disconcerting to many Japanese policymakers than those of China. Tokyo has witnessed a growing tendency for the United States to opt for the fashioning of an informal alliance among China, Japan, and the United States against the Soviet Union. Neither Peking nor Washington is contemplating formal treaty ties, and U.S. policymakers generally deny a commitment to the united front strategy—however, current actions belie their words. The U.S. drive to strengthen China both economically and militarily, coupled with the outspoken antagonism against the Soviet Union manifested by some key U.S. spokesmen, has not escaped

Japanese leaders. They are well aware of the fact that President Carter purposely urged Prime Minister Fukuda to conclude the friendship treaty with China at a time when debate over its terms was rife in Japan. And they know that various commentators are discussing the possibility of informal military consultations involving China, Japan, and the United States, together with a much broader range of cooperative or collaborative actions.

The U.S. position on this critical strategic issue has not yet been finally determined. While the united front strategy has strong supporters both in and out of government, those who favor an "equilibrium" strategy are not negligible. The latter strategy would strive for a roughly equal treatment of the two major Communist nations, avoiding any consistent tilt toward either Peking or Moscow. It would assume that we are entering an era of protracted, intensive negotiations, and it would take up each question on an issue-by-issue basis, determining the U.S. position on the basis of our perceived interests and those of close allies. Its criticism of the united front strategy centers on two concerns: (1) that it will lead to the further destabilization of Asia, presenting China in the middle and long term with strong incentives for expansion; and (2) that it will lead to the type of global confrontation with the USSR that will make it difficult if not impossible to resolve such critical issues as disarmament and that it will cause interference in the internal affairs of other nations.[19]

Meanwhile, many Japanese are increasingly nervous about current trends. To be sure, they have been anxious to expand their economic ties with China, and a certain euphoria has swept over Japan as over the United States about such prospects. But they do not wish to see Japan pushed into a position making confrontation with the USSR inevitable, and they believe that some individuals in the United States are committed to policies leading to such an end.

The central issue that we have been discussing is but one illustration of the fact that U.S.-Japanese relations will be deeply influenced by the international context in which they operate. First Western Europe, then after a much briefer period, the United States were forced or caused to abandon the role of being the predominant influence in the region as a whole. Today, a greater measure of self-reliance is incumbent upon every Asian nation. None can count with full assurance upon any external force coming to its assistance, either economically or militarily. Even where alliances continue to exist, they are far more porous, flexible, and permissive. The contrast with the 1950s is striking. In the age of monolithic Communism, lines seemed sharply drawn. The U.S. network of alliances, including that with Japan, was all-encompassing, and U.S. capacities were backed by an American consensus that made U.S. credibility high.

The cleavages among Communist states, the end of such monolithism as it existed, has affected the strategies of every nation and, most of all, those of the United States. No one can doubt that divisions within Communism have been of enormous benefit to most non-Communist states, especially in Asia. Recall the years when Sino-Soviet unity lent its support to guerrilla activities throughout Southeast Asia, abetted Kim Il-sŏng in his attempted conquest of South Korea, and led even the Japanese Communists to a hard leftist line. In contrast, the only hot war in Asia today involves the bitter struggle between the Vietnamese and Cambodians with both the USSR and the People's Republic of China heavily involved. And with the Communists so fragmented, the prospects of Communist guerrilla success seem slim at the moment, since the capacity to render external assistance is limited.

To a considerable extent, these deep divisions among Communist states offset the decline of U.S. power in Asia. An unstable, yet possible viable balance of weakness exists. Paradoxically, however, the Communist split has contributed new issues as well as advantages. A tendency has naturally grown both in the United States and in Japan to gamble on Communist nationalism. As one result, it has been impossible to reestablish any ideological or value base upon which to rest foreign policy, with the result that a consensus can never be achieved. This is particularly true for the United States whose people have always demanded an ethical basis for internationalism. They are not satisfied with broad appeals to end the rich-poor gap or abolish armaments, and the Carter administration's attempt to substitute human rights as the moral equivalent of a struggle against Communism has been repeatedly undermined by the realpolitik policies of that same administration.

This problem—the absence of a moral foundation—has been of less consequence in Japan and Western Europe since the people and governments of these nations were rarely attracted to such slogans as "make the world safe for democracy," nor was moral suasion ever a cardinal element in their foreign policies.

On another front, however, the dilemma touches Japan and others more directly. The balance of weakness presently prevailing in Asia includes among other things a fluid and indistinct concept of mutuality. The old ties among states with relatively common institutions, economic systems, and political values are now much looser, as we have noted. New ties with states like China are being fashioned, ties cutting across old ideological barriers. In this manner, largely without realizing it, both the United States and Japan are accepting a growing dependence upon events within the Communist world. Developments within China and, above all, the course of Sino-Soviet relations now constitute even more critical variables than previously in international politics—and in the future of the United States and Japan—because China is being incorporated loosely into what was once an anti-Communist alliance and the latter has lost its previous coherence.

How should one summarize the present complex scene and future alternatives? It is possible that the U.S.-Japanese relationship will remain a cornerstone of each nation's foreign policy despite the rapidly changing environment that surrounds that relationship and the elements of difference and tension that have recently emerged to trouble it. Our mutual interests in the economic arena are huge and likely to grow. For both nations, there are supplements to, but no substitutes for, this economic interchange. China trade, for example, is not likely to equal one-fourth of U.S.-Japanese trade for either nation even under the most auspicious of conditions. Cooperation and the resolution of difficulties in the economic sphere are thus vital to the interests of both nations.

Moreover, we continue to share those basic political values and a sizable measure of cultural respect for each other that help to give our relations a firmer foundation. There is no evidence, as we have noted, that either the United States or Japan will depart from the pluralistic democratic system or that either will cease to borrow extensively from the other's culture.

Finally, whatever the misgivings in Japan about U.S. credibility, there is no substitute—now or in the foreseeable future—for the U.S. security guarantee. Only the United States can serve as a countervailing power to that near-neighbor of Japan, the Soviet Union, and this fact is recognized clearly by both Peking and Tokyo. From the American standpoint, given the enormous and growing economic and political interests of the United States in the Pacific-Asian region, a strong, healthy, and independent Japan remains of vital importance.

For the first time in the postwar era, however, U.S.-Japanese relations cannot be taken for granted, despite factors noted above that weigh heavily in favor of continued close ties. As we have seen, on nearly every front are problems of varying degrees of severity. At the human level, there remains a lack of true intimacy in the relationship, a seeming inability to communicate freely, frankly, and continuously. Formal ties have increased—although some have lapsed—and one extraordinary deficiency lies in the paucity of Japanese experts in the top reaches of the U.S. government. At informal levels, connections are thin and generally comprise the same individuals, with little new blood coming into the scene. We are not equipped, in short, to deal with each other as true allies, especially in meeting the unexpected or the crisis.

Beyond this, a considerable hostility now flows within our respective business and labor circles. Given the fact that competition between the United States and Japan is likely to increase and that the constraints imposed by the domestic situation are apt to grow in both societies, the economic issues between us permit of no quick or easy solutions. As we have indicated, systemic and attitudinal changes of major proportions are required, and it will take both skill and luck to effect these in time to avoid further crises.

While our political systems are apt to remain compatible, moreover, nationalism in various forms is rising in both nations, and with it, the propensity to protect one's own. There is also a defensiveness, connected with a sense of internal problems that will not go away. And at another level, there are differences between us in strategic perception, at least in terms of current trends. Japan is not ready to accept the united front strategy and basically remains committed to a separation between economics and politics, a minimal-risk, maximal-gain foreign policy.

This commitment will continue to create unhappiness among those Americans who feel that Japan has at least as great a stake in a strategic equilibrium in Asia as the United States and should therefore bear an increased share of the burden. Such a concern might well grow in the event of a serious crisis. Even the use of U.S. bases in Japan would become extremely controversial under most circumstances, raising questions as to their value—except in the vital role of deterrent. The prospect of Japan becoming a full-fledged strategic partner is very slight. Thus, the issue of burden-sharing will remain.

Given these realities, the U.S.-Japanese relationship may well have to accommodate a higher degree of competition and tension than in the past. This is certainly possible, especially since there are no clear alternatives for either party at this time. Withdrawal from Asia is impossible for the United States, given its broad and growing interests in the region, although a thrust in this direction has taken place. Neutralism or Gaullism are equally unrealistic for Japan despite their emotional appeal and some tendencies toward the latter course. But the troubles that have emerged are real and there is considerable wariness in our relationship today.

Some assistance would be afforded if we accepted the idea of a Pacific Basin Community, thereby taking up many economic issues in a multilateral context. It would also help if both nations, particularly the United States, treated our mutual relations with the seriousness they deserve by developing a greater pool of expertise, in and out of government, and expanding the consultative process at many levels. Beyond these possibilities, however, the changes that we are each able to effect in our economic systems and policies, together with the compatibility of our international strategies, will in the final analysis carry the heaviest weight in determining our future bilateral relations.

Notes

1. A detailed study of the early phases of this alliance is to be found in Ian H. Nish, *The Anglo-Japanese Alliance: The Diplomacy of Two Island Empires, 1894-1907* (London: Athlone Press, 1966), followed by his *Alliance in Decline—A Study in Anglo-Japanese Relations, 1908-1923*, University of London Historical Studies, no. 23 (London: Athlone Press, 1972).

2. For a still useful, contemporary account of the Washington agreements, see Raymond L. Buell, *The Washington Conference* (New York: Atheneum Publishers, 1922).

3. Among various accounts of this era in English, see Robert J. C. Butow, *Tojo and the Coming of the War*, (Stanford, Calif.: Stanford University Press, 1961); James B. Crowley, *Japan's Quest for Autonomy—National Security and Foreign Policy, 1930-1938* (Princeton, N.J.: Princeton University Press, 1966); Nobutaka Ike, *Japane's Decision for War*, (Stanford, Calif.: Stanford University Press, 1967); and Sadako Ogata, *Defiance in Manchuria: The Making of Japanese Foreign Policy, 1931-1932* (Berkeley and Los Angeles: University of California Press, 1964). Of very considerable interest also is a five-volume translation of portions of a massive work, *Taiheiyo senso e no michi, kai sen gaiko shi* [The road to the Pacific war—a history of prewar diplomacy], edited originally by Hikomatsu Kamikawa and Jun Tsunoda, with the English selections edited by James W. Morley, vol. 1, *Deterrent Diplomacy—Japan, Germany, and the USSR—1935-1940* (New York: Columbia University Press, 1976).

4. For one among many examples of the official U.S. position, see the speech of Secretary of State Cyrus Vance before the Asia Society delivered on June 29, 1977. The following two sentences from that speech have now become ritualistic: "Of our allies and old friends, none is more important than Japan. Our mutual security treaty is a cornerstone of peace in East Asia." The Japanese official position was expressed by Ohira Masayoshi shortly after his election as Japan's new premier in December 1978 when he asserted that close ties with the United States would continue to be the foundation of Japanese foreign policy.

5. Under the auspices of the U.S. Information Agency, monthly polls have been taken for many years based upon the simple questions: which country do you like most/which country do you dislike most? While the results are not published, they have been

available to interested scholars. Separate polls, somewhat similar in nature, have been taken by various Japanese newspapers.

6. The *Asahi Shimbun* National Poll, conducted October 12-13, 1978.

7. For recent data relating to U.S. public attitudes regarding Japan, see George R. Packard and William Watts, *The United States and Japan: American Perceptions and Policies* (Washington, D.C.: Potomac Associates, 1978). When asked whether the United States should come to the defense of Japan with military force if it were attacked by the Soviet Union or Communist China, 43 percent of the respondents replied affirmatively, 40 percent negatively, and 17 percent with a "don't know" answer. The poll was taken in April 1978. Ibid, p. 29.

8. Data on this question are presented by Packard and Watts, pp. 31 ff.

9. Chie Nakane has written a very stimulating if somewhat unidimensional work highlighting respects in which Japanese society continues to require a special understanding of the processes of coalition formation, participation and decision making. See her *Japanese Society* (Berkeley and Los Angeles: University of California Press, 1972). For other Japanese perspectives available in English, see Tadashi Fukutake, *Japanese Society Today* (Tokyo: University of Tokyo Press, 1977); Takeshi Ishida, *Japanese Society* (New York: Random House, 1971); and Kazuko Tsurumi, *Social Change and the Individual—Japan Before and After Defeat in World War II* (Princeton, N.J.: Princeton University Press, 1970). For two U.S. studies, see Lewis Austin, *Saints and Samurai—The Political Culture of the American and Japanese Elites* (New Haven, Conn.: Yale University Press, 1975), and Bradley M. Richardson, *The Political Culture of Japan* (Berkeley and Los Angeles: University of California Press, 1974).

10. Studies of the contemporary Japanese economy or political economy have been so numerous in recent years that only a few can be signalled here as being especially germane to my themes, focusing upon the most recent: Isaiah Frank (ed.), *The Japanese Economy in International Perspective* (Baltimore: Johns Hopkins University Press, 1975); Kanju Haitani, *The Japanese Economic System* (Lexington, Mass.: Lexington Books Division, D. C. Heath, 1976); Chalmers Johnson, *Japan's Public Policy Companies* (Stanford, Calif.: American Enterprise/Hoover, 1978); Hugh Patrick (ed.), with the assistance of Larry Meissner, *Japanese Industrialization and its Social Consequences* (Berkeley and Los Angeles: University of

California Press, 1976); Hugh Patrick and Henry Rosovsky (eds.), *Asia's New Giant — How the Japanese Economy Works* (Washington, D.C.: The Brookings Institution, 1976); and Ezra F. Vogel (ed.), *Modern Japanese Organization and Decision-Making* (Berkeley and Los Angeles: University of California Press, 1975).

11. For recent studies pertaining to these issues, see William R. Cline, Noboru Kawanabe, T.O.M. Kronsjo, and Thomas Williams, *Trade Negotiations in the Tokyo Round — A Quantitative Assessment* (Washington, D.C.: The Brookings Institution, 1977); Robert S. Ozaki, *The Control of Imports and Foreign Capital in Japan* (New York: Praeger, 1972); Fred H. Sanderson, *Japan's Food Prospects and Policies* (Washington, D.C.: The Brookings Institution, 1978); and Yuan-li Wu, *Japan's Search for Oil — A Case Study on Economic Nationalism and International Security* (Stanford, Calif.: Hoover Institution Press, 1977).

12. For general studies on Japanese politics, useful in understanding broad trends, see Frank C. Langdon, *Politics in Japan* (Boston: Little, Brown and Company, 1967); Nobutaka Ike, *Japanese Politics*, 2nd ed. (New York: Knopf, 1972); Hiroshi Itoh (ed.), *Japanese Politics — An Inside View* (Ithaca, N.Y.: Cornell University Press, 1973); T. McNelly, *Politics and Government in Japan,* 2nd ed. (Boston: Houghton-Mifflin, 1972); J.A.A. Stockwin, *Japan: Divided Politics in a Growth Economy* (New York: Norton, 1975); and Joji Watanuki, *Politics in Postwar Japanese Society* (Tokyo: University of Tokyo Press, 1977).

13. On the conservative party, see Haruhiro Fukui, *Party in Power: The Japanese Liberal-Democrats and Policy-Making* (Berkeley and Los Angeles: University of California Press, 1970), and Nathaniel B. Thayer, *How the Conservatives Rule Japan* (Princeton, N.J.: Princeton University Press, 1969). For Japanese elections, see Gerald Curtis, *Election Campaigning Japanese Style* (New York: Columbia University Press, 1971), and for party structure and organization, see Robert A. Scalapino and Junnosuke Masumi, *Parties and Politics in Contemporary Japan* (Berkeley and Los Angeles: University of California Press, 1962).

14. On the Japanese Socialist Party, see Allan B. Cole, George O. Totten, and Cecil H. Uyehara, with a chapter by Ronald P. Dore, *Socialist Parties in Postwar Japan* (New Haven, Conn.: Yale University Press, 1966); for the JCP, see Robert A. Scalapino, *The Japanese Communist Movement, 1920-1966* (Berkeley and Los Angeles: University of California Press, 1967); and for the Kōmeitō, see James W. White, *The Sokagakkai and Mass Society*

(Stanford, Calif.: Stanford University Press, 1970). More recent developments are covered in articles appearing in *Asian Survey*, *Japan Echo*, *The Journal of Japanese Studies* and *Pacific Affairs* among other journals.

15. For this author's more extended discussion of these issues as they affect both the United States and Japan, see his *Asia and the Road Ahead* (Berkeley and Los Angeles: University of California Press, 1975).

16. A thoughtful earlier Japanese perspective is Hisahiko Okazaki, *A Japanese View of Détente* (Lexington, Mass.: Heath, 1974). For U.S. perspectives, see James E. Auer, *The Postwar Rearmament of Japanese Maritime Forces, 1945-1971* (New York: Praeger, 1972); James H. Buck (ed.), *The Modern Japanese Military System* (Beverly Hills, Calif.: Sage, 1975); John K. Emerson, *Arms, Yen and Power: The Japanese Dilemma* (New York: Praeger, 1972); James W. Morley, ed., *Forecast for Japan: Security in the 1970's* (Princeton, N.J.: Princeton University Press, 1972); Martin E. Weinstein, *Japan's Postwar Defense Policy, 1947-1968* (New York: Columbia University Press, 1971); and Franklin B. Weinstein, ed., *U.S.-Japan Relations and the Security of East Asia: the Next Decade* (Boulder, Colo.: Westview Press, 1978).

17. Personal discussion with Kiichi Saeki, Nomura Research Institute, November 1978.

18. See, for example, Michael Pillsbury, "A Japanese Card," *Foreign Policy*, Winter 1978-1979, pp. 3-30.

19. For a more extensive discussion by this author of recent basic security alternatives facing the United States in Asia, see Robert A. Scalapino, "Approaches to Peace and Security in Asia: The Uncertainty Surrounding American Strategic Principles," *Current Scene*, August-September, 1978, pp. 1-18; and Robert A. Scalapino, "Strategic Issues in U.S. Policies Toward Asia," *Politique Internationale*, January 1979.

10
Locomotive Strategy and U.S. Protectionism: A Japanese View

Leon Hollerman

In the summer of 1976, the Organization for Economic Cooperation and Development (OECD) Secretariat proposed that three leading industrial nations—the United States, West Germany, and Japan—should adopt expansionary fiscal and monetary policies. Expansion, it was argued, would not be inflationary because of the presumed existence of unutilized capacity in the designated countries due to the world recession of 1974-1975. Moreover, in stimulating their own economies, the major industrial nations would act as locomotives, hauling other countries out of the recession.

The locomotive strategy was adopted by the United States; it urged that Germany and Japan do likewise. For their own domestic reasons, however, those countries preferred to follow a specifically noninflationary path to recovery. The contrast in results was interesting. In the United States, the real rate of growth of GNP dropped from 6.0 percent in 1976 to 4.9 percent in 1977. In Japan, the real rate of growth of GNP was 5.1 percent in 1977, higher than that of the United States.[1] In Germany, GNP grew at 2.5 percent during 1977. In terms of inflation, the contrast was even more dramatic, especially toward the close of 1977. It became clear that rates of inflation in Japan and Germany were declining while inflation was rising in the

This is a slightly revised version of a paper originally published in the Summer 1979 issue of *Pacific Affairs*.

United States. The rate of increase in wholesale prices of nonfood manufactures during 1977 was 6.6 percent in the United States, as compared with approximately 0.5 percent in Japan. Furthermore, while in 1977 Japan's real rate of growth of GNP was twice as great as that of West Germany, the latter's rate of increase in wholesale prices of nonfood manufactures was more than twice as high as Japan's.[2]

From these figures, it could be concluded that Japan has been making a sound contribution to stable and noninflationary growth in the world economy. However, its performance has failed to receive the approval of the United States. Together with the OECD Secretariat, the United States has put persistent pressure on Japan not for stability but rather for more expansionary action. Japan's "sincerity" in performing its locomotive assignment has been measured by a specific international test: to what extent has its trade account surplus been reduced? In applying that test, the United States has clearly been preoccupied with its own trade deficit and with the political onus of its failure to correct it. This has been made explicit in the form of U.S. protectionist measures, directed primarily against Japan. Japan's failure to discharge its locomotive obligations as interpreted by the United States has been used to rationalize these protectionist measures. U.S. pressures on Japan for further expansionary policies and for the adjustment of the United States–Japan bilateral trade balance have been inappropriate, inconsistent, and counterproductive.

The Locomotive Strategy Is Inappropriate[3]

At the outset, it may be noted that Japan's present economic difficulties are in large part structural as well as cyclical. These structural difficulties reduce the effectiveness of macroeconomic instruments designed for the mere "expansion of the economy." Japan's structural problems include the following:

1. The seniority-wage system (*nenkō joretsu*) as combined with "lifetime" employment security cuts across the grain of Japan's present demographic transition. As the population ages, older, high-wage employees become an ever-increasing propor-

tion of the work force, raising the cost of production and squeezing profits.

2. In Japan's industrial transition, the tertiary sector increased from 40 percent of the GNP in fiscal 1960 to 50 percent in fiscal 1975. This trend will continue. With regard to the growth of GNP, the income multiplier effect of investment in service industries and trade is lower than that in manufacturing.

3. Within the secondary sector, the gap between strong and weak industries is progressively widening. Labor-intensive, pollution-intensive, and energy-intensive industries such as electric furnace and open hearth steel, aluminum smelting, shipbuilding and synthetic fibers have been designated as eligible for reallocation assistance under the Structurally Depressed Industries Law (passed by the Diet in May 1978). Other depressed industries include chemical fertilizers (ammonia, urea, and calcium phosphate), cotton spinning, ferroalloys, corrugated cardboard, polyvinyl chloride, and sugar refining.

4. In various specialties, relatively inefficient small enterprises are regionally concentrated. Examples include stainless steel flatware and textile weaving and dyeing. Increased competition from newly industrializing countries as well as rising import barriers abroad have had a particularly adverse impact on these specialized regions.

5. The scarcity of land is a basic and increasing structural bottleneck.

6. In contrast with Japan's unrivaled international marketing network, its domestic distribution system (which serves partly to substitute for public social security in providing subsistence to marginal workers) is backward and inefficient.

These structural problems cannot be overcome by mere "expansion of the economy." Moreover, as Gottfried Haberler has observed, while the locomotive strategy says "expand," it really means "inflate." The pressure on "strong currency countries to expand faster is tantamount to an attempt to eliminate the inflation differential by inflating the low-inflation countries rather than disinflating the high-inflation countries."[4] By pressuring Japan to relinquish its sound, independent monetary policy, the United States is a destabilizing force in the world economy.

With regard to the merchandise trade account, it may further be noted that the surpluses of Japan are different from those of OPEC (against which no apparent U.S. pressure has been applied). They were achieved by means of competition rather than oligopsony. Moreover, during the past thirty years, Japan has had trade surpluses only seven times. Three of those surpluses (1965, 1966 and 1970) were minor. Only four times (1971, 1972, 1976 and 1977) were they major.

The repertoire of pressures placed on Japan includes a numbers game. The statistics of Japan's trade surplus, for example, are often quoted on an IMF basis, which excludes the cost of insurance and freight. On the IMF basis, Japan's total trade surplus in 1977 was $17.5 billion. The buyer of imports, however, has to pay the cost of delivery as well as the cost of manufacturing the merchandise. Accordingly, Japanese customs statistics report imports on a CIF basis. The value of exports, on the other hand, as measured by the return to producers, is correctly reported in the Japanese customs statistics on an FOB basis. In terms of the latter, Japan's total merchandise trade surplus in 1977 was $9.7 billion; this is half as much as the figure quoted on the IMF basis.[5]

Depreciation of the dollar in terms of the yen also plays a role in the numbers game. On a yen-denominated basis, the increase in Japanese exports has already tapered off. In March 1978, for example, the yen value of total customs-cleared exports was 3.1 percent greater than that of March 1977. As reported in dollars, however, it was 23.0 percent greater.

The numbers game, however, can be played both ways. For the sake of consistency, Japan's GNP, as well as its foreign trade statistics, might be reported in the United States in terms of dollars. In that event, Japan's growth rate would promptly be restored to "miraculous" levels and its locomotive assignment would be more than fulfilled. From a Japanese point of view, another example concerns the large quantity of Japan's imports that are purchased from U.S. multinational corporations but shipped to Japan from physical points of origin outside the United States. Japan's merchandise trade account with the United States would actually be in deficit if these transactions were included.[6]

It is ironic that the United States now espouses the locomotive theory after so recently having advocated the adoption of floating exchange rates on the ground that this would promote a greater degree of national economic independence. As opposed to independence, its interest in the locomotive strategy at the present time seems primarily inspired by the wish to be rescued from the balance of payments consequences of its own inflationary policies. It might also be noted that prior to abandonment of the Bretton Woods system, when the United States was in balance of payments surplus, it demanded that deficit countries assume most of the burden of adjustment. When it was in deficit, it demanded that surplus countries assume the burden. In this respect, the United States at present maintains consistency in its economic policy.

From a Japanese point of view, the locomotive strategy as expressed in the demand for expansionary monetary and fiscal policies is fundamentally inappropriate because it misperceives the dynamics of recovery from the recession phase of the business cycle in Japan. In the post-1960s, recovery in Japan has been export-led. Thus the demand that Japan simultaneously increase its growth rate and sustain a decline or even a deficit in the current account of the balance of payments compounds the inappropriate monetary and fiscal prescription.

During Japan's economic miracle of the 1960s, when the overheating of the economy gave rise to balance of payments deficits, recessions were induced by contractionary monetary policy designed to constrain imports and increase exports. Since economic growth was propelled during this period by a spontaneous tide of capital investment, after adjusting the balance of payments the authorities could terminate the recession simply by relaxing monetary policy and unleashing the demand for capital investment once more. In the post-miracle period, however, the nature of both recession and recovery has changed. The recession of 1974-1975 was induced by causes other than the balance of payments constraint and a tight money policy. Instead, as mentioned above, it resulted from structural as well as cyclical factors. The tide of investment demand no longer swelled spontaneously. Thus the mechanism of recovery was changed as well.

In the post-miracle era of reduced capital investment, moreover, the nature of the recovery process in the Japanese business cycle has come to be dominated by traditional institutional characteristics of the economy. The breakeven point of Japanese producers occurs at a high level of output due to traditionally heavy, fixed costs. These include heavy interest charges resulting from high, debt-equity ratios in the financial structure and a heavy burden of personnel expenses due to "life-tenure" employment. The economy is also characterized by high-saving ratios due to inadequate retirement provision, inadequate consumer credit facilities, and other factors. In addition, the present recession has been marked by a phenomenal inventory accumulation that was generated by the commodity scare following the oil crisis of 1973. These are among the principal factors that combined to precipitate in 1976-1977 the greatest supply-oriented export phenomenon in Japan's history.

There has been argument about whether or not in the past Japan's historical growth was export led.[7] There can be no argument, however, about the fact that recovery from the recent and still prevailing recession in Japan depends upon exports. Thus in expressing its "substantial concern" about Japan's trade account surplus, the U.S. government appears oblivious of the nature and dynamics of Japan's recovery process.[8] At the same time, its inflationary monetary policy and budget deficits have been the principal source of the trade difficulties that it blames on Japan.

In Japan, the need for a sound recovery, leading to stable long-term growth, is recognized as preferable to short-term "reflation" based on expansion of the money supply. Despite its intrinsic economic instability (as can be seen in the variance of its principal economic indicators and the markedly uneven performance of major industrial sectors), Japan has adhered faithfully to long-term objectives. In the United States, vastly more stable and more self-sufficient, economic policy has been dominated by short-term political commitments. This is a luxury Japan cannot afford.

Besides inflation and trade deficits, U.S. problems include unemployment and a decline in the value of the dollar. In various degrees, Japan has been accused of being responsible for each. However, even at the theoretical level, the interrelation among these economic difficulties is not entirely understood. The inadequate degree of verification of empirical relationships can be seen in the failure of forecasters to anticipate either the inflation of the early 1970s or the recession of 1974-1975. Uncertainty among the theorists has thus compounded the uncertainty created by variations in short-term government policies in creating a poor environment for business investment or consumer spending.

Concerning the relation between exchange rates and inflation, for example, it is argued that with a decline in the value of the dollar the cost of imports rises, imparting an inflationary effect to wage goods, to import-competing home goods, and to the import content of output. Thus the decline in the value of the dollar leads to a rise in the general price level.[9] On the other hand, it is maintained that the inflow of competitive merchandise is antiinflationary inasmuch as it exercises a restraining influence on the price of import-competing home goods.

The exchange rate does more than bring supply and demand into balance with regard to flows of goods and services. It must also bring into balance the flow of financial assets. The latter are highly volatile and affected drastically by changing expectations. Suppose, in accordance with the locomotive theory, an expansion of the money supply takes place in the United States. This may be accompanied by a decline in the interest rate. The latter would tend to promote an outflow of portfolio capital, having a negative effect on the balance of payments. The outflow of capital would also have a depressing effect on the exchange rate. Devaluation of the currency (under floating rates) would presumably (with a lag) promote an increase in merchandise exports, having a positive effect on the balance of payments. The effect of the decline in the interest rate, however, while having a negative effect on foreign portfolio investment, might have the opposite effect in attracting foreign direct investment as a result of the expansion in the money supply. This would have the effect of improving the balance of payments and raising the exchange value of the home currency. But an offsetting effect would be imparted to the trade accounts where exports would be reduced because of the rise in the exchange rate.

Suppose, however, that the increase in the money supply created rational—or irrational—expectations of further expansion of the currency. Instead of declining, the interest rate might rise because of the premium for inflation.[10] The uncertainty created by inflationary expectations would discourage the inflow of both portfolio and direct investment. This seems to be what happened in the United States during the latter half of 1977, contributing to the decline in the value of the dollar.[11] At the same time, inflation raised the price of U.S. merchandise, tending to offset the decline in the value of the dollar as a stimulus to exports.

The effect of attempting to produce economic locomotion by means of expanding the money supply, therefore, has distinctly uncertain results on the balance of payments under flexible exchange rates. Expansion by means of fiscal policy introduces a further set of complications and divergent effects on the balance of payments. For example, fiscal expansion raises the interest rate, which attracts foreign portfolio capital and improves the balance of payments. The rising interest rate may also depress domestic direct investment, thus tending to offset the fiscal expansion. How fiscal expansion would interact with monetary expansion in producing the desired results in the balance of payments is highly problematical. With so unclear an outcome even in the U.S. economy — which U.S. forecasters presumably understand better than the economy of Japan — it seems inappropriate to urge the locomotive theory of expansionary macro policies on the Japanese.[12]

Combined with its pressure on Japan for the adoption of the locomotive strategy has been the implementation by the United States of protectionist policies against Japan.[13] In doing so, the United States has practiced both avoidance and evasion of its ostensible commitment to an international free market system. In conniving with the Japanese government for the establishment of "voluntary" export quotas by Japan, the United States avoids General Agreement on Tariffs Trade (GATT) rules for the payment of compensation which compulsory unilateral import quotas would require.[14]

In the United States, business as well as government has resorted to protectionist policies directed against Japan. While declaring allegiance to a competitive, free market economy, U.S. business has "through an array of esoteric and highly technical manoeuvres" waged a campaign of legal harassment against Japan. "American protectionism is becoming much more sophisticated, without policy makers or the press fully aware of what is happening. Those interest groups desirous of action to moderate or impede imports are now engaging in a procedure of harassment through as many avenues as possible and all under the law."[15] Legal harassment of importers has emerged as an important nonmarket method of profit maximizing.[16] Recent changes in the law tend to encourage such harassment.[17]

At the macroeconomic level, an assumption concerning the existence of a high degree of interdependence among national economies is a basic ingredient of the locomotive strategy. However, according to statistics in the OECD *Economic Outlook* for December 1975, a 1 percent increase in autonomous expenditures by Japan would have a 0.1 percent effect in increasing the GNP of the United States. In the other direction, a 1 percent increase in autonomous expenditures by the United States would produce a 0.35 percent increment in Japan's GNP. These figures show that interdependence in terms of GNP is slight at the margin. Accordingly, the amount of increase in Japan's GNP that would suffice to significantly improve the U.S. balance of payments would be wholly disproportionate to the results desired by the United States.[18]

Confusion between macro- and microeconomic issues constitutes still another aspect of inappropriate U.S. pressure on Japan. If the nature of the U.S. trade deficit is analyzed in detail, it is seen to be concentrated in a relatively small number of commodity categories. During 1977, U.S. oil imports were valued at $41.5 billion, one-third of total imports. In trade with Japan, about 40 percent of the deficit was attributable to imports of motor vehicles. It is especially inappropriate that Japan should be asked to reflate its entire economy for the sake of providing local relief to a comparatively few U.S. firms, mainly oligopolies, that are unable to meet the competition of imports. In Japan, such firms would be required to achieve structural reform or would be forced to merge.[19]

Although, in promoting the locomotive theory, the United States contemplates that by reflation of its economy Japan's competitive export power would be blunted, it takes an equal if not greater interest in the expansion of Japanese imports. Here again there is confusion between micro and macro considerations. The fact that the ratio of imports of manufactured goods to total imports is lower in Japan than in most other industrial nations has been cited as evidence that Japan practices import restrictionism. However, because of its unbalanced natural resources, about 80 percent of Japan's imports consist of industrial raw materials and food.[20] Therefore it is inappropriate to compare the above ratio with the corresponding ratio for most other industrial nations.[21] Expansion of the economy would do little to change the ratio. Benefit to the United States, moreover, would be limited by the fact that exports of key manufactured products in which it possesses a comparative advantage are not highly correlated with the phases of the business cycle in Japan.[22]

Despite pressure and inappropriate criticism of its orthodox preferences, Japan has actually acquiesced to a considerable extent in setting targets for the expansion of its economy. In talks between Robert Strauss and Nobuhiko Ushiba in January 1978, Japan agreed to strive for a 7 percent real GNP growth rate in fiscal year 1978 (beginning April 1, 1978). As passed by the Diet, the government budget for 1978 was approximately $225 billion.[23] Under programs for local government finance, additional expenditures of approximately $155 billion were planned for the fiscal year. The budget for fiscal year 1978 includes the device of incorporating in the 1978 accounts revenue that properly belongs in the 1979 accounts. Consequently, whereas the nominal deficit is 32 percent of the General Account, the actual deficit is 38 percent. This is a far higher figure than that to be found in the budgets of other industrial nations.[24] The rising ratio of deficit expenditure in Japan in recent years and the rising cost of the government debt required to finance it implies increasing fiscal rigidity and loss of government capacity for flexible response to future economic contingencies. In this case, "imitation of the West" does not necessarily bode well for Japan's long-run economic prospects.

In addition to expansionary fiscal policies, other measures have been adopted by the Japanese government in response to U.S. pressure for adjustment of the trade balance. As mentioned above, it imposed export restraints on designated commodities.[25] Effective in March 1978, prior to the conclusion of the Tokyo Round negotiations, tariffs were reduced on 124 items, including reduction to zero of the tariff on passenger cars. Nontariff barriers and residual import restrictions were removed, credit for import financing was expanded, cooperation was extended to restrict excessive competition in export financing, foreign exchange control procedures were relaxed with regard to standard methods of settlement, stockpiling of key import commodities was increased, and the yen was appreciated to an extraordinary degree after September 1977. Recovery strategy included the adoption in March 1978 of a seven-point program. It provided for (1) increased spending on public works, (2) reduction of interest rates[26] and expansion of consumer finance, (3) promotion of private investment, (4) creation of jobs for the unemployed, (5) relief for structurally depressed industries, (6) relief for small and medium sized industries, and (7) promotion of capital outflows through direct foreign investment.

It must be acknowledged that, in addition to external pressure, business interests in Japan, as represented by Keidanren and the Japan Economic Research Center (JERC), have likewise demanded that the government abandon "orthodox" recovery methods. To the extent that it has complied, the government has assumed a high degree of risk. Given the relative instability of the Japanese economy as compared with that of the United States, Japan's capacity to tolerate potentially inflationary policies is correspondingly limited. In contrast with the period of "miraculous" growth rates in the 1960s, when capital spending was the chief dynamic force in the economy, during the present period of lesser growth, recovery primarily depends upon the expansion of consumer demand. Renewed inflationary expectations on the part of consumers could fundamentally jeopardize prospects for further recovery.[27]

Apart from the risk to the stability of the economy, there is the further risk that the desired results of these expansionary policies may not appear quickly. Fiscal expenditure, for example, is being concentrated primarily on the expansion of infrastructure, such as the construction of bridges between

Shikoku and Honshu across the Inland Sea and the construction of Shinkansen railway lines. These projects take shape slowly. A large proportion of the expenditure for public works, moreover, is used for the purchase of land, which has a low multiplier effect and creates minimal new demand for imports.

The desired results of yen appreciation likewise appear with a lag. In June 1978 the rate of exchange rose to ¥ 210 = $1, representing an appreciation of 46.7 percent in the value of the yen over the rate established in accordance with the Smithsonian agreement of December 1971. It constituted an appreciation of 71.4 percent over the value prevailing for twenty-two years prior to that agreement. Yet in the course of the progressive appreciation of the yen, the U.S. trade balance with Japan steadily deteriorated. This outcome can be seen as the result of various factors. In the first place, the supply-oriented export process mentioned above was of great importance in pushing Japanese exports over the exchange rate barrier. The slack domestic market in Japan impelled firms to seek markets abroad even at prices that barely exceeded variable costs. Second, the so-called J-curve effect may in some cases tend to increase rather than correct the trade imbalance in the short run: a rise occurred in the value of exports from Japan booked at lower yen-dollar rates but shipped at higher rates, while a corresponding decline occurred in the value of imports.[28] Third, in other cases, contrary to the J-effect, Japanese exporters attempted to maintain their competitive positions by absorbing part of the revaluation themselves and reducing their profit margins.[29] This procedure, typical of the many firms heavily overstocked with inventory, helped to maintain the physical volume of exports.[30]

Fourth, for some commodities, the role of nonprice factors (such as quality, reliability, design, promptness in delivery, availability of credit and after-sales services) tended to outweigh the importance of price in Japan's competitive position. Fifth, buyers of complex equipment tend to be tied to their original suppliers for replacement parts. Sixth, where import content was a significant component of exports, the reduced price of imported raw materials due to the revaluation enabled producers to hold the line on price increases — a counterproductive effect of yen revaluation from the U.S. point of view. Seventh, due to superior technology in industries such as steel, motor vehicles, and consumer electronic products, many firms were able to match world prices profitably despite the higher value of the yen. Eighth, many U.S. subsidiaries or joint ventures in Japan continued to sell to their U.S. parent firms regardless of the rate of exchange. In the short run, for a variety of reasons—some quite contradictory to one another—the level of Japan's exports was maintained if not increased despite the revaluation.

In general, the impact of yen revaluation was effective in reducing the exports of small- and medium-sized firms in Japan far sooner than the exports of major manufacturers.[31] Small-scale makers of textiles, sundry goods, flatware, and toys have been forced into bankruptcy in unprecedented numbers. According to Deputy Minister of Finance Michiya Matsukawa, it takes about a year and a half for yen appreciation to be reflected in the balance of trade.

In the short run exports did not decline, and the United States was also unsatisfied with the extent to which Japan's imports increased as a result of yen revaluation. In the first place, the fact that Japan's GNP growth rate was below its "miraculous" peak resulted in a corrrespondingly reduced demand for industrial raw materials from the United States. Second, as mentioned above, after the oil crisis of October 1973 and the worldwide threat of impending commodity shortages in 1974, Japanese producers had engaged in reckless stockpiling. In 1978, these inventories were still being worked off. Third, the recessionary effect of the revaluation on many small- and medium-sized export firms reduced their output and thus its import content. Fourth, anomalies in the traditionally organized distribution system of Japan were a further factor restraining the increase in imports. The reduced cost of imports due to yen appreciation is often appropriated by the relatively long chain of dealers and brokers instead of being passed on to consumers.[32] Quotas have a further restrictive effect on agricultural imports.[33] With reference to citrus fruit and beef, these have been the subject of a running controversy between the United States and Japan for about two decades. On the other hand, Japan's purchases of agricultural products from the

United States amounted to more than $4 billion in 1977. No other nation purchased half as much. In these circumstances it might not be unreasonable to accord Japan the privilege of deciding for itself the assortment of agricultural products it wishes to purchase.

The Locomotive Strategy Is Inconsistent

With the modest exception of 1959, Japan had a deficit in merchandise trade with the United States in every year between 1945 and 1964 inclusive. During that period, the United States responded to Japan's appeal for help with good counsel: it advised Japan to resolve the deficit by means of multilateral trade.

In former days, moreover, when world trade was governed by more liberal policies, it was thought to be correct and even admirable behavior on the part of a country suffering a recession to reduce its appetite by tightening its belt, thus generating an export surplus that would cure the recession. It is ironic, having followed that classic prescription—while simultaneously liberalizing its trade and exchange policies—that Japan is now accused of being an irresponsible member of the world community.

It is not considered irresponsible on the part of the United States, however, to urge on Japan expansionary macroeconomic policies that have been widely condemned as a means of making short-term gains at the expense of long-term inflationary costs. Moreover, while liberalization is being implemented in Japan, the rest of the world—including the United States—is becoming more protectionist. By its increasing protectionism, the United States promotes inflation, which it professes to abhor. And while complaining about the decline in the value of the dollar (which makes U.S. imports too expensive), the United States accuses Japan of "dumping" (which makes imports too cheap). The Japanese feel that they are being made a scapegoat for the failure of the United States to achieve a rational energy policy and to distract attention from other political as well as economic failures of its leadership.

Despite a professed commitment by the U.S. government to

free market principles, its economic intervention has progressively increased. In its relations with Japan, this inconsistency is particularly acute. The term "Japan, Inc." is used pejoratively to refer to supposedly undue government intervention in the economy of Japan. Yet the U.S. government attempts to utilize the very practice it professes to deplore by serving the Japanese government with insistent demands for its further intervention and administrative guidance to reduce exports and increase imports. Negotiations by U.S. officials for the establishment of "voluntary" export quotas in Japan, moreover, are in violation of U.S. antitrust laws.

By the use of protectionist tactics in its attempt to impose the locomotive strategy on Japan, the United States is thus involved in various types of inconsistency. Some of these are based on misperception of reality in Japan, some on economic or political opportunism in the United States. At various times, the U.S. government has attributed Japan's trade surplus to an "undervalued yen," to "export subsidies," to "nontariff barriers," or to "dumping." In attempting to resolve its own trade deficit, it insists that Japan must maintain a natural rate of economic growth in excess of that of the United States.

In 1978, the U.S. government reversed its complaint that Japan has preserved an undervalued yen and complained instead that the Bank of Japan failed to support the dollar. With regard to implementation of the antidumping law, various inconsistencies have been noted.[34] Concerning nontariff barriers (NTBs), absurd arguments have been presented, such as the argument that the Japanese language constitutes a nontariff barrier. The Japanese language presents problems, but it certainly is not an instrument of commercial policy. In the meanwhile, the United States maintains its own NTBs. Among these are the Orderly Marketing Agreements and trigger prices mentioned above. The United States imposes quotas on imports of various agricultural and mineral products and maintains the American Selling Price system for customs appraisal of certain chemicals. It is also a party to the International Multifiber Agreement, which imposes quotas on imports of clothing and textiles.

The Locomotive Strategy Is Counterproductive

In support of U.S. demands, the London *Economist* asserted, "Japan's surplus is a problem. . . . The solution is to put pressure on Japan to reflate or upvalue."[35] Protectionism (or the New Protectionism,[36] as it is sometimes called) has been added by the United States as an ingredient of the "solution." This solution, however, creates further problems. As mentioned above, the demand for restraint of Japanese exports requires more intervention on the part of the Japanese government. Thus in effect it is a demand for reversal of the liberalization program that has been implemented (likewise under foreign pressure) in Japan during the past decade. This "reverse course" jeopardizes the survival of the multilateral free market system—such as it is—in the world economy. For various well-known reasons, the coming decade may afford the last chance for the preservation of that system. As a key country, Japan's policies will have a significant effect on the outcome.

Overruling the market system by means of "administrative" solutions introduces adversary relationships on the domestic as well as on the international plane. One reason for this is the attendant politicization of economic activities. Administrative or political response to the promptings of pressure groups arouses domestic adversary relationships both at home[37] and abroad.[38]

Politicization likewise arouses international adversary relationships. For example, Japan knows that concessions to the United States in the form of "voluntary" export restrictions will be followed by demands from other countries for similar concessions as they have in the past. The same implication applies to the United States. Coercive pressures on Japan for correction of the trade balance may invite reciprocal demands by other countries for correction in the U.S. bilateral balance with them.[39]

The counterproductive pressure on Japan in behalf of the locomotive strategy implies a further inimical result. For the New Protectionism (the means by which that pressure is being applied) serves to validate and reinvigorate the propensity for cartelism, which is traditional in Japan. Cartels are consistent with the feudal remnants within Japanese capitalism.[40] They are consistent with endemic "scale optimism" on the part of both business and government. They are consistent with the liquidation of small- and medium-sized firms and the increase of economic concentration now taking place in accordance with government policy for the structural reform of industry. (That policy, as well, is being unconsciously encouraged by the New Protectionism.) They are consistent with strategy to avoid disruption of Japan's enormous capital investments in high technology industries. And of course they are an obvious Japanese response to the cartelization of the European Economic Community (EEC) now proceeding under the direction of its Commissioner for Industry, Viscount Davignon.[41]

Corresponding to "organized trade" and "fair trade," the Japanese version of the quiet life associated with the suppression of competition is discreetly known as "agreed specialization," a concept derived from respectable academic sources. In its academic form, agreed specialization by means of regional integration has been proposed as a "second-best" solution for the problem of industrialization within developing countries.[42] As evident from the failure ratio of experiments in regional integration, however, this means of promoting horizontal trade in manufactured goods has not gone very far among the developing countries. In Western Europe, on the other hand, where horizontal trade already predominated in commerce among advanced countries, regional integration stimulated it further through the formation of the European Free Trade Association (EFTA) and EEC. In his writings on a Pacific Area Free Trade Association (PAFTA), Professor Kiyoshi Kojima has advocated a similar arrangement among the United States, Canada, Japan, Australia, and New Zealand. In the world as it is, however, prospects for the realization of that proposal are distinctly dim.

The transition of EEC, in the meanwhile, is ironic. At the outset, it was an inward-looking group that academicians acclaimed because of its outward-looking aspirations. Short-term trade diversion was to be overwhelmed by long-term trade creation. Within a large island, the market system was to be nurtured; eventually this would strengthen the market system elsewhere. The present cartelism of EEC is not consistent with its early promise.

Similarly, while Kojima's concept of PAFTA emphasizes the

possibilities of horizontal trade in a free trade context, Japanese oligopoly firms see it in the context of cartelism. The term "agreed specialization" may be interpreted from either point of view. And while Japan is not welcome as a member of any free trade community of its industrial peers, membership in cartels is another matter. On this plane, association with Japan is not precluded. Arrival of the New Protectionism has opened the way for an alternative to PAFTA, namely Japan's accession to emerging international cartels.

For years, Japanese publications have referred to the merits of "international division of labor by mutual agreement" among industrial countries. For example, Yoshizo Ikeda, president of Mitsui & Company, has been described as a "proponent" of such agreements.[43] In its 1974 White Paper on International Trade, the Ministry of International Trade and Industry (MITI) declared itself in favor of promoting the industrialization of developing nations in order to promote horizontal division of labor in manufactured goods between them and Japan. In its 1978 White Paper on International Trade, MITI urged Japanese industries to arrange international division of labor not only between industrialized and nonindustrialized nations but among the industrialized nations themselves.

The New Protectionism now rising in the United States can hardly fail to encourage the institutionalization of protectionism abroad. In particular, as Japan's leading trade partner, the United States may propel Japan into the widening orbit of EEC cartels.

Notes

1. The index of industrial production in Japan rose at a faster rate than that in the United States during the period 1975-1977. Moreover, the rate of growth of GNP in Japan exceeded the rate of growth of industrial production during that period.

2. Morgan Guaranty Trust Company, *World Financial Markets*, February 1978. During fiscal year 1977, Japan's wholesale price index declined 1.8 percent, its greatest decline in twenty years.

3. In a general sense, the inappropriateness of the locomotive

Locomotive Strategy/U.S. Protectionism: A Japanese View 207

strategy has been recognized by the emergence at a meeting of the IMF Interim Committee in September 1977 of its rival, a "program for coordinated reflation," otherwise known as the "convoy" strategy. As Gottfried Haberler remarks, "The main advantage claimed for the new approach seems to be that if many countries expand at the same time, there is less danger that some of them will run into serious balance of payments problems." "Reflections on the U.S. Trade Deficit and the Floating Dollar," *Contemporary Economic Problems 1978* (Washington, D.C.: American Enterprise Institute for Public Policy Research, 1978), p. 230.

4. Ibid., p. 212.

5. Correspondingly, in terms of U.S. Department of Commerce statistics, which report both imports and exports on an FAS basis, the surplus to Japan in trade with the United States is overstated and the deficit to the United States is understated. This reporting problem disappears if the balance of payments is discussed in terms of the current account rather than in terms of the merchandise account. According to Japanese customs statistics, the 1977 trade surplus with the United States was $7.3 billion.

6. According to a survey performed by Mitsui Bussan, the volume of Japan's imports from U.S.-affiliated enterprises outside the United States was $18.9 billion in 1975 and $21.5 billion in 1976. As adjusted for the proportion of United States equity participation in such enterprises, the figures are reduced to $8.9 billion and approximately $10.0 billion, respectively. *Nihon Keizai*, Tokyo, July 8, 1977. Japan's imports of crude oil accounted for approximately 70 percent of these amounts.

7. Historically, the growth rate of Japan's exports has greatly exceeded the rate of growth of world trade. Its exports grew more than twice as fast as world trade from the 1880s to World War I, ten times as fast during the interwar period, and about three times as fast since World War II. Among those who have discussed the "export-leading" hypothesis of economic growth in Japan are W. W. Lockwood [*The Economic Development of Japan* (Princeton, N.J.: Princeton University Press, 1954)], M. Shinohara [*Growth and Cycles in the Japanese Economy* (Tokyo: Kinokuniya, 1962)], and H. Kanamori ["Economic Growth and Exports," in L. Klein and K. Ohkawa, eds., *Economic Growth: The Japanese Experience Since the Meiji Era* (Homewood, Ill.: Irwin, 1968)].

8. United States Department of States, *Gist*, "U.S.-Japanese Relations," June 1978.

9. In testimony before a Senate banking subcommittee, Anthony

Solomon recently stated that for each percentage point decline in the dollar, inflation might be increased by a quarter of a point in the United States.

10. *Real* interest rates at the present time are low, thus making it particularly inappropriate to attempt to stimulate investment by means of an expansionary monetary policy.

11. The value of the dollar is also affected by trading in dollar assets held outside the United States. At present, the total of such assets exceeds $500 billion. When holders of these assets entertain adverse expectations about the inflationary prospects of the dollar, they convert their dollar assets into nondollar form. This has a depressing effect on the rate of exchange. In this connection, it should be mentioned that the presumed linkage between the U.S. trade deficit and the decline in the value of the dollar is generally misperceived. U.S. imports from Japan and from OPEC, its principal creditors, are paid for almost exclusively in dollars. As such, therefore, these are not foreign exchange transactions and place no pressure on the value of the dollar. Adverse pressure on the dollar arises when Japanese or OPEC recipients of trade dollars are induced by inflationary U.S. government policies to exchange them for other assets.

12. Compounding the task of U.S. forecasters is the fact that in Japan interest rates are determined primarily by the government rather than by the market.

13. For example, in July 1977 an Orderly Marketing Agreement became effective in which Japan was limited to the export of 1.75 million color television sets to the United States annually for a period of three years. In addition to the quotas on specialty steel product imports imposed by the Ford administration, the Carter administration created a "trigger price" system on steel imports effective in February 1978. These measures were aimed principally at Japan. Ironically, the restrictions on imports of steel tend to make U.S. automobiles less competitive with cars from Japan.

14. The United States has furthermore proposed that "the other country's export restrictions" be added to the emergency "safeguard" restrictions now being negotiated at GATT. This would have the effect of giving GATT "recognition" to Japan's voluntary export restrictions, making them involuntary. *Yomiuri*, April 14, 1978.

15. Harald B. Malmgren, "Significance of Trade Policies in the World Economic Outlook," *The World Economy*, October 1977, p. 24.

16. At the instigation of the Zenith Radio Corporation, the Justice

Department conducted an antitrust investigation of Japanese television exports to the United States. "During their investigation, antitrust lawyers reviewed 35,000 documents submitted by Japanese and U.S. TV makers to support their respective claims in the matter." After an entire year of study, the head of the antitrust division said, "I don't find any basis for proceeding further to begin a full-scale investigation." *Wall Street Journal*, April 13, 1978.

17. Title II, Chapter 1, of the Trade Reform Act of 1974 provides for relief from import competition where imports either cause or *threaten* to cause "substantial" injury to domestic producers. In the previous law, the Trade Expansion Act of 1962, it was necessary to demonstrate that increased imports were "in major part the result of trade agreement concessions" before import relief measures were undertaken. "Substantial" cause is now defined as not less than any other cause, whereas in the previous law "in major part" was defined as a cause greater than all other causes combined. U.S., Senate, Committee on Finance, *Summary of Trade Reform Act of 1974*, November 20, 1974, p. 5.

18. For further discussion of the interdependence issue, see Thomas D. Willett, "It's Too Simple to Blame the Countries With a Surplus," *Euromoney*, February 1978.

19. It is symptomatic that in the United States, not only sick industries, such as steel, but also thriving automobile firms, such as General Motors, complain bitterly about import competition from Japan.

20. The great increase in the import cost of raw materials due to quintupling of the price of oil reduced the ratio of manufactured goods imports to total imports into Japan from 30 percent to 20 percent after 1973.

21. It is particularly inappropriate to compare the ratio for Japan with the ratio for EEC countries, which report 80 percent of their imports in the form of manufactured goods. Most of these manufactures are exchanged in intra-EEC trade, which in a significant sense is "domestic" trade. The ratio of manufactured goods to total imports received by EEC countries from non-EEC sources is approximately 20 percent.

22. In commodities where the United States does not possess a comparative advantage, its difficulties in exporting to Japan do not necessarily arise from the recession in Japan or from Japanese nontariff barriers but rather from competition by low cost producers, such as Taiwan and Korea.

23. This figure includes (1) the appropriation in the General Account (or budget proper), amounting to ¥ 34,295 billion; and (2) the loan and investment program (or "second budget"), funded chiefly by the postal savings and other reserve accounts held by the Trust Funds Bureau of the Ministry of Finance, amounting to ¥ 14,888 billion.

24. In the United States, the federal deficit during fiscal year 1978 was approximately 12 percent of the budget.

25. Exports of automobiles, for example, will be limited in fiscal year 1978 to a volume less than that in 1977. Each manufacturer is requested to submit a quarterly shipping schedule and "necessary requests" will be made to the manufacturers concerned. MITI Press Release, NR-166 (78-13), May 12, 1978. Surveillance of exports of other commodities (including steel, television sets, and ships) was also to be implemented. However, as Prime Minister Fukuda pointed out to U.S. Cabinet members at his breakfast meeting in Blair House on May 2, 1978, "Although exports to the United States in 1978 will decrease quantitatively, whether this will become linked with a decrease in monetary terms will depend on the U.S. side's efforts to have its antiinflation and dollar-stabilization measures produce effects." *Mainichi*, May 13, 1978.

26. In March 1978, the Bank of Japan reduced the discount rate to 3.5 percent, the lowest rate since World War II (with the exception of an interval in the immediate aftermath of the war).

27. The inherent instability of the Japanese economy, among other factors, helps account for the defensive reaction on the part of consumers in the form of a high ratio of savings in relation to disposable personal income. The ratio for Japan during 1971-1976 was 24.6 percent, as compared with 14.6 percent for West Germany and 7.4 percent for the United States.

28. In the case of the United States, depreciation of the dollar gives rise to the opposite effect because the import bill goes up at once while exports expand only gradually.

29. Reinforcing the effect of tenured employees contributing to the fixed cost of production and thus to the supply-oriented export phenomenon is the fact that Japanese firms feel that their primary obligation is to their employees rather than to their stockholders. Therefore, they do not emphasize profits from the point of view of the stock market performance of their shares.

30. In terms of real effective exchange rates, the index unit value of manufactures exported from Japan (March 1973 = 100) was 90.7 on May 15, 1978, as compared with an average of 88.8 during 1973-1977. The standard deviation of the index, computed for the March

1973–December 1977 period, was 6.7. Morgan Guaranty Trust Company of New York, *World Financial Markets*, May 1978.

31. Approximately 40 percent of Japan's exports are produced by small- and medium-sized enterprises. They export 32 percent of total exports directly and about 8 percent indirectly, as subcontractors.

32. A Japanese government survey of thirty-three principal consumer import commodities compared prices in December 1977 with those in December 1976. In fifteen cases, both import and retail prices were reduced; in six cases import prices dropped but retail prices remained constant or increased; in eight cases, import prices rose but retail prices remained constant or declined; and in four cases, both import and retail prices rose. Mitsubishi Economic Research Institute, *Monthly Circular*, May 1978.

33. For example, a box of Sunkist oranges yields $4 to the grower in California. At the retail level in Japan, the same box is sold for approximately $88. Import quotas for oranges are granted to distributors in accordance with their political contributions to the Liberal Democratic party. Thus it is not only the Japanese agricultural lobby that helps maintain residual import restrictions.

34. These include, for example, reports that implementation of the antidumping law has been designed to give favorable treatment to imports from Poland. *Journal of Commerce*, February 21, 1978.

35. June 24, 1978, p. 85.

36. New Protectionism emphasizes nontariff barriers and government assistance or subsidies to domestic industry. It includes the concepts of "organized free trade" and "fair trade." The latter, according to George Meany, means "do unto others as they do unto us, barrier for barrier, closed door for closed door." *Business Week*, December 26, 1977. The former, which implies cartelization, was contained in French proposals within EEC in July 1977.

37. In the United States, a typical example is the competition among the states for larger shares of the concessions granted by Japan in the agreement of January 13, 1978, between Minister of State for External Affairs Nobuhiko Ushiba and the President's Special Representative for Trade Negotiations, Ambassador Robert S. Strauss. In commenting on that essentially political agreement, Senator Abraham Ribicoff, chairman of the Senate Finance Subcommittee on International Trade, observed that while increased beef and citrus exports to Japan will benefit agricultural states, "there is little in the Ushiba-Strauss package to benefit the industrialized states, whose labor-intensive industries feel threatened by import competition."

38. In Japan, farmers resent government concessions to the United

States with regard to the liberalization of agricultural imports inasmuch as the trade surplus has been caused chiefly by exports of manufactured goods. At the government level, this issue has provoked interministerial conflict between officials having jurisdiction over agriculture and officials having jurisdiction over industry. Opposition political parties, moreover, have adopted an increasingly protectionist position in response to acquiescence of the government to U.S. demands. This threatens the policies of the ruling Liberal-Democratic party and its chances of remaining in office.

39. As remarked by Mauricio Gonzalez, director of the Dominican Republic Export Promotion Center in the United States, "Latin America is very interested in the outcome of the trade talks between the United States and Japan. If the U.S. has the right to equilibrate its balance of trade with Japan, then we also have a right to equilibrate our balance of trade with the U.S." *Journal of Commerce*, February 13, 1978.

40. The first cartels began to develop in Japan with the Spinning and Paper Manufacturing federations in 1880. U.S., Senate, Committee on Finance, *Implications of Multinational Firms for World Trade and Investment and for U.S. Trade and Labor*, February 1973, p. 849. They have never been wholly absent from the scene up to the present day.

41. Eurofer, the legalized EEC steel cartel, which sets market quotas and minimum prices, is apparently a model for similar cartels that have been proposed for shipbuilding, synthetic fiber industries, automobiles, chemicals and shoes. *Business Week*, March 27, 1978.

42. Roy Harrod, "Economic Development and Asian Regional Cooperation," *Pakistan Development Review*, Spring 1962, as quoted in Kiyoshi Kojima, *Japan and a Pacific Free Trade Area* (Tokyo: Tokyo University Press, 1971), p. 52. For such countries, at a similar stage of development, of similar size, and of similar factor proportions, agreement about the direction in which investment should be channeled would provide each with the benefits of specialization, including both (static) gains from the reallocation of resources and (dynamic) economies of large-scale production.

43. *Mitsui Trade News Supplement*, December 1975.

11
The Politics of Economic Relations Between the United States and Japan

Leon Hollerman

In the deflationary stagnation of the 1930s, governments typically resorted to protectionist policies in international trade. In the inflationary stagnation of the 1970s, they have done likewise, but more besides. The New Protectionism constitutes merely a single aspect of the recent politicization of international economic relations. Whereas protectionism as such is essentially passive, defensive, and inward-looking, politicization may appear in an active or invasive mode as well. Politicization may take the form not only of barriers to imports but also of pressure applied by one country against another for purposes of economic advantage. Thus it possesses a greater potential than protectionism alone for frustrating the attainment of an economic optimum in the world economy.[1]

In relations between the United States and Japan, political manipulation has progressively displaced the role of economic rationality in recent years. I would like to identify some causes, manifestations, and results of this syndrome.

Causes of Politicization

A basic cause of the politicization of U.S.-Japanese economic

This is a slightly revised version of a paper originally published in the *Journal of Contemporary Business*, Vol. 8, No. 2, Spring 1979.

relations is misperception or misrepresentation of the relation between economic cause and effect. For example, in a visit to Tokyo, Mr. Richard Holbrooke, U.S. Assistant Secretary of State for East Asian Affairs, asserted that the U.S. trade deficit with Japan is a key cause of inflation in the United States.[2] On the contrary, a strong consensus of professional economic opinion maintains that U.S. inflation has been caused chiefly by inappropriate monetary and fiscal policies in the United States and that the trade deficit is a consequence rather than a cause of the inflation. It may be of interest that during the decade 1960-1969, when the ratio of Japan's trade deficit to its GNP was approximately the same as the ratio of the trade deficit to GNP in the United States during 1972-1977, the rate of increase in Japan's Wholesale Price Index averaged less than 1 percent annually.

Since the great depression of the 1930s, Keynesian demand-oriented economic policies have been dominant in the United States. In Japan, on the contrary, since World War II, supply-oriented policies have prevailed. In terms of productivity, the result is expressed in widely quoted statistics concerning the performance of industrial countries. Among eleven major nations, Japan achieved the highest rate of growth in manufacturing productivity (8.8 percent per annum) during the period 1960-1977, while the United States ranked lowest (2.6 percent per annum). During 1978, United States productivity grew at less than 1 percent, one-tenth of the rate of increase in Japan.[3] Recent attempts to reverse demand-oriented policies in the United States have concentrated on the restraint of government spending. Resistance to such restraint has notably politicized the issue.

Behind the neglect of supply capacity in the United States, however, lies a more fundamental matter, which has been described as the problem of "governability." Expansion of the role of government has occurred partly because of adverse externalities in modern economic societies with which only governments rather than individuals can cope. The role of government has expanded also due to rising expectations concerning the attainment of utopian goals, such as social justice, social welfare, preservation of the environment, increased leisure, and a high standard of living. To a considerable extent, these goals are mutually inconsistent, at least in the short run. Attempts to achieve them simultaneously have generated conflicts such as that of freedom versus bureaucracy, egalitarianism versus hierarchy, participation versus exclusion. While pursuing utopian goals, moreover, the "Now" generation is not inhibited in its demand for immediate satisfactions.

The special interest groups that have politicized economic demands of one sort or another have come to dominate the decisions of government. Labor unions, for example, now regard import restraints as a means of promoting job security and thus as an instrument of social welfare. Labor's short-term gain is outweighed by the long-term loss of income for all that could be attained through international specialization in accordance with comparative advantage. Ironically, while advocating policies that undermine U.S. competitive power, the unions complain against the consequent export of American capital, which "financ[es] foreign competitors of U.S. industries."[4]

In Japan, declining industries such as agriculture and textiles have likewise through political pressure promoted protectionist policies on the part of the government. However, it is interesting that labor unions in Japan are becoming increasingly critical of protectionism that raises the cost of food. Politicization of the food issue by Japanese unions, in contrast with the political activities of American unions, may thus strengthen rather than weaken the market system.

In United States–Japan relations, as well as in the world community at large, economic uncertainty has greatly increased in recent years. Uncertainty is associated with risk, which induces the politicization of demands for economic security. Among various sources of uncertainty has been the failure of economists to make adequate forecasts. Having accomplished the "miracle" of the 1960s, the Japanese economy paused in the mid-1970s. Following World War II, economists failed to predict the miracle, and during the miracle they failed to predict the pause.[5] In the United States, changes in the rate of growth, the level of employment, the balance of payments, the level of investment, and the rate of inflation have for the most part come as a surprise to economists. Uncertainty arising from the difficulty of anticipating politicized economic decisions of the government has in turn been a major cause of the inability of economists to make adequate projections. This situation has the makings of a vicious circle.

Another vicious circle arises from the fact that many individuals who have speculated in real assets and placed themselves heavily in debt to do so have a vested interest in inflation. They plan to pay their debts in continually depreciating currency. When private fortunes can be made in speculative acquisition of old assets, innovation, new investment, productivity, and competitive power consecutively decline. Employment and exports decline as well; government spending increases. Then the money supply expands and a new round of inflation begins. Government revenue rises due to the progressive tax rate structure, giving the government a vested interest in inflation as well. The inequities and social and political conflicts created by inflation are of a highly politicizing nature.

Within government itself, economic decisions are subject to bureaucratic politics. The officials in charge of relations with various regions do not invariably have consistent policies and they change their minds frequently. Moreover, in the Carter Administration there exists a considerable lack of coordination among Treasury, State, Commerce, and the Special Trade Representative with regard to international economic affairs. In the power struggle among these agencies, the possibilities for politicization of U.S. economic affairs are abundant.

In the evolution of a new international economic order, the advent of floating exchange rates has contributed to economic uncertainty. As compared with uncertainty under fixed rates, the increase in uncertainty under floating rates arises in part from the potentially more disruptive role of monetary, as distinguished from real, effects of shocks sustained by the economy. In particular, such shocks are immediately reflected in capital movements, which are magnified in a floating-rate system. Under the Bretton Woods system, exchange rates were pegged rather than permanently fixed, and repegging was also potentially disruptive. However, with the advent of floating rates capital movements have become a larger and more volatile component of international commerce than under the Bretton

Woods regime. These capital movements, including speculative activity, are reflected in exchange rate fluctuations, which in turn may affect the flow of trade and other real variables. Reallocation of the factors of production may also be induced. In that event, demands for import protection would also increase. Theoretically, however, given inappropriate monetary and fiscal policies, it is not clear whether resource reallocation would be more subject to disruption under pegged or floating rates.

The belief that modern society progressively creates structural problems that cannot be solved by the market system has contributed to the politicization of economic affairs. An increasing amount of interaction among economic, political, and military factors as well as increased interdependence on the international plane contribute further to the same effect.

The United States deficit in trade with Japan has clearly been magnified as a result of increased economic interdependence. Japan's recession in the mid-1970s generated supply-oriented exports together with a decline in demand for imports, while the United States in recovering from recession during the same period increased its demand for imports from Japan. The combined effect of these countercyclical movements was an enormous trade imbalance. As the debtor country, the United States declined to adopt appropriate domestic measures to adjust its balance of payments. Instead, it attempted to force Japan to carry the brunt of the adjustment by reducing its trade surplus. Pressures imposed upon Japan toward this end were contrived by politicizing the problem.

United States Pressures on Japan

In its physical resource structure, the Japanese economy is unbalanced; in its dependence on the world economy for the essentials of existence, it is highly vulnerable; in its demographic and industrial transition, it faces formidable bottlenecks and constraints. Traditional instruments of social and economic control are losing their grip. Thus the potential instability of the Japanese economy is very great. Psychologically, Japan is beset by fear of being isolated in the world community. In these circumstances, it is highly sensitive to pressures from the outside, especially from its partner and only military ally, the United States.

Its partner's policies, however, illustrate the aphorism that nations do not have friends, they only have interests. In the short-term interest of reducing its trade deficit, the United States has applied increasing amounts of direct and indirect pressure on Japan. At the macroeconomic level, the "locomotive" strategy was invoked as a means of forcing Japan to abandon its independent monetary policy. At the microeconomic level, U.S. producers have been able to harass U.S. importers by invoking legal procedures. In this connection, it is noteworthy that, for domestic political reasons, the United States declined to adhere to the antidumping regulations prescribed for members of GATT in the Kennedy Round. With reference to the U.S. Antidumping Act and the Countervailing Duty Law, Noel Hemmendinger has pointed out that "For both substantive and procedural reasons, the laws against so-called unfair trade give just cause for complaint to both American importers and U.S. trading partners and need amending."[6]

In September 1977, a U.S.-Japan Trade Facilitation Committee (TFC) was formed for the purpose of resolving complaints made by United States exporters against Japanese trade practices such as the following: "restrictive regulations or actions such as 'Buy-Japan' procurement practices, arbitrary administration of product safety and health standards, official pressure ('administrative guidance') on Japanese end-users to buy Japanese rather than foreign-made products, and customs procedures."[7] Although the TFC was formed jointly by the U.S. Secretary of Commerce and the Japanese Minister of International Trade and Industry (MITI), it made no provision for reciprocal complaints by Japanese exporters against restrictive U.S. trade practices.

The tactics of United States officials in applying pressures on Japan have been openly acknowledged and discussed. For example, on March 29, 1979, U.S. Special Representative for Trade Negotiations, Ambassador Robert S. Strauss, abruptly "broke off" talks with Japanese officials on a proposed government procurement agreement, calling their offer "wholly inadequate." As reported in the press, "Mr. Strauss, who has used such 'shock tactics' several times previously in his negotiations with Japanese officials on trade issues, said 'the time for negotiation has expired.'"[8] In discussing Japan's compliance with U.S. demands, Senator William V. Roth announced that "time is running out." Representative William Frenzel declared, "Congress is not going to tolerate a continuing high imbalance in U.S. trade with Japan."[9] Congressional sources also announced a proposal for imposing a surcharge of 10 to 15 percent on imports from Japan.[10] And in Congressional testimony, Ambassador Strauss stated that the U.S. trade deficit was "unacceptable."[11] This version of the source of the deficit implied that it was being forced on the United States from the outside.

Another U.S. tactic is to threaten Japan with dire consequences if it fails to comply with given demands. Referring to its proposals, the Jones Task Force report states, "Japanese officials and industrialists are unwilling to take these hard steps, so we must make them more attractive by posing less acceptable alternatives."[12]

A similar device is to widen the scope of demands on Japan so as to facilitate acquiescence on the core issue by means of subsequent U.S. withdrawal on irrelevant or inappropriate peripheral matters. This gives rise to the "bandwagon" effect described below. The core issue at present is simply the U.S. assertion that the creditor rather than the debtor is responsible for the adjustment of a deficit. Surrounding this central proposition, the Carter Administration sent an "eleven-point proposal" to the Japanese government in January 1979, containing an assortment of demands.[13]

In attempting to impose its views upon Japan, the U.S. government has sent a stream of important officials to Tokyo. For example, Secretary of the Treasury Michael Blumenthal conferred with Prime Minister Ohira on March 5, 1979. One of his arguments concerned the importance of resolving the U.S.-Japan trade problem before the then impending summit meeting to be held in Tokyo in June 1979. The implied threat of a confrontation on the host's home ground was calculated to embarrass the Japanese into submission.

The pressures placed upon Japan by the Carter Administration were magnified by virtue of their occurrence in the context of pressures previously applied, in particular by the Nixon Administration. Richard Nixon repeatedly applied political pressures against Japan and used economic pressures for political purposes. Nixon's "textile war" with Japan was the product of his political commitment to textile interests during the presidential election campaign of 1968. That issue was further politicized by becoming involved with the reversion of Okinawa to Japanese sovereignty. In July 1971, the first of the three "Nixon shocks" (concerning the way in which his visit to China was announced to Japan) was a traumatic episode. A former United States ambassador to Japan told me in 1978 that, prior to Nixon's trip to China, the U.S. State Department and the Japanese Foreign Ministry had a very good relationship, but since then "things have never been the same." The second Nixon shock was the "New Economic Policy" of August 15, 1971.[14] The third Nixon shock was the U.S. soybean embargo of June 1973. This occurred at a time when the United States had almost a monopoly of the world supply of soybeans. The embargo prohibited deliveries even on contracts that had already been concluded. In explaining this policy, Pierre Rinfret, a former Nixon economic adviser, said that the U.S. embargo on soybeans was intended less as a solution for domestic shortages than to "teach Japan a lesson in international relations." He said, "We wanted to show something to the people who thought our economic strength was low. And frankly, the Japanese have been increasingly cooperative since then."[15]

Effects of Politicization

In the period of economic recovery following World War II, Japan repeatedly asserted the principle of "separation of economics from politics." In those days, Japan interpreted its "partnership" with the United States to imply that the United States would provide aid and understanding to Japan. At present, the United States interprets "partnership" as a commitment by Japan to share the burdens of the United States. As a major industrial nation, the interactions among Japan's economic, political and military affairs have become increasingly complex. Thus repeatedly in Japan's relations with the United States, it has become necessary to seek a solution to economic difficulties by "raising the problem to the political level."[16]

The politicization of Japan's economic relations with the United States has been reflected in the domestic affairs of both countries and in third country relationships as well. The Commission of the EEC has reinforced U.S. pressures by proposing that the Community impose controls on imports from Japan. In launching its proposal, the Commission leaked a controversial report written by its director-general of external relations, Sir Roy Denman. The report referred to Japan as "a country of workaholics" who live in "what westerners would regard as little more than rabbit hutches...."[17] In the midst of mounting U.S. political pressures against Japan, it was interesting that in March 1979 China "temporarily" suspended contracts with eight Japanese trading companies in the amount of approximately $2 billion. Within the United States, textile producers joined the bandwagon: the long-term textile agreement with Japan was revised in January 1979; however, in the following month, sensing an opportunity to demand more concessions from Japan, they induced the government to request quantitative restrictions by Japan on its exports of three additional products.[18] The U.S. leather industry was prompted to demand that Japan reduce its import quotas on leather goods, a quota established in behalf of the *burakumin*, a disadvantaged minority group. U.S. banks, perhaps in response to increasing Japanese competition in Southeast Asia and elsewhere, have taken the occasion of the U.S.-Japan balance of trade argument to press for relief against alleged discrimination against foreign banks in Japan.

The politicization of U.S. economic relations with Japan reverberated ironically in the Carter Administration's campaign to secure Congressional approval of the GATT Tokyo Round agreement. Prior to submission of the supposedly liberalizing agreement to Congress, the administration favored the constituents of key congressmen by providing increased import protection for various products, including textiles, steel, fasteners, footwear, chemicals, dinnerware, sugar, and dairy products.[19]

Within Japan, politicization of the U.S. economic relationship has had other effects. Special interests in Japan attempted to use the United States as a stick with which to beat their own government. For example, in promoting its program for government assistance to business, Keidanren (The Federation of Economic Organizations) endorsed the U.S. demand that Japan should not adopt a tight monetary policy.[20] A more devious method of applying pressure on one's own government is practiced by government officials who have contacts with colleagues in the adversary government. Officials in MITI have been known to put pressure on their own prime minister by providing ammunition to their opposite numbers in the U.S. Treasury Department.

Politicization of its economic relations with the United States has not been wholly without redeeming merit even from the point of view of the Japanese government. In responding to the U.S. attack on Japanese exports, it has been able to pursue its policy of phasing out backward or declining sectors and to reform the structure of industry. The onus for bankruptcies and liquidations can be passed to the United States. Prior to the battle of the trade balance, it used the same tactic during the "textile war."

Since the end of the occupation, moreover, it has been the policy of the Japanese government to attempt to diversify its markets and sources of supply and thus to reduce the degree of its dependence on trade with the United States. The present demand of the United States for restrictions on Japan's exports is completely compatible with that policy.

It might be noted that some barriers erected by the United States against imports from Japan have had an adverse effect on the exports of South Korea and other countries. These barriers provide such countries with a grievance against Japan as well as against the United States. They have also proclaimed their fear of being overrun by Japanese competition that has been rechanneled in their direction.

The history of the postwar period does not encourage the belief that nations have the ability or the will to coordinate their economic policies within a multilateral world market system. Under pressure, Japan has accommodated the United States on many occasions. Increasingly, these pressures reflect the politicization of their economic relations. The rise of the New Protectionism is a conspicuous example. Further results which may be anticipated include the growth of bilateralism, discrimination, and retaliation. The prospect of such developments does not bode well for the future of the free world market economy.

Notes

1. Barriers to imports are erected in response to the pressures of special interest groups, resulting in redistribution of income from consumers to producers and from export industries to import-competing industries. Protectionism as such is thus primarily a domestic rather than an international issue.

2. *The Journal of Commerce,* New York, March 13, 1979. The Jones Task Force report to the Vanik Subcommittee on Trade makes a similar assertion. It states that "trade deficits with the Far East have become a major (perhaps *the* major) cause of the recent downward pressure on the dollar, and thus they contribute substantially to domestic inflation." Subcommittee on Trade of the Committee on Ways and Means, U.S. House of Representatives, *Task Force Report on United States-Japan Trade,* 95th Congress, 2d Session, January 2, 1979, p. 1. In his State of the Union message, President Carter's version was that "skyrocketing hospital costs" are "the largest contributor to inflation."

3. *Notes From the Joint Economic Committee,* Congress of the United States, Volume 5, Number 7, March 2, 1979.

4. *IUD Bulletin,* Industrial Union Department, American Federation of Labor-Congress of Industrial Organizations, Vol. 9, No. 1, First Quarter, 1979.

5. Likewise in the early 1960s, economists completely failed to anticipate the then impending spectacular growth of South Korea.

6. The reasons are explained in his paper, "Recommendations for Amendments in U.S. Laws to Provide Relief From Unfair Trade Practices," in *Unfair Trade Practices,* Subcommittee on Trade of the Committee on Ways and Means, U.S. House of Representatives, 95th Congress, 2d Session, September 5, 1978, p. 100.

7. Internal memorandum, "U.S.-Japan Trade Facilitation Committee," Industry and Trade Administration, U.S. Department of Commerce, May 1978.

8. *Wall Street Journal,* March 30, 1979. The immediate target of the government procurement negotiations was the Nippon Telephone and Telegraph Company (NTT). Its counterpart in the United States, the American Telegraph and Telephone Company, is a private corporation that invites bids from whatever source it chooses, principally "from its subsidiaries, over which it has exclusive control." *Asahi,* Tokyo, February 16, 1979. Pressure on NTT to accept foreign bids has been regarded as "high-handed" interference in Japan's domestic affairs. See *Nihon Keizai,* Tokyo, April 1, 1979.

9. *The Journal of Commerce,* December 18, 1978.

10. *The Journal of Commerce,* January 6, 1979. The proposal was not implemented.

11. Testimony before the Joint Economic Committee, January 25, 1979. In the same testimony, however, in soliciting Congressional approval of the results of the GATT Tokyo Round negotiation, Ambassador Strauss revealed that important trade concessions had been granted by Japan on another issue. "The average Japanese tariff on industrial imports from the United States will be 2.3 percent, while our own tariff on imports from Japan will be over 4 percent. After these cuts are fully put into effect, Japan will have one of the lowest tariff structures of any developed nation."

12. *Task Force Report on United States–Japan Trade,* p. 16.

13. *The Journal of Commerce,* January 31, 1979.

14. The New Economic Policy was adopted in response to the first U.S. trade deficit since 1893 and to accelerating attacks on the dollar. A 10 percent tariff surcharge was imposed on most U.S. imports, convertibility of the dollar into gold was suspended, and other remedial measures were taken. The import surcharge was regarded as a special hardship by Japanese exporters of steel, automobiles, textiles, and sundry goods.

15. *The Journal of Commerce,* October 18, 1973.

16. Japan's relations with other nations have also become politicized. The Japanese government was reported to have warned Vietnam that it would halt economic assistance to that country if Vietnam allowed the Soviet Union to use Cam Ranh port and airfield as a permanent military base. *Wall Street Journal,* April 19, 1979.

17. *The Economist,* April 7, 1979, p. 61.

18. *The Japan Economic Journal,* February 27, 1979.

19. *The Journal of Commerce,* March 1, 1979.

20. In a press conference on March 12, 1979, this point was emphasized by Toshiwo Doko, Chairman of Keidanren. United States–Japan Trade Council memorandum, March 23, 1979.